THE EDGE OF EXTINCTION

The Edge of Extinction

TRAVELS WITH ENDURING PEOPLE IN VANISHING LANDS

JULES PRETTY

COMSTOCK PUBLISHING ASSOCIATES
a division of
CORNELL UNIVERSITY PRESS
Ithaca and London

First published 2014 by Cornell University Press
Printed in the United States of America

Library of Congress Cataloging-in-Publication Data

Pretty, Jules N., author.
 The Edge of extinction : travels with enduring people in vanishing lands / Jules Pretty.
  pages cm
 Includes bibliographical references.
 ISBN 978-0-8014-5330-4 (cloth : alk. paper)
 1. Nature—Effect of human beings on—Moral and ethical aspects. 2. Human beings—Effect of environment on—Moral and ethical aspects. I. Title.
 GF80.P73   2014
 304.2—dc23   2014017464

Cornell University Press strives to use environmentally responsible suppliers and materials to the fullest extent possible in the publishing of its books. Such materials include vegetable-based, low-VOC inks and acid-free papers that are recycled, totally chlorine-free, or partly composed of nonwood fibers. For further information, visit our website at www.cornellpress.cornell.edu.

Cloth printing   10 9 8 7 6 5 4 3 2 1

For

My father, John Pretty (1932–2012), and mother, Susan

and

Gill, Freya, and Theo

Without my journey
And without this spring
I would have missed this dawn.

—Masaoka Shiki (1856–1902)

Traveling this high
Mountain trail, delighted
By violets.

—Matsuo Bashō (1644–94)

CONTENTS

PREVIOUSLY

I often rise before dawn and sit on the pine bench in the garden. In winter's cold, plumes of breath greet first light. All is silent. In spring, the liquid songs of robins and blackbirds welcome the sun. In summer come swarms of midges, then at dusk bats stitch in and out of shadows. I water the plants, fill the bird feeders. In autumn if I am still, deer come, delicately stepping beneath the apple trees. Above may circle buzzards on thermals, lately come to the valley, and jackdaws and rooks daily beat with purpose toward the east, tumbling playfully back at dusk. The garden is nothing special. Wild and not wild. Nothing stays the same. It is droughty, then sodden. Sheets of drizzle, then sun. Blankets of snow. Clear cold nights bringing a family of tawny owls. Then in spring, nightingales singing from the same trees. Animals come and go; plants sprout, grow, are swamped, die back. Yet how is the economy to recover if we were all so irresponsible? Seriously, how can it survive if we sit around and do not spend more?

The notion of the inevitable benefits of all material progress is a modern invention. Hunters and foragers, many farmers and herders too, tend not to hold that their current community is any better than those of the past or at other places. Past and future are no more or less valued than current time. But economic development too easily justifies the losses of both species and special places, as we expect losses to be offset by creating something much better. Our environmental problems are thus human problems. Disconnection from the land, in the form of non-regular contact, already has the capacity to damage and even destroy cultures. Yet many talk of the need for escape, to get away from it all.

Something important remains elusive to many moderns. It is much happiness. We do not have clear answers, but the proportion of people in industrialized countries describing themselves as happy has not changed since the 1950s, despite a trebling of wealth. At the same time, the incidence of mental ill-health has grown rapidly. We solved, largely, infectious diseases; then came cancers. Our lives were extended and treatments improved; then came obesity, and problems of cardiovascular disease and diabetes. Dementias have become more common in the elderly. The reasons are largely simple: bad lifestyles, wrong foods, too little physical activity.[1]

Evolutionary history is framed by losses and gains. The same goes for humans and our cultures. Ways of living emerged that were adapted to local ecosystems. Wild places, farms, grasslands, gardens: none were invariant. And whether hunter or farmer, we changed things, and in return our minds have been shaped by the land. Then came the industrial revolution, and the invention of machines that released abundant energy from coal. Within half a century, oil gushed from wells, and it changed the world yet again. Then consumer culture transformed the old equations about people and land. Global connectedness now illuminates the upsides of consumption, and aspirations are converging. But now come considerable environmental and social side-effects, so serious they threaten this finite planet's capacity to resource all our wants. Conventional economic growth encourages a race to the top of consumption, even though large numbers of people currently have no prospects of escaping poverty or hunger. We still call this progress.[2]

Yet reason and evidence have not compelled us to care enough for nature. A good future will not be a return to something solely rooted in the past: we need medical, farm, and transport technology, certainly computers and modern communications. But a hybrid vigor might be created through *both-and* Zen practices rather than *either-or*.[3] A new green economy in which material goods have not harmed the planet would be a good economy: even better if production processes could improve natural capital. The great majority of nonindustrial cultures that maintain links to the land have done so through local cultural institutions, often manifesting in nature a variety of spiritual symbols and stories that command respect. If we wish to persuade people to manage the planet sustainably and consume in different ways, then we will have to embed twenty-first-century lifeways in a new texture of beliefs, emotions, and experience. We will need moral teachings and wisdom about the environment and our duties as individuals. Through a different kind of consciousness of the world, perhaps our impact can be changed.[4]

In such a barbarian green economy there would be regular engagements with nature, whether in gardens or wild places, city parks or fields, many people doing things together in rituals that make these behaviors valued and worth repeating, people giving to others and making intergenerational links, and communities investing time in activities that build contentment and well-being. We may need to break the current rules, bring the wilds inside the city walls, introduce new behaviors, create different aspirations.

There is some journeying to be done. Paths to be explored, and new ones made.[5] Each year, the pine leans a little further. After night, the dawn comes. There is mud, but the birds are singing. The waves come and go, but the ocean is still there.

Each new day begins in the Pacific along the north-south dateline. The earth spins, and the sun appears to travel from east to west. That is why I chose to start in the east and migrate west, across continents to explore how and why people still live close to nature, land and sea. I sought clues for moderns about ways of living that will not condemn cultures and economies to extinction. I walked and traveled by pirogue, snowmobile, skiff, canoe, airboat, horse-trap, cable car, jeep, car, van, truck, train, and plane. Sleep came in tents and farmhouses, cabins and house-boats, bleak administration blocks and occasionally distinctive hotels. And food shared included muttonbirds and mutton, pike and catfish, moose and porcupine, crawfish and flounder, noodles and breakfast grills. In some places there was much beer, vodka, wine; others were dry. Extinction has already been a reality for many species, but I saw close-up sharks and kangaroos, horses and sheep, elephants and lions, gun dogs and catfish, swallows and curlews, alligators and coyotes, and all the while the land was being narrated by corvids. Extinction has denied many human groups and languages a future. It now threatens the ways of life of the afflu-ent, even though many ignore the signs.

I walked with local Māori people along the coasts of the Pacific, climbed newly accessible mountains in China with thousands of others, and journeyed into petroglyph-rich deserts of Australia where oil and gas have come but the locals are extinct. I traveled with nomads across the continent-wide steppes of southern Siberia, walked and boated in the inland swamps of southern Africa rich with wildlife, and journeyed out onto the Arctic cold with ice-fishermen in Finland. I explored the coasts and inland marshes of eastern England and the coastal glens of Northern Ireland, and trekked with Innu people across the taiga's snowy forests and lakes of the Labrador interior. The passages continued in the Americas on the small farms of Amish horse-cultures that thrive alongside the failing cities of the rust belt, then with Cajun swampers of the Deep South's largest inland swamp, and finally in the deathly deserts of the West, to the lowest places where live the Timbi-sha, and to some of the highest, ending up at the Pacific Ocean again.

I met and traveled with people defending nature-based cultures, proud of their relationships with the land, and willing to join with the modern world only on their terms. Lessons for moderns may lie in some of the stories from these places.

People on the land like to tell stories. Perhaps ripples will travel far.

This is not the first day, nor the last.

NOTE ON WEIGHTS AND MEASURES

I have allowed weights and measures to be both imperial and metric. Mostly distances are in miles, but sometimes kilometers, and on a smaller scale, variously feet, yards, and meters; areas in hectares, but acres where local people still think that way; weight in kilograms and pounds, tons and metric tons (tonnes); volumes in liters and gallons; and speed in miles or kilometers per hour, or knots at sea. These renamings of terms, and the subsequent and inevitable confusion, echo many of the changes in name and identity that places and people on the land have undergone.

THE EDGE OF EXTINCTION

1

SEACOAST

Ngāi Tahu, Aotearoa (New Zealand)

10° West of Date Line[*]

The sun rises from the east over an ocean that covers one-third of the planetary surface. Cross the line, as the sun appears to do, from east to west, and you repeat the calendar day; cross from west to east and confusingly a day of your life seems to disappear. It is a jagged imaginary line from Wrangel Island to the Antarctic, in the middle a panhandle recently created to absorb Kiribati, Tokelau, and Samoa into the same time zone as the western ocean. Humans came late, spreading eastward from Asia some five thousand years ago in the world's first oceangoing vessels. Later the Lapita carried by canoe domesticated pigs, dogs, and fowl, also taro, yam, coconut, and banana, traveling on to Fiji by 1300 BC, Tonga and Samoa two hundred years later, to Hawaii and Rapa Nui (Easter Island) by AD 700, and onward to South America to carry back kumara, the sweet potato, and gourd by AD 1000. Thor Heyerdahl was both right and wrong in 1947. People did travel from South America by sea, but they had come that way first. And they didn't blunder around in a reed and balsa raft. Those navigators and canoe makers knew what they were doing, even though ocean distances must have seemed interplanetary.

The world's last substantial landmass, apart from Antarctica, to be peopled was Aotearoa, now New Zealand, in about AD 1300. Using subtropical weather systems, Polynesians made heroic crossings from the Cook and Society Islands. When the Europeans came to the Pacific, first Ferdinand Magellan in 1521, then William Dampier, Abel Tasman, James Cook, and many others, they could not believe the indigenous people navigated without instruments or charts. Yet in this vast ocean, where there are six thousand square kilometers of water for every one of land, it was the navigators who were the most honored. The Europeans came with astrolabes and compasses, yet had no means of calculating longitude until the mid-1700s. By contrast the Pacific navigators had knowledge of stars and sun,

[*]Day begins at the Pacific Date Line.

swell patterns, clouds, homing birds, deep phosphorescence, wave refraction and reflection, currents and sea marks.

For three hundred years, the Pacific was reckoned to be a vast wilderness to discover and conquer. And to bring back booty. Locals were variously called hostiles, swindlers, heathens, and murderers, or were elevated into romantic myth. Most books about the Pacific and its navigation contain no reference to the locals' capacity to populate remote islands in the first place, or to continue to move around. Many of those on the expeditions were oddly incurious. There were clues: Cook's *Endeavour*, a converted collier thirty-three meters in length, was smaller than Fijian canoes that could carry 250 people. Cook wrote of canoes traveling at speeds of twenty-two knots; his ship could make six knots at top speed. The knowledge of the navigators was detailed, precise, and derived from experience, though in modern times fell away before recent revival by the Polynesian Voyaging Society.[1]

Navigators need to know the whole sky, and would have both sidereal star and wind compasses in their minds. At night, horizon stars can be used to steer by for a short time. The belt of hunter Orion, for example, always rises due east and sets due west, but as stars rise four minutes earlier every day, the sky needs to be known throughout the year. A night of sailing thus requires knowledge of the position and bearing of some ten to twelve horizon stars. Another method centers on knowledge of swell patterns, the waves that have traveled hundreds of miles beyond the wind systems that generate them. These are generally long, slow undulations, and the best navigators lie in their canoes and direct helmsman by what they feel of the swell. Navigators can also read the resonance patterns when reflected off distant land or refracted around islands. One technique is to leave a rope trailing behind the canoe, so that if a wave pushes the canoe off course, the rope remains true to the original line of travel. Canoes could also follow migratory birds, such as long-tailed or shining cuckoos, or shearwaters.

There is thus a zone of land indicators around every island. Some birds will travel only ten or twenty kilometers from land; others typically thirty. Terns and noddies are known to visit passing canoes at night, and then fly directly toward land, thus gifting a bearing to the navigator. Many birds also fly toward fishing grounds in the morning, and back to land in the evening. Clouds move more slowly over land, as if stuck, indicating islands over the horizon. If green beneath, they are above a lagoon; if bright, then above white sand or surf. Sea convection clouds over islands can be 150 kilometers away. In *A Pattern of Islands*, Arthur Grimble recorded sea marks or *betia* in Kiribati, then the Gilberts, stable lines of leaves or rubbish caught forever between currents. Many navigators also use deep phosphorescence, manifested in the form of streamers, flashes, or glowing plaques of light that are often common on dark, rainy nights, and always point toward land. Many journeys of discovery were search and return that relied on trade winds reversing at different times of the year. Sailing against or across the wind meant a relatively easy return;

but traveling downwind would require return by a different route, and thus needed knowledge of other islands.

Still, though, two great islands between the southern latitudes of 34 to 48 degrees remained undiscovered. Pharaohs and their pyramids had come and gone, the Roman Empire too, William and the Normans had arrived in Britain, dispatched Harold and stayed, and still Aotearoa remained off the human map. Then a group of Polynesian navigators and mariners looked south and west from the central Pacific, and set off in their great canoes with outriggers to cross sixteen hundred miles of open ocean. The originating homeland became known as Hawaiki, and the people settled the two islands of endemic ground birds, dark fern forests, deep harbors, and crumpled mountains. According to Māori *whakapapa* genealogies, settlement occurred twenty-four to twenty-seven generations ago, confirming those first arrivals at about seven hundred years before today. Some say there was one great arrival, others that there were waves. Some may have been pushed onward by conflict, others guided by migratory whales.

It was too cold for coconut, breadfruit, and banana, but taro, yam, mulberry, cabbage trees, kumara, and gourds thrived. There were extinctions: moa and other species of large land birds were gone within two hundred years. In 1642, Tasman was the first European to arrive on the west coast, then 140 years or so later came Cook to stake his country's ownership of New Zealand. Cook's three voyages of discovery in the 1770s, as they were called, produced a new map of the Pacific, though this son of a Yorkshire laborer was to meet his end on the Sandwich Islands. But unlike many Aboriginal groups in Australia, Cook's arrival did not bring the end for the many Māori cultures.

The waves of new colonialists took lands and resources, brought their own plants, animals, and language, yet within seventy years had signed the crucial Treaty of Waitangi in 1840 that formalized political and institutional space for Māori peoples. But still the Māori population fell dramatically, the result of disease, loss of land and resources, and despair: from eighty thousand in 1840 to half that by 1900. During the twentieth century, kā Māori people shifted from being almost all rural or coastal based to nearly nine-tenths urban by 2000. For urban Māori, identity tends now to be toward generalized Māori rather than the particular tribe or *iwi*. Māori in New Zealand, though, obtained the vote from 1902; Aboriginals in Australia had to wait until the 1960s.

My navigators will be members of the Ngāi Tahu *iwi* of South Island, and from the local university in Dunedin.[2] The Ōtākou *marae* was the first Māori village encountered by Presbyterian settlers and whalers who had ventured into Dunedin's deep fjord of a harbor. They rendered Ōtākou to Otago. I sleep at Tahu and Megan's spare bungalow overlooking the slate-gray harbor, and had intended to rise early to walk the hills. In vivid dreams populated by cabbage trees, mutton-birds, wild harvest, and sacred lakes, I find myself wondering why it is so light so early in the country when it had been dark ten miles away in the city. In those becalmed dreams, all urgency has gone. Eventually I lean over to check the clock and find it is four minutes before our agreed departure time.

I leap up and bolt a warm coffee, breathe deeply, and step quickly down the hillside.

Tahu is relaxed. He is sitting at the kitchen table completing his weekly article on laptop. His hair is prematurely gray, Megan's tousled brown. Their daughter is at school, younger son running around. No one's in any hurry.

I remember how Pacific time can slow like this. I ran a course in a village in eastern Fiji. In sweltering humidity we sat in the chief's house with three other leaders opposite a new *bora* communal barn, its steep roof being freshly thatched almost to the ground. The sea breeze hurried the curtains, and palm trees bent and quivered. The azure sky was deep and unending. We had brought peppery yaqoma roots, also known as kava, *Piper methysticum*, and these were pounded in a large communal bowl. For most of the humid afternoon, the ceremony continued, coconut bowls of muddy brown liquid exchanged and drunk, one clap of hands from the receiver, three by the giver, then two more by the receiver on completion. We exchanged murmured speeches. We the visitors could then enter the village; I stayed with the chief's party. The kava filled the afternoon that was both long and too short. Outside plates rattled in bowls, chickens squabbled, a child called, leaves rustled. The wooden house was painted cream and blue. I remember watching white cumulus start to drift over. Each day started in the same way, and proceeded with a measured South Seas' pace. "Small is the voice of a chief," said Arthur Grimble on the Gilberts to the northwest.

From the kitchen window and beyond a picket fence, I can see white horses dashing across the two-mile-wide harbor flanked by scalped hills. The native vegetation hugs the hills, the imported stands out, explains writer Khyla Russell later. We drive north on the inside of the peninsula for formalities at the marae. This seems a straightforward arrangement, but there had been many prior discussions. You do not just come to the land without acknowledgment of history and intentionality. My coming had provoked talks about how formal or informal should be the arriving. There is always a proper way. You do not just show up like Cook and the others. The previous night at Edward Ellison's six-hundred-acre farm, in the family since 1880, we had shared a meal of salty muttonbirds, with mashed potatoes and greens, and glasses of red wine from a South Island winery, the wood fire blazing in the stove.

We arrive at the marae, meeting place and spiritual center for the community. It is for encounters, a creative space alive with ancestors. Above the door is written *Tamatea*, the name of the legendary traveler from Hawaiki. Everything begins and ends here, where nature and culture cohere. At the gate, brick-red carvings span the entrance, and a plaque notes their centennial memorial in 1940, a hundred years after the treaty was signed here, and we walk up the curved path to the cream hall with sweeping red roof that almost meets the ground. All the pillars, eaves, and windows are carved with spiral forms and stacked ancestors standing on one another's shoulders. In this bitter southeasterly that tugs and pulls, it still puts me in mind of that communal hall in Fiji. Inside, a stage is hidden by crimson curtains, and electric heaters hanging from the ceiling glow. A stained-glass window depicts a Māori soldier with bayoneted rifle, khaki shirt rolled above elbows, shorts and long socks with dark shoes. The sky is blue, and at the top is a face with bulging eyes and tongue outstretched. On the left is a roll of honor with one Ōtākou name under the Boer War, fourteen for 1914–18, and on the right another sixteen from 1939–45. Many are repeated, including three Ellisons, Robertsons, and Forsyths.

The group gathers on a line of chairs beneath the stage, and I sit tentatively in the audience with Megan, Edward's daughter. Tahu welcomes, Khyla stands to add more, her lips blue with *mata*, two parallel lines down her chin, curling back in spirals. I stand to give thanks, announcing myself to the Māori ancestors here in the marae. I'm left with a feeling that I could have done this better. We chat about memories of the hall. Of playing badminton, and of community events with all the kids sleeping on mattresses and the grown-ups drinking outside. Death is a theme. It brings people together. Bodies are brought inside the marae before going to the cemetery next door. Everyone gets used to death, to living with ancestors.

"Sometimes you only know someone when they're dead," observes Tahu, as others nod.

There used to be a school associated with the marae, but it's closed now. Yet the country's first Māori doctor and lawyer were from Ōtākou, right here.

With a slow stride, we walk north along the thin strip between coast and cliff. Wrapped in coats and hats we talk along the bay. Long waves race through the narrow opening in the harbor. On the beach oystercatchers pipe mournfully and crouching shags gaze at the water. Other waders skitter as the waves rise and crash and retreat. On the hills above the houses and gardens are cabbage trees tall and branched, and clumps of golden gorse, a pest here, the parched pasture cropped by rabbits and sheep. We turn into Riki and Eleanor's and stroll up the garden to where they run forty sheep on the hill.

By a thin stream that drains into a seasonal pond, Riki has built a fifteen-foot arch of rare kauri wood and carved an intricate pattern depicting ancestors and marking this particular piece of homeland. These native kauri, *Aganthis*, can reach fifty meters in height with trunk diameters of five meters or more, and normally live for six hundred years, the oldest a couple of thousand, rivaling the great sequoias of California on the other side of the Pacific. It's a hard wood, says Riki, yet soft enough to carve. There is something dependable about very old trees.

Some have seen off whole civilizations, stuck where their roots first took hold. When the Europeans came, they logged kauri for ship masts and spars; only a tenth of the original forests remained by 1900.

At the far end of the bay, we stop at the house of elders Paul and Natalie, and cramp in the front room warmed by a portable gas heater. The metal-framed windows are soon covered in condensation. Paul has a shock of white hair above broad face, his torso seeming to speak of rugby forward. Natalie glides around the room, smiling. They rent land out for cribs, small houses, but there's a constant dance over rents. The edge is over commerce: is it right to be making a living, or is it the density of social relationships that matters most? Family members, for example, want housing rent-free, and almost everyone is family in some way. Paul was helping in the construction of a community garden with John Reid of Lincoln University when they discovered *riwai* potatoes growing wild on a tiny ledge by a cliff towering above. It's now part of their *kotahitanga* cultural revitalization program.

Paul comes out in cardigan, blue jeans, and black slippers to wave us off, and we return past the tussocky grasses on the sand dunes. Riki points to the spit jutting out from Aramoana on the far side, a name forever marked by an appalling disaster. Towering container ships heading to Dunedin harbor sweep in a tight semicircle, and invasive wash floods these dunes with aggressive waves. *Beware*, says a sign, *there is danger to public.* Young George smiles from inside padded jacked and hood, describing how well they surf these industrial waves in small boats. But never tell their parents, he chuckles. Today, natural waves thrash the shore.

Riki is salt-scorched and wind-tanned, one of the deepwater fishermen whose battle for resources is far from over. There may be treaties, but implementation and protection of rights is still political. Lives close to the land have changed too. The Ngāi Tahu hold 80 percent of the land of Te Waipounamu, the Greenstone Isle, South Island. But conflicts continue. In this harbor are important beds of *tuaki* cockles. The Ōtākou hapū wish to declare a harvesting moratorium to protect stocks. But a commercial cockler on the north side will have none of it. He's taking 650 tonnes a year on his research permit, not bothered by concepts like rotation patterns. Now average shellfish sizes are getting smaller. The company commissioned research on the sustainability of the cockling, but when the results were published, it dismissed them. The Ōtākou *rūnanga* assembly has still chosen not to take up its quota, preferring to protect the stock. The government minister responsible for fishing rights is felt not to care for Māori views. He's the one who will arbitrate.

Riki's own fishing territory is one hundred miles south at Bluff. We look at the map. The straits between there and Stewart Island are notorious for vicious wind and tide. They get only about a hundred days of safe fishing a year, and Riki often takes risks in weather that regularly brings fifty-to-sixty-foot waves. For the first time ever, Riki's boat lost a trawl net yesterday, the glittering catch cast free. It will cost them thousands of dollars to replace. The flatfish should never run out though, he says. But again, quotas are set in distant Wellington, and there is little desire from there to listen to localized conditions. Māori fishermen are allocated one-third of the regional quota.

"Have you ever been asked for your views?" I ask.

"Never," he rolls his eyes. "If we catch the wrong fish, we're also supposed to pay the government."

⁓

Across from Bluff, though, is the place for the annual cultural event central to Ngāi Tahu. Māori have always been part cultivators, part hunters, gatherers, and fishers. The wild harvest, *mahinga kai*, has cultural significance, as it is about obtaining unique foods from specific locations at particular times, which are then shared, bringing people together. On Rakiura / Stewart Island, it is the annual harvest of *tītī* in late autumn that does precisely this.

Over that dinner of *tītī* muttonbirds in gravy, Ngāi Tahu elder Edward Ellison, tall and balding, cream shirt buttoned at wrists, explains. The 1840 Treaty of Waitangi legally bound in agreement the British crown and Māori chiefs. It allowed the colonists to settle, and granted Māori full, exclusive, and undisturbed possession of their lands, estates, forests, and fisheries. Despite the apparently unequivocal language, room for interpretation was later assumed. There is long-standing skepticism across New Zealand over whether Māori can manage their own resources, despite the irony that ecological problems are widespread elsewhere in modern society. The harvest of young sooty shearwaters, *Puffinus griseus*, between the beginning of April and end of May takes place on thirty-six *tītī* islands around Rakiura, and *whānau* extended families hold exclusive rights to birding areas. These *manu* are deeply valued: once allocated, they stay with each family forever.

The shearwater is an apex marine predator, spending much of the year over the South and Central Pacific. Shearwaters nest in southern New Zealand, also in Australian Tasmania, New South Wales, and Victoria. The population of these dark brown petrels is reckoned to be forty to sixty million birds. Each year Māori families spend four to six weeks down on their *manu*, harvesting the young birds from burrows at night, and plucking them during the day.

The trip revitalizes everyone, explains Eleanor, rubbing delicate hands. Even though the work is physical, people can look ten years younger by the end of the trip. Mobile phone contact is only possible from the roof, and so everyone gets used to the personal reconnections, the being there rather than not somewhere else. The harvest is thus not just about gathering food, it is about reaffirming family, friends, wider social links as well as ancestral ones, and being out in a wild place that helps wash away other pressing troubles.

But there is a problem. There seems to be a long-term decline in *tītī*.

Henrik Moller of the University of Otago began working with Māori on Rakiura in 1994.[3] The combination of scientific methods and knowledge and *māturanga* traditional knowledge had led to new insights, including one on climate change that is yet to be accepted by the scientific community. The research relationship has not always been easy, as preconceptions on methods and worldviews differ. But trust was steadily built. Birders claim that there is a greater breeding density closer to the edge of islands, and that fledging birds emerge from burrows earlier on western sides of islands: both were shown scientifically to be true. Birders prefer to take fat chicks, but scientists are troubled: they know that survival from fledging to breeding age is closely correlated with chick weight. Recently, fat chicks have become rarer, but the reason is not known. The scientists now acknowledge that birders' *māturanga* relates not just to the harvest but to a wider understanding of ecological patterns and relationships. Birders then took a great leap and offered Henrik diaries that had been kept for up to fifty years, many of which contained details of weather, tallies, harvest effort, and unusual weather.

This unique data led to a breakthrough. Statistical analyses revealed a link between harvests and the onset of El Niño years. Climatologists with knowledge of the Southern Oscillation had never before made a link to traditional knowledge of birders. Crucially, it was found that low harvests in April–May predict the onset of an El Niño shift later in the same year. It is not known why, but something must be happening out in the Pacific prior to breeding. El Niño changes the abundance of anchovy and sardines; *tītī* can dive down to sixty meters' depth to catch prey. It could be food; it could be wind patterns. Birds that lock wings to travel enormous migratory distances must somehow find their breeding sites, and be well-enough fed to make it.

At the time of my visit, Henrik is saying an El Niño is on the way. But no one believes him. Later, in November, he sends an e-mail at the time of severe weather conditions in eastern Australia and the washing up of thousands of *tītī* along coastlines. Everyone will be helpless if the problem originates in the vast Pacific. The El Niño was going to be a bad one.

These shearwaters survive by ocean navigation, as do other important wild foods. The freshwater short- and long-fin eels are important wild food. They too engage in their own *heke*, or migratory journeys, traveling out from freshwater rivers and lakes to swim to the waters of Samoa, Fiji, and Tonga to breed at about twenty years of age. The elvers' return takes six months. But where coastal wetlands have been lost, or rivers blocked, or others polluted with dairy farm runoff, the eels cannot now escape to sea or return. Many habitats are permanently amended or lost. At Lake Ellesmere on the Banks Peninsula, Ngāi Tahu, who have rights to the lake bed but not the inflowing waters, have opened up the water to the sea. But how to collaborate with dairy farmers who have become increasingly intensive to remain competitive on the world market? How to find a new model that allows farming and wild foods to coexist? Edward observes that his aunt Mary, born in 1899, said it was the *mahinga kai* foods that got them through the depression of the 1930s.

The value of wild food has never declined: sixty species are still eaten and shared. "If the land is changed," he says, "then this also changes the way people see themselves."

Many hundreds still go to the islands off Rakiura. The traditions remain strong, and thus the transfer of knowledge is not at threat. But Edward notes that there is much to do elsewhere. Advocacy and involvement in environmental issues is toward habitat restoration, particularly of inland waterways and lakes, and recovery of native vegetation. Some 15 percent of the population of New Zealand is Māori. For many, alienation from the land has created social and identity problems, and Māori in general are recognized as suffering more health problems than the rest of the population. Government chose to call its policy "Closing the Gap," but this echoes policies elsewhere: indigenous people can be saved by being more like, in this case, the *pakeha*—those of European descent. Ngāi Tahu, though, have grown in number from fifteen hundred in 1901 to nearly fifty thousand in the early 2000s. There is much that can be done.

After our walk along Harrington Point Road, Tahu, Megan, and I go in search of blue penguins. At Pilots Beach we see pathways pattered through the grass, and burrows under lupine bushes. But no gift of yellow eyes peering out. No seals or sea lions on the deserted beach, either. All is quiet. This was once Measly Beach, where Māori afflicted by the 1835 measles epidemic came to bathe, and die, and also Hobart Town Beach, where whalers set up their huts and homes. We climb up to Taiaroa Head and its eighty-meter cliffs facing eastward over ten thousand miles of ocean. It's the wrong time of year for *toroa*, the royal albatross: they are out in the Pacific sailing the trade winds, their own long-lived narratives of migration on three-meter wingspans. Here more spotted shags are circling, sweeping up on the wind, rendered motionless, winging wide again. Waves are pounding rocks below. We're looking toward Chile, but see no dusky dolphins, no southern rights or humpback whales. Inside the harbor the water is many shades of gray and sandy yellow; outside the Pacific is pure aquamarine. There's nothing like this color at all in our own northern seas. The clouds are breaking up, whipped sideways by this howling wind. This bay is *Waiwhakaheka*, the place where the bodies are thrown into the sea.

———

Later Khyla takes me over the top road of rolling hills and widely spaced farms to meet with Hugh Campbell again. We set off for Blueskin Bay to go floundering with John Fairweather, rural sociologist from Lincoln University, who's been doing this from his gimcrack crib overlooking the water for a good half century.

The boat is lowered into the estuary, and across the mudflats comes the wheeping of waders. The oars creak in the rowlocks and the sun drops to the edge of the distant inland hills. The wind is direct, sharp. We step out on the sticky mud shore, wavelets slapping quietly. John takes one end of the nylon net and rows out in a great semicircle back to the shore fifty meters further up. He's comfortable in his white boat, out on these waters so many years, wearing chest waders and brown woolen hat, sharp gray beard with no mustache. I've borrowed a battered red jacket and Wellington boots. We pull the white nylon ropes attached to the gray net, now clogged with a fine crop of sea lettuce, fingers numb with salty cold. The flounders are identical in hue to the mud, distinguished only by two surprised eyes.

John unsheathes a curved knife and pulls a wooden block from the red box. He guts each flounder, slices off the head, food now for the squabbling gulls. We set the nets several times, and the sun flashes free of cloud for several minutes to light the hills over Doctors Point. The cold waters are briefly golden. Waders peep and cry again. At his lodge, John gives me the blue feather of a pigeon. Later, in the way of these things, I gave it to an elderly gypsy in Essex, and tell him about those marshes and mudflats. Hugh grills the flounders that evening, which we eat with a fine red wine. These are things that should go onward the same.[4]

On the plane north, I sit next to an elderly woman from a farm in Middlemarch, who says at the end of our conversation, "We still think of England as home."

Khyla visits. I meet her at the rail station, and we sit in my garden drinking tea among summer flowers. At her home, it is wet and wintery. Here bees and hoverflies buzz the quiet afternoon away. On the way back, people stare at her striking blue *mata* on neck and jaw.

Then Edward e-mails to say it has been a wet spring too. The paddocks are now unusually green. Hugh and John are continuing their work on creating sustainable food systems for the South Island, reclaiming both modern and traditional practices, of interweaving the farmed and wilder parts of the landscape.

2

MOUNTAIN
Huangshan, China

62° West of Date Line

The land was vacant for more than a thousand years. Then the people came back. They walked out of mists, through bamboo groves, up granite steps, and into the heavens. And looked down on seas of clouds where ancient pines grew from rock faces, and waterfalls poured past pagodas offering green tea and noodles. For centuries, only painters and poets were permitted by emperors; for the last half century only party leaders came, also keeping the mountains to themselves. But Huangshan, these Yellow Mountains of Anhui, made famous by those artists, was opened up in the 1990s, now declared a World Heritage Site. It has been reclaimed. A typical day may see ten thousand walkers, during the holiday weeks in October and May up to thirty thousand.

It is said you will not want to visit any other mountains once you come here. Not entirely true: you will do if you want to be alone. Yet Huangshan has sacred beauty combined with a very public claiming. The tops are not high, the seventy-two granite peaks reachable, the highest, Lotus Peak, at 1,860 meters. Like the Great Wall and Yangtze River, Huangshan is now one of the great symbols of China. And now it is available not just on silk and canvas. People are coming to the land. It was Rob Macfarlane who planted the idea of walking these mountains, but we couldn't match up timetables. I went alone; he was to go west to sacred Minya Konka instead.[1]

Long before the Tang emperor Xuan Zang gave Huangshan its name in the eighth century, enduring traditions in Chinese landscape painting were emerging. Confucius had said that "artistic skill is the nearest equivalent to the truth." Landscapes and sceneries were not to be copied; rather painting was a way to approach nature, to link natural beauty with wisdom and knowledge. Writing about 300 BC, Zhuangzi promoted ideas of being in nature to discover inner tranquillity. In the Song dynasty, thirteen hundred years later, Guo Xi indicated that landscapes should be "marchable, visible, accessible, and livable." Meet these criteria, and a landscape would be a masterpiece. And so emerged traditions in which landscapes had mountains, but also roads and tracks; streams and rivers, but also fishing boats; trees but also woodpiles; lakes, but also pavilions and arched bridges.

Above all there was blank space in compositions. Space for imagination: around fish, birds, trees, between foreground and distant hills, all giving the sense, as Lin Ci has put it, that "there was a presence of an ever existing landscape." In this way, the *shanshui* mountain and water style of landscape painting came to fuse remote peaks and foreground detail, to put people and nature together harmoniously, to show lands crossed by tourists, traders, and poets, among morning mists, cold forests, beckoning valleys, wide skies. They provoke a longing for the tranquillity of the wild, nature shaped and used by people, landscapes that offer a deep spiritual connection.[2]

I step on the world's fastest train not far from the Pacific Ocean. The gleaming maglev tube of glass and metal accelerates to 430 kilometers per hour, bulleting past so many hundreds of forty-story tower blocks, in the shadows of which old houses and quadrangles of distinction are being bulldozed to piles of bricks. History is also disappearing beneath raised highways. The train lunges past intensively cultivated fields and polytunnels, the region's vegetable basket, and on to the city center. On the metro are beggars sitting by live TV ads. The young are comfortable, the old weather-beaten, dragging sacks and plastic-wrapped goods, looking bewildered. Men in shiny ill-fitting suits stand beside the young displaying many global brands. At the railway station square, groups of people wait on concrete plinths and piles of sacking. High up are great public screens, for advertising rather than political slogans. A winter's sun filters through low cloud. I had been here nearly thirty years before, and only Shanghai's grand railway station seems the same. Marble halls, glass frontage with tall windows, a plush waiting room for the military, another for the rest with hundreds of seats. There is a subdued anticipation, then a sign, and everyone rushes down corridors to the platform. Then, it was a clunking, gushing steam train; now another modern one.

⸻

Shanghai at that time in the early 1980s was gray and wet. I walked through the backstreets near Fuxing Park at the heart of the old French Quarter. In the market, penned ducks awaited their end, and women in rubber aprons gutted fish while musty grain sacks were loaded onto trucks. Redbrick and gray apartment blocks surrounded tiny courtyards and groups gathered from the rain under large black umbrellas. On the sheen of the wet streets, there were no cars. Not one. Just many cyclists serene under plain plastic capes. Often, people would simply stop to look at us, the new outsiders, curious about what changes a new political era was going to bring. On the terrace of the old hotel, net curtains billowing, we sipped strong coffee and listened to a waitress playing on the grand piano. That night we stayed in and watched a quintet play traditional folk music, and in my notebook I naively wrote *I shall carry their image forever.* Time has passed, and I cannot remember them at all.

Now I had come to talk about an agreement with Nanjing University, founded in AD 258. We visited a new campus, out in the dense mists of the same neighborhood as the new MG car factory. Controversy in the UK when this symbol was sold to Nanjing Motors, but now the company advertises the MG as *England's Best Car.* The campus is carved out of fields and farms. Broad boulevards, ranks of dorms and blocks of labs, and a giant library. By entrance pillars four stories high, bicycles are parked in long lines. Thirty students in two facing lines pass footballs to each other in the fog. Back then, we had an official visit to the main university, before an evening of illusion. Those notebook pages have many dry notes about departments, courses, and students. But there was nothing on the still painful memories of the Cultural Revolution. Between 1966 and 1976, the university lost it entire stock of textbooks, two hundred million burned by fervent believers of only one single small text. The challenge for those students was the complete lack of materials and information.

The main campus in the city still has wide boulevards and red-tiled pavilions. Now they are hemmed by skyscrapers that house all academic departments. The evening meal is twenty-five courses, many opportunities to try terrapins and lake fish, portions of chicken feet, duck, and hairy crab. Red wine today, but then smiles and the slow twisting of the cap of a bottle of mao-tai spirit. Thirty years earlier, we the youth who thought we knew it all became cross when authorities tried to force on us too many tourist sights rather than factory visits, or entertainments that were falsely designed. In many ways, it was good to be naive. Life is clearer when young, before you start to navigate the gray areas in between.

I recall in Suzhou an excruciating dance and song evening of Western music, yet it wasn't ill-meant. The day before we had crowded into a Nanjing theater for a magic show. Outside the road was crammed by a mad scrabble for tickets, and the auditorium all of a chaos of active participation and thick with shouting and cigarette smoke, a girl cut in half and appearing seconds later behind us, smiling and waving. In the raffle, a friend with winning program number was called onstage in front of TV cameras that had mysteriously appeared. How must this have been for an audience only five years out of the upheavals of the Cultural Revolution, and watching agog as the Gang of Four had gone to open trial earlier that year in front of 880 representatives of the people. Jiang Qing, Mao's last wife, was one of two sentenced to death. As she was dragged away, she shouted, "Revolution is glorious. Revolution is no crime!" China then was so completely unknown to us all; the rest of the world must have seemed just as much a mystery for our hosts.

The dawn comes up wet and clears the dense fog that had enveloped Nanjing for days. The bus waits in a sodden car park for the last of the travelers. A woman wrapped in plastic sweeps up rubbish. A crew-cut man rides by on a bike, cigarette glowing in the gloom. The wind catches his blue cape and sweeps him into the traffic. I make a dash for the nearest toilet, down among nearby flats. Two sets of Chinese characters—male, female. I choose wrongly. The toilets are entirely public, as they were then: no separate cubicles, just a row of seats. When the bus leaves the city, tail lights glisten on the road, and cyclists all in bright capes sailing on and somehow the host of vehicles keeps on missing them. A quarter century ago, everyone wore blue or green Mao suits; today the traffic lights have blinking time counters. On the bus there is much chatting into mobile phones. There is no uniform in our group, except that everyone is smartly dressed, pink-padded jacket, black leather and roll-neck sweater, hiking gear, city gear, all sorts. One thing is common: everyone smiles. The driver seems content not to use windshield wipers, and through the fog of condensation we pass raised arterial roads, golden gingkos and avenues of green plane trees.

The hours pass. A man and woman are standing in a field, looking to the horizon; nearby a new road has four lanes and simply ceases at a ditch. In every village, all houses have solar water-heaters. On a two-lane road a woman sweeps the roadside, alone. Houses are wet and gray. A flock of ducks absorbs into a wood, a lake is clogged with water hyacinth, and we pass fields of patchwork vegetables and others white with lotus flowers. Walking alongside ditches are farmworkers hefting heavy loads. A chimney belches black smoke over yellow paddy and spindly poplars. Inside the bus, the video is switched to karaoke, and the passengers sing along in unison. Then as we approach Tangkou, the driver changes to *Crouching Tiger, Hidden Dragon*, and Ang Lee's tale of the hidden mysteries that lie beneath the surface of people accompanies us up to the hill station. The rain still patters down, but now on bright autumnal maples and cherries, and quivering bamboo forests.

Tangkou reminds me of hill stations I have known: Dehra Dun with bed tea in dull light before a dry Himalayan dawn; Kericho among the Kenyan tea estates dripping with water; Murree's cliff of wooden houses in Pakistan; Mendi's highlands of Papua wrapped in the smoke of grassland fires. Each one relentlessly cold, though all in the tropics or subtropics. Here the shower argues between scorching hot or ice cold, but the lunch of noodles and meats is good. We are to spend the afternoon in the valleys and bamboo forests where the dueling martial arts masters of *Crouching Tiger* fought. Ang Lee chose here to film his surprise hit in 2000, and it's now an additional reason for people to visit. We leave Tangkou's sodden valley of rushing rivers and autumn trees in full blaze of reds, oranges, and greens fading to yellow, and a driver in a hurry takes the two of us and two of the Nanjing group to Phoenix Valley and the Nine Dragons Valley. Then we find we can slow down. It's autumn: not the end of summer or the beginning of winter. Just autumn.

My navigator Miss Guo tells me that during the previous month's annual holiday week you can hardly move on these paths as lines of people shuffle up the valley and then back down. She is above average height, with long black hair, frame-free glasses, wears a tartan scarf wrapped tightly above an aquamarine jacket. The valley is quiet today. In the drizzle, occasional visitors crouch under pale blue umbrellas, or wrap themselves in translucent capes, and then snake upstream, around still ponds. On a slab of granite are three red pictographs, and we pat them four times, left hand for men, right for women, for luck and long life. Yet the symbol dates from only 1990: new rituals are being created. Elsewhere are ancient poets' huts and lookouts that give out on these burbling streams and bamboo bowed with moisture. The rocks themselves are animated. Four women lying in the river; a great pig, very much a pig and not a rock, gazes down on them. A seal, turtle, dragon's son, and on the roofs of pagodas, *shi yi* jigsaw animals of all types. There are real animals in these humid forests too: black bear, wild dog, civet, boar, Sitka deer, and the clouded leopard. Things happened here too—a princess came, a dragon lay down. People are here for both the nature and the stories. I find I'm drawn to take two kinds of photos—those deliberately with no people, misty mountains, red-gold trees among the green bamboo and pines, limpid ponds, water falling across the porphyritic granite. And others of people, usually posing for pictures themselves. Every spot demands an electronic statement of record.

At the entrance to Nine Dragons Valley, one of the most famed waterfall complexes in China, where golden carp swim in a pond fringed with dripping camellia, I find other signs. A grove of bamboo with names and symbols carved on every one. It has become frowned upon to carve names on trees at home, and old carvings have warped as trees have expanded with age. But here the filigree carvings look entirely appropriate. Much graffiti is about establishing identity; some also sets out to shock; some simply to decorate. Further up the valley by an infinity pool that leaps away into the sky, a chain fence by the path is clipped with thousands of brass locks, each with names etched into the surface patina, some burnished with rust. The cool water is itself clear to the riverbed, reflecting only serene trees and gray clouds.

The water is not so pure as to have no fish. Insects disappear and ripples silently advance on the shore. At the Mellin ruins a board indicates that a prime minister of the Qing dynasty studied here. At the valley head, in a corner of pink feldspar and quartz washed smooth by a dozen trails of water, I hold up a stone dragon's egg, fashioned by these mists and mountains. Back down the valley, guides with megaphones now shout their stories that ebb and flow across the hillsides, far beyond the huddled groups that wetly stand and listen. Still water drips, splashes, flows over rocks and stones, cleansed by the forests. Side valleys are filled with smoky clouds. That night, I put on extra clothes and pull up the only blanket, listening to the rain drizzle on the trees outside. When finally it stops, the eaves drip-drip onto the terrace in the darkness. A cock crows, the drips continue; dogs begin competitive barking.

—⟨⟨⟨⟨ ⟩⟩⟩⟩—

The day already seems old when we pull up chairs for breakfast of rice soup, hot relishes, and salty brown eggs hard-boiled in tea. Outside still only a half light, and constant dripping. Before we catch the first of two buses, the dawn's gloaming reveals the hill station and forested hillsides wreathed in mist. At Yungu gate, it has cleared, and bus drivers in air-pilot-style uniforms stand proud beside a rank of new coaches, hands thrust in pockets. The seven-kilometer walk will raise us up a kilometer to White Goose Ridge station through bamboo, oak, chestnut, and pine forest. The path is stone, the steps shallow at the start. One thing is soon clear. This is not a solitary Saturday morning ramble. Others have come. It is land democracy at work. People are doing this because they can, and because not long ago they could not.

As we walk, we are overtaken by four men carrying a large metal pump. We pass a thin man with gray hair, blue jacket, and shirt unbuttoned for air, with four swinging sacks of grain on two yokes held in cross pattern. I had thought the going was getting hard. The clouds close in, the steps now steep like a staircase. Then wiry men with a steel girder appear. They too have shoulders of iron. The beam is six meters long, and each has a split bamboo on his shoulders to take the weight. Ingenious double yokes and twisted ropes mean that when the men walk in a line the girder itself is aligned with the direction of travel. But when maneuvering around steep bends, they can twist and still take the weight, forcing this great lump of metal up a thousand meters of altitude. Soon we come upon four men carrying another, and then a much longer one hoisted by a dozen. They heave and haul, and chant their count, *yi, er, san*, and push and grab another step, and then another. It is the visitors bringing money who are giving this local economy a boost: they smile and joke, and seem to show no animosity toward us, the walkers with small backpacks. Everything in this mountain economy is hauled up or down by them. The laundry, the noodles in pots, bottles of water, beers, roof timbers, wastes. Everything. Enough to silence any of our creaking joints.

We apparently pass the Fascinating Pavilion, and Two Cats Watching a Mouse. The famed domes and bosses are out there, and we cannot see them in the mist. But even as we climb, there are hints. A bulging slab of granite a hundred meters high, a single pine gripped on its perch by improbably large roots. Green forested slopes, another pine on a weathered pillar, then all disappear again. A young engraver stands by a stall, brass locks laid on his table. There are many wooden carvings and bright walking sticks. On we climb, along with more porters carrying wicker baskets of rice and meat. By the time we reach the top at 1,770 meters, we're on smiling terms with all the Nanjing bus party. We have to accept the clouds and this shrunken landscape, and dismiss the hope. Yet this will make the later revelation all the more astonishing. Perhaps the clouds will roll back like theater curtains precisely because we are calm. But maybe not. We have to accept things as they are.

We settle for lunch in a café perched over the edge of a cliff. Mountain tasting—unlike Santoka, we have more than water. Hot noodles over cloud and thin air. Resting our feet, we eat, and then take a cup of local Maofeng tea. In the corner, music videos proclaim on the TV. Photographs on the walls seem to mock; they're of views that could be here. But weren't.

Wrote Bashō:
> In a way
> It was fun
> Not to see Mount Fuji
> In foggy rain.[3]

Soon we will explore many of the fifty kilometers of paths that wind through pine forests, over humpbacked bridges, and around vertical faces again decorated with clinging and distinctly individual pines. In the clouds, all is hushed. No singing birds, no bellowing deer, just wide spaces of silence and the murmuring of visitors emerging from the mist and then absorbed by the rain.

We walk to Mount Huangshan Peak, and also Beginning to Believe Peak, Refreshing Terrace, Flower Grown Out of a Writing Brush Rock, and Monkey Watching the Sea. The paths and steps twist into tunnels, over ridges, down and then up steep slopes. All sense of direction is quickly lost in this cloud. We stop at Black Tiger Pine, a Huangshan pine. Hundreds of pictures are taken, people standing formally in front of a wall of cloud. All are proof of the visit, some kind of mark being left. And there are others too. Near Cloud Dispelling Pavilion, where we wait with no luck for the dispelling, I count the locks that have been attached to a chain-link fence by a great drop. There are sixty sections with about forty locks on each, all with names engraved. We were here, they all say. Through such gestures we believe we can influence the world. Good business for the engravers, too, at forty yuan a piece. Somewhere in the abyss will be the keys, thrown over symbolically.

I had thought that ten thousand people on these mountains on a weekend day would be too much. But I was quite wrong.

That this invasion is to be celebrated was confirmed when we came to the sprawling Beihai Hotel looking out over its North Sea of cloud. This is where the national leaders came to stay. They had spectacular views from behind bulletproof glass. We can just see the sitting room through panoramic windows and elegant curtains; large armchairs in a row, the ceiling richly decorated with gold. We are down below, beneath the sight lines as if sheep beyond a ha-ha. Gods up there, the rest mere mortals. A large red billboard depicts a smiling Deng Xiaoping. At the time we came on that youth visit, the public was not permitted to climb this mountain. Since then it has become China's Kinder Scout or Yosemite. As far as I can make out, every other walker on these hills is Chinese. Huangshan is no new creation. It is one of five sacred mountain areas in China, with millennia of poems and paintings produced for public consumption. People knew these places through art, not experience. Now they come and take their own photos. You cannot argue with that.

Today, though, Dogen's eight-hundred-year-old koan seems appropriate: *There are mountains hidden in the sky. There are mountains hidden in mountains. There are mountains hidden in hiddenness.* The clouds and mist are in, the pictures on café walls and in guidebooks could be of a mythical place, or perhaps heaven. At first, it's hard not to be disappointed. Yet this is good enough. We have climbed a kilometer up into these clouds, and visitors mostly remain shadowy ghosts in the mist, lines of blue or yellow capes advancing to a sacred place, then to another. We too walk from place to place. These are special mountains: just water and mountain.[4]

Technology has come too, another dramatic change from the early 1980s: mobile phones, music, headphones, texts bleeping. Some visitors are dressed for a mountain, to my eyes; yet others swing plastic bags as if on an afternoon stroll in a city park, with formal footwear, jackets and ties. At first, the temptation is to feel superior, but this is wrong. We should cheer. People of all types willing to spend a couple of days on a mountain range half as high again as anything in Britain. They'll go home changed by it too. Every guidebook or web advice I have seen, though, is sniffy, suggesting the experience is diminished by the numbers of people. How often we frame being in nature in terms of opposites, of not being in the other modern world. As if we had escaped from jail, but only for a short remission. We say we will get away from it all, escape the rat race, forget the pressures, relieve the stress, knowing we have to go back. Here, though, is a hint of the welcome combination of this place and the other.

Then something extraordinary. We check into our rooms at a small hotel bedded into granite, thinking ahead to the predawn rise tomorrow. Through the room and corridor windows, I see some blue.

Guo appears: she's seen it too.

We dash back to the nearest trail, bubbling, pointing. We see a hint, half a minute of a thousand-foot drop and hills emerging from cottony clouds. It is almost impossible to believe this was just beyond us all day. A precipice dropping several thousand feet to forest and a tiny river. But, then, the mist closes up again, and we wait. And rain starts, and we wait yet more, hoping for another break. Dogen said we should see an ounce and a pound with an equal eye. Two people huddle, under a single umbrella, looking away from each other.[5]

And then it all unfolds, and the mountainscape is such a surprise it is almost impossible to believe. I had thought Huangshan were just mountains people liked to visit, that had charm, some history, and were solely a destination.

Now I understand. Above the seas of clouds are domes of granite with towers, slabs of glistening rock, yet more towers. Bright green pines sprout from vertical rock faces, then twist skyward. Distant hills pop out of the mist, hovering in the sky. Walkways earlier crossed with ease now are above terrifyingly thin air. The drops stop the heart. Foregrounds dark, mid-grounds of hills somehow avoiding gravity, backgrounds of pale blue promontories of sloping forests. An ocean of cumulus, far below us. Through the green pines, a pavilion perches on top of a vertical face of pink granite, where we had stood so casually wrapped in cotton. We scamper through tunnels and over ravines wide enough for only a single person, down steps steeper than in a house. And we keep smiling at these wonders of all this world. To enjoy the magnificence of most mountains, you look up. In Huangshan, you look down upon the peaks and clouds.

The land makes us think of ourselves, here on a rock face and its thousand-year-old carved steps. Or there under a pine, or misty in the enclosing cloud where every sound is damped and I feel we must do no more than whisper. And then the clouds close in for good, and heavy rain is hard upon us. I zip up jacket, and walk on. The spectacle is perhaps greater because it had been denied for most of the day, and we long gave up worrying that we were missing something. One guide had said, this is the first day it's been wrapped in cloud for, well, ages. It's been sunny all month. Just like the captains of whale- and dolphin-watching trips who state that this is the first day they can ever remember when the animals did not come. Yet blank days are a central part of engagement with the world. Go to a zoo or gallery if you don't want one.

Near the red *no smoking* signs painted on the ground, a group of weary porters stand and smoke, their loads of large windows lashed to bamboo with green ropes. The corner of one pane is cracked.

At dinner of spicy dishes, Guo is receiving texts. She has no siblings, but does have a sister. It's another generational change, cousins now like sisters and brothers to this generation of single children. Her cousin was married today to a doctor. She sighs. I get texts from home too. The busy restaurant is alive with chatter, the hotel packed, wet capes shaken, corridors full of comings and goings and shouted greetings, warm food and cold beer, anticipation now of dawn and sunrise over the mountains. In my room, the phone rings as I write up my notes. A woman asks in passable English, "Foot massage, sir?"

In the pitch dark, we drink coffee and pour hot water into pots of noodles, and then set off with flashlight shining back from the close cloud. It is 5 a.m., and raining. We ghosts all wear clear capes, stepping gingerly along the wet steps. It's better not to know in this gloom about those precipices and vertical drops. Black umbrellas of pine loom by skeletons of Huangshan oak, chestnut, ancient juniper, dogwood, and rowan. There are 1,650 species of plants here, a third trees. A number of individual juniper and pine are older than a thousand years. I wonder about the clouded leopard, hungry in these hills. The sky becomes slightly less than black, and now gray advances. In an hour we no longer need torches. On a peak is a hotel with a geodesic sphere on its roof, and red computer-display pictographs are bright in the foggy gloom. They give the percentage chance of seeing a sunrise.

I look around. It has to be about zero.

We're here to watch the sun appear, but the gathered figures in yellow, blue, and pink will be disappointed. Hollow-faced visitors shed capes in the hotel lobby, the air a mixture of sweat and rain. Though we are utter strangers, we feel joined by this common experience. A smile, a nod, a wriggling out or in of over-clothes in the murky foyer, a wish for an open café for something warm to drink at this dawn. Outside the gloom offers to lift, and crowds gather with cameras. Now comes a mountain wind, whipped up and bringing a harshness to the morning, tearing at clothes and hair. Capes snap and fingers freeze. But the wind shifts the cloud, and there's a collective gasp and a rush, and there before us is a view of an astonishing landscape. Peaks jut out of seas of cloud, pines by steps carved into domes of granite, mists wreathing a pavilion. And then we walk.

It takes us five hours to reach Jade Welcoming Pine. On west-facing slopes, winter trade winds set in, and the temperature plummets. Thousand-feet slabs of granite look at first untouched, but then my eye is drawn to lines of tiny steps stitched into zigs and zags with the precision of the prints of some deliberate creature. There are sixty thousand steps carved into Huangshan's orogenic granite, some cut fifteen hundred years ago. Under Lotus Peak, we lean into wind in a gully, and above are the turtle and snake rocks guarding this entrance to heaven's gate. The steps are slick with ice. It is November and there could be snow to cover the land like the clouds and mist. Only a low stone wall separates me from hell. I am reacquainted with vertigo. I look at my feet as I walk, and try to forget there is a view. No whispering winds today: they batter us, roaring over mountain faces, tearing at loose clothes and capes, tugging whole children. Hands search for holds on the rock, happily finding metal rails. Progress is slow.

And then a couple of men in suits stroll past. Coming toward us is a group of gray-haired women in street footwear. The ice, the drop. They smile.

The Welcoming Pine, Ying Ke Song, is near to the top of Yuping aerial tramway. Queues jostle for photos in front of the thousand-year-old pine tree. Like a cascade or slant-style bonsai, its purpose is contemplative. Everyone seems to be following Bashō's famous call on his narrow road to the deep north, when he also wrote *go to the pine if you want to learn about the pine*. This one and others, somehow surviving the punishment of the axe for centuries.

At the shack, the coolers are packed with green-and-red cans of beer. Above is a gold plaque with Chinese and English lettering: *civilisation seller*, it appropriately states. I had a strong sense we were creating something as we had walked step by step. Perhaps this is why so many people wish to have the formal photographs. Not of the place, but of the people at the place. A young soldier erect in gray-green greatcoat waves red-raw hands to marshal the eager crowd. I take pictures of people taking pictures in the biting wind. Perhaps it is all as simple as this: a personal experience in nature is all that matters, especially if the place itself has some kind of special historical or cultural significance. Some may appear ill-prepared, tightly holding the hands of tiny children. But they are here, rather than there.

We look down, and see all the steps are icy on this side of the mountain. We decide on the cable car. We wait seventy-five minutes in a remarkably patient queue, and then see only five instead of six people are being loaded per cab. Near the front of the queue it is starkly clear why. The ascending cars are swaying wildly. We are trapped, and climb aboard. There is worse. The six-minute journey has been slowed to thirty. Too much time to be in this wind. The vertical drop is 760 meters, and we descend alongside a sheer cliff face, giving us all a vivid sense of impermanence. In the battering wind, there is too much to dwell upon, and far too much time. It is a lesson in slow terror.

We make it. Yet the queue at the Mercy Light Temple at the bottom is enormous, again patient, snaking around metal fences and down the steps. Tired and edgy, we sit down to watch the squabbling Tibetan macaques in the trees. I cannot see that all the visitors will get up today. Or perhaps want to, if they only knew. The ground is reassuringly solid.

We walk out some kilometers along a riverbank. Leather-faced laborers queue for soup, and sit on the metal beds of a cramped dormitory, the outer walls splashed with dirt and oil. They are impassive as we walk by. The bridge over the river will bring many identical days for them. The sound of poverty will be the long hours worked beneath the faded red and gold pavilion on the only spur remaining of the ancient bridge. The ground is covered with a yellow layer of maple leaves, the trees bare. We anticipate something to eat, but find ourselves diverted to a teahouse. Tubs of green teas are opened, and hot water poured for tasting. Stomachs grumble. Eyebrows are raised, lips pursed. The bus awaits, its engine off.

Much later, back in Nanjing, I am taken for a proper foot massage. Painful tight spots in calves and feet are probed. Both women are from Anhui, and left school at fifteen years of age, drawn to the bright city from those mountains. I catch the night bus back to Shanghai Pudong, and doze on metal benches in the gleaming airport. It does not matter how many days or hours are spent in nature. The one act is to be there, perhaps to forget and find ourselves, as Dogen observed. The Huangshan landscape has been largely unchanged for a couple of thousand years. Another reason why the people come.

The land changes us all.

3

DESERT COAST
Murujuga (Burrup), Australia

64° West of Date Line

We went walking with sharks. We didn't intend to, yet at low tide the boat beached in the glittering bay, and we jumped in to tug it across the sandbar. Dark shadows of reef sharks raced in. We kicked up sand and water as they circled. The sky was clear, the water warm, our legs exposed. We were in the Indian Ocean, kilometers off Australia's northwestern shore and a fraction north of the Tropic of Capricorn. A land and sea continuously inhabited for 50,000 years, less the last 140 or so. The Yaburara left petroglyphs and rock art, but were massacred in 1868. Related groups survived, but the Yaburara themselves are gone. They might have known what to do about reef sharks around your ankles. Perhaps they could have made things right.

The mining region of the Burrup peninsula, fifteen hundred kilometers north of Perth, is also known as the Dampier archipelago. Its proper name is Murujuga, hip bone sticking out. It's a parched land of boulder slopes and ridges, steep-sided valleys and spinifex plateaus containing perhaps a million petroglyphs. When modern hominids walked out of Africa, their first route was down the coastlines of Asia to the continent of Australia. Then over fifty thousand years, they created the greatest concentration of rock art in the world, among their campsites, quarries, shell middens, standing stones, and rock shelters. They watched the edge of land and sea ebb and flow. In the last ice age, fourteen thousand years ago, sea levels were 130 meters lower, and there were no islands off this shore with sharp continental shelf. The forty-two islands of today's archipelago were simply hilltops, today's underwater trenches dry valleys. By seven thousand years ago, the sea had risen to today's levels, and many settlements and rock motifs had gone underwater.[1]

Fifty millennia in one place suggests a lived experience of deep time. Fresh water must always have been scarce, but there was the advantage of being at the edge of many habitats. From the sea, they harvested fish, mollusks, turtles and their eggs, dugong, and shellfish from the intertidal zones. From the land, wallaby, kangaroo, other macropods, emu, thylacine, and more recently dingo. Acacia and eucalypt trees gave resin and seeds, and there were edible tubers of bush potato and pencil yam. And finally, a grass that gives the whole region its desert character: spinifex, technically a grass of sand dunes, but also the name used for the spiny-leaved *Triodia* porcupine grass, the seeds of which were collected and ground to make cakes, the resin used as an adhesive for spears, the grass itself used for shelter and fish traps, and burned for smoke signals, as it gives off dense black smoke.

This mode of living could still be the same, we might suppose, had not settlers steered to these shores three hundred years ago. In 1699, buccaneer William Dampier sailed his *Roebuck* here on a global circumnavigation, named islands and bays, and wrote of smoke rising from the land. Burning is a sign: it indicates that the land is healthy, both used and managed. No place on this continent was not fashioned and kept productive by traditional land management. Burning is often called firestick farming, and it is instructive that Aboriginals adopted the imported term farming, as they never separated ideas of the wild from the domesticated or managed. Settlers, though, were never able to appreciate that active management helped a dry land.

Deborah Bird Rose of Macquarie University has observed that the term *wild* is seen today as meaning a kind of willfulness gone wrong, a loss of connectivity with land. One man told her that a properly burned land looks cared for, but that "big fires come when that country is sick for nobody looking after with proper burning." After burning, you can walk in the grass without fear of snakes and the nuisance of skin-burrowing grass seeds and their twisting awns. It enables people to find tracks and burrows, and fresh growth provides new food for kangaroos and wallabies. "Any bloke hungry in this country just silly," said another elder from Yarralin in the Northern Territory to Bird Rose. Knowledge and active management are key to staying healthy in a dry land. In this way, no environments are pristine.[2]

Later visitors in the 1840s described huts covered in spinifex matting, and in 1865 Jefferson Pickman Stow was the first to be shown by a group of men and boys the petroglyphs of fish, reptiles, mammals, and birds. A turtle, he wrote, had "the merit of being dashed off with a free hand." For a brief period, settlers observed a "traditional life almost undisturbed." But it was not to last. Local people were employed on farms and in mines as laborers, many indentured. And then the end came swiftly.

A policeman was speared in an incident, as an official account records, relating to the abduction of a Yaburara woman. The police swore in a posse of settlers and hunted down the whole tribe. The resulting Flying Foam massacre killed five to ten people, say those records; later analysts have estimated upward of a hundred were killed over eight days that February. Either way, no Yaburara survived. There are no ruins, no abandoned buildings, to mark their former presence. Like so many evildoers, that posse recedes faceless into history. No one will remember them.

The current land claimants and custodians are the East and West Ngarluma people, the Yindjibarndi, and the Yaburara Mardudunera, who all have cultural associations with the Dampier archipelago and peninsula. In 2003, the federal court concluded that no native title pertains in the region. Industrial development was free to expand.

Few narratives have found a way to celebrate some of the shared endeavors of both indigenous people and new settlers. Cattlemen, ranchers, miners, bagmen, fugitives, rustlers, all battled their way across new frontiers, made heroic efforts and lived in hardship, and yet rarely thought to ask local people for help. The pre-contact population of Australia was 750,000 people in many hundreds of language groups. Yet under national policies of breathtaking narrow-mindedness, Aboriginals were not permitted to vote until 1967, nor to travel from their outstations without permission. The census did not even ask their numbers until this time, nor were they permitted to have money or buy alcohol. Like many indigenous groups in both industrialized and developing countries, their designated settlements are places of misery, poverty, and abuse. In the 1980s and 1990s, government in Australia funded a program of new housing, yet somehow the units came to be called "dog boxes." People lived and slept outdoors, retreating into the boxes only in storms and the cold.

National studies and some politicians have pointed to domestic violence and internal social problems, rarely recognizing these breakdowns are not unique to indigenous societies. Modern ones are similarly afflicted. The only question is why such problems are used so regularly to frame debates about indigenous people's apparent inability to look after themselves when their land has been taken away.

If there is an answer, it is being kept secret from those same policy makers who believe they know best. Here's one: let people live on their land, where the organizing matrix of identity, knowledge, respect, and action can keep both people and land healthy, and above all give meaning. But industrialized governments don't seem to believe it. Their civilization is so good, they say, why should anyone else want to live differently? But living like us, you'd like to remind them, probably means the end of the world as we know it.

Under a tropical blue sky streaked with high cirrus, we navigate the eastern shore of the peninsula in search of ancient memories and dreams. I have come with one of the country's foremost environmental philosophers, Glenn Albrecht of Murdoch University and his wife Jill and in-laws Hilary and Sam, and we do not have to search hard. Glenn coined the term *solastalgia* to refer to the pain or sickness caused by the inability to derive solace from your local environment. It is the lived experience of powerlessness and loss of hope about the current state of your home environment. By contrast, he defines *soliphilia* as manifest in the interdependent solidarity needed between people to overcome the alienation present in contemporary political systems. Glenn is shaped by much life outdoors, with gray goatee beard, dark eyes beneath sunglasses, amulet around his neck, swept-back wiry hair, and almost permanently quizzical smile.[3]

As civilizations across the planet rose and fell, as nomads took to cities and as cities themselves collapsed under their own bureaucratic weight, as animals and crops were domesticated to bring new ways of living, so in this corner of an ancient continent did the first people continue their ways of living established tens of thousands of years earlier. Yet as we pass red boulder slopes and creek lines of gums, patches of blood-red peas, so appear factory buildings, gleaming white gas tanks, cracking-towers of silvered pipes, ranks of dusty trucks with snapping flags, and beyond the slopes, the tops of cranes digging in a way we probably do not want to be confronted with. Behind a long fence surely unnecessarily topped with barbed wire is a land of giant concrete pipes, awaiting deployment. The workers in this newly industrial land are but ants by the monster machines.

From the meadows of arrow-sharp spinifex, the rocks look as if they have emerged from the land. Up close they have a dark shiny patina, the edges worn smooth by millions of years of weathering. We dodge dense spiderwebs strung between bushes inviting entanglement, and stand at the base of a hill. A miner bird calls a greeting, then all is silent. The morning air is still, yet heat rolls off the iron-clad landscape. We wait, and then our eyes start to see. Petroglyphs appear. These are not paintings. There may once have been ocher and other bright colors, but here now are patinated intaglios created by deep and shallow pecking on the rocks, by grooving, abrasion, pounding, carving, and incising. All remove the outer weathered surface of granophyre to reveal a paler color of unweathered interior.

Sam says, "I seem to remember a thylacine is up to the left."

There are said to be a dozen depictions of thylacine on the Burrup. It died out on the Australian mainland five thousand years ago, and survived in Tasmania until the 1930s, maybe later, some believe and hope.

In the shadows is a white stick figure pecked into a dark surface, one arm holding three crescent shapes. Glenn and I clamber, rock men in search of signs, in a land of miners and train drivers and oil men. Here is a two-meter emu with neck outstretched toward the sky, and now our eyes are accustomed. Animals and birds, fish and turtles are about to come forth. A miraculous power emerges from this land. I feel we should sit all day and through a moonlit night and listen to the intentions of the artists themselves. By a patch of gum, we find a fat-tailed macropod, perhaps *Palorchestes*, three meters long, with long neck and tapir-like heavy head, four tapering legs that seem to step across the rock face with dainty care. There is no such marsupial today. It became extinct eighteen thousand years ago. The style also seems to suggest a particular individual rather than a species.

The rock slopes seem remarkably stable, though some individual rocks clang with the sound of anvils when stepped upon. They have mostly settled onto the land. We find bustards and echidna, kangaroos, whales and turtles, spotted stingrays, snakes and water pythons, emu feet walking, boomerang shapes held by goannas, crocodiles, or perhaps spotted lizards, and single scimitars with circular objects, perhaps the sun moving across the sky. One rock has six circles and an inner circle or sphere—more planets, perhaps. It is the density of depictions and sheer range that stops the breath. The shirt clings to my back as I pick my way across the gallery of boulders. An iguana, its head turned east and tail west, legs in the air. Or has the rock, perhaps, fallen and turned the image on its back? Rock circles, not crop circles, intersecting. When I lift my gaze, there in the valley is the new fertilizer factory, placed by a blocky power station.

As the sun climbs and the shadows deepen, we begin to see humanoids. Some have found iconic status, and occur elsewhere in the world too. A woman who seems to hover above the ground, arms outstretched but cocked at the elbows, and from each hand extends lines to the ground. Maybe some kind of force emerging from the soil, or spells cast by the figure; perhaps they are just long fingers. An ancestor who dreamed up the world? Her eyes have no expression to them. You feel as though this should be special, and yet it exists as just one image of many. The faces with owl-like eyes are thought to be older, the exaggerated hands and feet seem earlier in design. One with triangular dress and three lines orbiting the body like satellites, one leg longer than another, could be dancing as she hangs in the air. And one with a pointed head that tapers to a line that stretches from the far edge of a fractured rock. By a patch of vivid green grass, we count a dozen petroglyphs on twenty rocks. Macropods, crescents, iguana-dragons. The light dazzles off the patinated surfaces.

The trench of time makes us pause. People had been living here five times longer than since the invention of agriculture. The lighter petroglyphs are more recent, the darker ones have had time for the ferruginous coating to reappear. The air shimmers over the rocks. Between two hills we walk up a creek line filled with white-barked river gums. Clear water bubbles over rocks gray with stromalitic biofilms. Clumps of yellow spinifex line the banks. The air is cooler by the water, the moisture carrying the fresh scent of menthol. A bird warbles and I spin around to search for it. Red and blue dragonflies dart above the water, and papery butterflies of black on white spiral into the eucalypts. A flock of rusty-red rock pigeons double-snap wings and glide away. A rock monitor with banded tail watches, tongue flickering for scents.

Emu feet tempt us up again. Pecked into a cracked rock are four lines of twenty bird feet pointing to a long-beaked echidna, *Zaglossus*, extinct from Australia for nearly twenty thousand years, but still found in New Guinea. We squint into the sun, and there in the shadow at the top of a dizzying rock face are climbing men. Ladders and figures ascending a mottled rock face. This is not the fabled climbing men panel, but still there are dots on panels and figures to one side, heads disconnected from bodies. A round-headed snake man waits with short arms and legs but a long twisting tail. In the shadows of one rock pile, I sit and wonder about the illustrators. Did they come here to create the animals, perhaps to bring them to the hunt? Or were they just waiting, passing time with graffiti? Could anyone depict an animal, or were the authors chosen in some way? Perhaps it is instructive that there are no trees or grasses or tubers. Plants are on the land, in their place, but animals on land and in sea need to be found, encouraged to come to the hunter. They are representations of animals present, symbols to invoke an animal's presence, mythical beings, ways to tell stories or teach children, or something much more important. The animals were drawn by humans, but Aboriginals say the gods put themselves on the rock.[4]

I climb further and another miner calls, and I find a striated foot-long piece of red wattle. Air-dried, driftwood, at ease. By a turtle petroglyph, there is a cache of bones deep among the rocks. And among the wallaby leg bones, vertebrae, jawbones, I see a midden of cockles. Some shell middens have been dated to eight thousand years ago. Perhaps they just left the bones and shells for this moment of discovery. There is no whisper of wind, utter silence, just the sun thumping off the rocks.

I pick up a dried jawbone and some cervical vertebra, and hold them up to the light. At this very place, early people must have sat, carving animals, waiting for them to be drawn to this oasis. Eating shellfish and turtle carried from the sea and mangrove shores. I call over Glenn, and we climb still further, and beyond the factory can be seen cranes, towers, pipes, and flues, storage tanks, linked together and looking like they may take off at any moment. A further creation myth has been made here. This is the beginning of a long chain that feeds industrial society, that is in turn driven by patterns of overconsumption. Authorities resist formal recognition of these remarkable petroglyphs. Too much international celebration, especially World Heritage designation, would not be good for roads, factories, and mines, they believe. Bad for growth.

We tire in the heat. Then find the mandarin. Perhaps a postcontact figure, or an original spirit man. At the top of a slope with a great bustard crowing to the sun, and more men with crescent boomerangs, there is a tall man with broad shoulders, long coat, short legs, fat fingers, and a hat with wide brim. Was this a sailor who visited this shore, or an imagined figure? There may have been contact between Pilbara residents and people from other continents. Maybe they decided to record their presence. We find spiders, whales, dolphins, geometric shapes, saucers or perhaps hats, striped fish, lizards, more macropods, thin and fat tailed, a long-necked turtle, and falling stick figures with splayed fingers and toes. Mythic beings on the edge of maps.

And finally, here it is. Not gone after all. A carnivorous quadruped with striped flanks. The thylacine, or Tasmanian tiger, more like a wolf than a feline. We walk out from the shade of more gums, and there beneath a wattle tree is a live kangaroo grooming among the yellow grasses. It pauses, looks up, and lopes away.

—⬥⬥⬥—

Iron ore mining and salt extraction began here in the 1960s, then new port facilities were built during the late 1960s and 1970s, and the northwest gas field discovered in 1978. Roads were graded and new towns dropped onto the coastal plain. Karratha sprawls ahead of us across the flats between the rugged Jaburara Hills and the sea. We are now climbing past outcrops of red rock and clusters of marble-trunked gum trees, the ground made of no soil but thousands of crunched shells and glittering mica. Trees have grown up around older buildings, but the new neighborhoods are surrounded by low walls and seem disconnected from the land. Sam works for a gas company, which is what brought him and Hilary here.

"How many of your colleagues come out on the land?" I ask, reflecting on how the town looks like a space station tethered to a rocky desert.

"Not many," he says. "Actually, none."

We all live with these contradictions. Gas brought him here, then he brought new in-laws, and Glenn brought me. We all learned something new from those petroglyphs. Maybe this will help to save them too.

Only the town's telecom mast and church tower are higher than a single story. Tropical cyclones Bobby, Gertie, John, Kirstie, and Olivia tore up this coast in the 1990s, Monty, Clare, and Glenda in the 2000s. Strong winds, storm surges, tropical rain. No place or time to be far off the ground. Jutting into the ocean is the strip of dark hills and red rock that is the peninsula. A metal plaque on a slab of pink granite, unveiled in 1973 by the Western Australia premier, marks the spring that feeds the West Pilbara drinking water supply. An oasis in this elemental landscape. To the west is the edge of the salt pans, fifty square miles of them, attractive blue like a great swimming pool.

Among the grasses are many vivid Sturt's desert peas, scarlet flowers with their black bosses on sage-gray stalks, collected from this very place by William Dampier in 1699. Enticed out across the flats, my feet and legs are stabbed and sliced by the sharp spinifex edged with silica. The ground is carpeted with black marbles of ironstone. At the shore, what look from a distance like inanimate rocks turn out to be fossil brain corals and banks of ancient limpets that accreted between ocean and hot shore. Some jagged lumps of coral sit out on the brown sand, each in its own pool of water where the sand has been scoured away. A patch of blue appears below a bank of angry racing clouds. A wader cries across the muddy shore, and it is enough for me to forget this tropical location. It speaks of the wide marshes of home.

At a bridge we stop and look down upon a cutting. Four railway tracks link one horizon to the other, the sleepers like steps. On one, a thousand empty boxcars clatter by, on another each rusty container is filled with ocher ore, and this single train has three engines to power it from strip-mining scars three hundred kilometers away to this port. Each trainload delivers $30 million worth of iron, and a full ship leaves port daily. Gas plants are being rushed into the landscape, bringing more cranes, tanks, silvered pipelines, and wasteful flares. All this front-end damage, all to create so much end-of-system damage too. Will these ever become ruins themselves?

There have been programs to check if air pollution is damaging the petroglyphs, and less was found than in a city. No surprise. It is a windy peninsula projecting into the Indian Ocean. The problem is not pollution, it's development itself. There have been no formal planning permissions, no processes for accounting for Aboriginal heritage; sites are chosen by helicopter survey. In the 1980s, 349 registered archaeological sites were damaged, and another 1,619 engraved boulders moved to temporary compounds. They are still there. There are 250 to 1,100 petroglyphs per square kilometer in the region, but arguments persist over what to call a site. Destruction of a site doesn't sound so bad; but a site may contain several thousand images. In their review of the Dampier archipelago's archaeology and rock art, Caroline Bird and Sylvia Hallam concluded that "the sheer quantity and richness of the archaeological sites in the project area would normally have led to a reconsideration of the overall plan for industrial development. It did not. Irrevocable damage continues."

This is the most important and distinctive rock art installation in Australia, possibly the world.

The contrast with the original land ethic is painful. Dreaming is an accommodating worldview. It does not reject others who may be different. It accepts diversity. Such pluralism is quite different from many of the world's major religions that have adopted hierarchical monocentrism. In heterarchies, you can learn the system from any point, and every viewpoint is just as valid as another. No one is boss; everyone is. In such systems, nothing is external. The world and mind are all one piece. Dreaming is thus a kind of map of metarules about relationships that define balance, respect, and communication. Each country is best and finest for each group; each country is the center of its world, while acknowledging that the center of the world for another group is indeed somewhere else.

It is conceivable that these rock images are the Dreaming, not representations. This puts their destruction at least on a par with deliberate damage to cathedrals or mosques, to temples or monasteries.

"We have to go to sea," says Sam. Out to the islands that once were hilltops above inhabited valleys.

—⁓⁓⁓—

The boat slaps across the waves at twenty-five knots, a surging wake trying to catch us up. The industrial shore sprawls far along the Dampier Peninsula. Beneath a mottled and cracked sky of turtle shell, we motor north past salt pans, alongside giant ships fussed over by cranes and other kinds of lifters and loaders. By their names, it is clear many are heading for China. Beyond a forest of cranes a gas tower flares orange in the dull morning light. Ships that have come from far, will go far too: Jumbo Shipping, Austral-Asia Line; *Chikuzen Maru, Stellar Navigator*. The Energy Frontier is swollen with four white spheres of propane tanks, and we lay off at a safe distance. A whoosh of gas flares, wasteful orange vivid this gray morning.

It's a good place for shipping, protected from onshore weather by the islands of Enderby, East and West Lewis, Rosemary, and Malus. We motor up the coast to Conzinc Bay, where the ocher ore of iron is being loaded. To the south are the bright piles of white salt; further north liquid gas plants feed more ships with domes. Gas is piped in from the ocean, hundreds of kilometers away, compressed into liquid and exported. Somewhere fertilizers are being loaded. Beyond are the boulder slopes and the region's other history. Rays of sun begin to pierce the cloud, and light a flotilla of ships lined up along Mermaid Sound. Down south at Geraldton, a whole new port is being planned by the Chinese: access to resources guaranteed. From this remote coast, new trade lines link gas, iron, oil, and fertilizer to distant consumers.

The boat swivels, and lifts again on the white wake, and we pour across Enderby Sound. We abandon industry and go in search of animals of water and land. Glenn grins in the wind, and says we will have fine wine later. The clouds now disperse, and light now sparkles on the water, and the sea turns from brooding green to tropical blue. Then to port two dolphins rise out of the water and ease back in. Then another emergence, and gently reabsorbed. They don't jump, just appear to be swimming in the air. They nip toward us, and there is tinsel flittering in the air as flying fish leap from the water and scatter across the boat, gliding into distant waves. The dolphins follow.

The islands out here in the Indian Ocean are also boulder slopes and bristly grasses. At one island, we turn slowly into a creek lined with mangroves and motor quietly away from the sea into a rippled lake of shallow blue-green water surrounded by wiry forest. We peer down into the glassy water, and see turtles jetting into the fringing mangroves with great speed and much grace. The anchor clatters to a bed of shells and fossilized trilobites. I jump into the cool water and gasp. The air fills with concert-hall birdsong: warblers, a *kee-kee* of kestrel, chatters, calls, cackling laughs. This sanctuary already feels far from the industrial shore. I swim along the mangrove fringe. Shoals of glittering fish dart and jink, moving in tight synchrony. There are batfish and pink-green wrasse, and angelfish trailing graceful streamers. Underwater I pull hard at the mangrove roots locked into the hard bed, and they do not move an inch. No wonder they are excellent shoreline protection from cyclones. I read later that mangroves are migrating south along the Australian coast, and are bringing crocodiles too. Cyclones too may become more common. In Arnhem Land, storms have bubbled up from land rather than at sea. This coast has always changed, but probably not this quickly.

As the tide ebbs, we exit over the creek's sandbar with a meter to spare, and leave the moist inland air behind. We head north to search for dugong, seeing no more than shadows deep in the water column. On the shore of one island, our eyes are drawn to smears of guano on rocks by a cave. And warming in the sun is a herd of small wallabies. I had wondered how it was the islands looked grazed. At a bay of yellow sand on the eastern side of Rosemary Island, we moor and wade ashore.

The crystal-clear turquoise water is that which inhabits everyone's dreams about atolls in the tropics. Among the scarlet peas creeping down from the vegetation zone are skittering footmarks of waders, and at the waterline there is a zone of clinking cowries. We walk along the sand, the sun now at its highest. On the promontory is a densely woven nest six feet above the low scrub. With water either side, it's a perfect place for the ospreys. Two adults and a juvenile now weave circles around us, dropping sharply and climbing on thermals, keening loudly, white with dark knuckle feathers and wingtips. An onshore breeze ruffles the grasses. We retreat to the hot beach and shimmering rocks, watching the birds swoop to the nest, their ivory heads bright in the noon light.

We eat lunch on the boat. We sit back in the shade with beer cool from the Eskie, and squint through the dazzling light at the water and island shore. Glenn, Jill, and I set off for the far end of the bay, stopping to investigate mosaic patterns of sedimentary rocks and hard red granites. One rock is sheared in a straight line, leaving a tabletop surface. Later I sit alone on the beach, silently watching the warm waves crump on the shore, just watching and nothing more. We tarry too long, though we don't know it yet. Inland there are petroglyph sites, some under the sea too. I swim a hundred meters along the shore, making enough of a disturbance to ensure stingrays flit away. Even as we swam, I wondered about predators and dangers. Yet hull up on the horizon I could still count a dozen giant ships queuing for their gas and ore.

We set off for a reef in the middle of the bay, and swim among swarming shoals of fish and alien corals. The fish seem quite unaffected by our presence; few humans can have come here. They do not dart or move away, though a yellow and neon-blue stingray flashes across the sand. The fish assume iridescent color when I swim toward the sun as the light refracts through them—neon blues, yellow, reds, silver grays, dense blacks. A moray eel lies curled in a crevice of coral. There are 230 species of scleractinian corals here, turbinaria, faviid, porites, many with geometric patterns that defy description. Fingers of mauve and pink coral reach up toward the surface. I start counting the number of fish species, then give up.

The tide continues to fall, and the newly full moon rises into the blue sky. We set off for the southern exit from the bay. Ahead is a distinct sandbar, but there should be a passage. Sam jumps off to pull the boat, and I join him at the bow. We are in a few hundred mils of water only. I begin to discern subtle differences in color that represent depth and opportunity. Darker blues are good. Yellow not. Then off to one side we see a dark shadow twist and curl. Then to the right too.

Just reef sharks, no more than a meter in length. But what has brought them to us if it is not potential food? We don't believe the first two sharks are fishing for humans, but when more appear, we scuff the water and sand and make as much fuss as possible. The sharks press in, a dark and watchful smoke of bodies. A dilemma: to admit defeat and jump aboard, or keep at it, and be eaten. We look at each other, and push harder through the soft sand. But there is no way through. Deep water lies half a kilometer away. We turn the boat and retreat to the north, growing more confident about the sharks. Yet by now the two easterly bay exits are also blocked.

If the tide beats us, the boat will stay here for hours yet, beyond dusk and deep into the tropical night. The water deepens, becomes shallow again, and then it's a meter deep and we're leaping aboard and motoring away into the rising wind. The sharks are foiled. We head for the shipping lane. Now the boat powers up, and slices through the dark sea, white spray crashing either side.

Onward, to the industrial shore.

STEPPE
Tuva, Russia

85° West of Date Line

An eagle soars faint in the thin air, far above the rippling grasslands. A single cloud is static on the dome of the cobalt sky, fixed to a distant shadow on hills away to the north. Over a gravel wash bubbles a stream, recently frozen. Carpets of spring flowers are turning pastures yellow and purple. A herd of heavy-headed Siberian horses grazes as buttons of sheep and goats trail up an olive-green slope. The mountain steppe of Tuva has been home to nomadic herders since livestock were domesticated. Life is lived according to the way of that white cloud.[1]

I came first to the capital Kyzyl huddled by the rushing Yenisey River, still crammed with tumbling ice floes. It feels a frontier town, even though dropped on the steppe nearly a century ago. On the rim of every horizon are snowcapped mountains. It has taken three days to get here. In the Russian capital no one smiled: fourteen million people packed into a city the size of London. Edge cities of Odyssean tower blocks sprouted around the periphery. I counted a hundred towers in one neighborhood, thirty-five in another. The midnight flight to south Siberia was delayed, the plane switched, and eventually we squeezed into an ancient Tupolev 154. The heat poured out of metal strips embedded the length of the narrow fuselage. Few could sleep; the cabin staff too were grimly sweating. Released into the smoky industrial city of Abakan, capital of Khakassia, we drove four hundred kilometers south on one of only two roads into Tuva. There is no railway, and the airport operates only occasionally in summer. If ever there was an appropriate time to use that problematic word *remote*, this may qualify.

Siberia is vast, a twelfth of the world's landmass, thirteen million square kilometers of southern steppes of pastoralists, central taiga forests of hunters and reindeer herders, and ice-coasts of northern fishers and hunters.[2] It's Russia's equivalent of America's West: a territory inhabited by indigenes who lived on a land almost certainly rich with natural and mineral resources. There had long been a profound Russian longing to populate their East. For outsiders, though, an enduring myth held Siberia as a kind of hell. Exile became a common punishment from the 1700s, and much later it was chosen for the gulags. Russia's political approach to its internal frontier territory was exemplified in 1822, when the Statute of Alien Administration in Siberia defined all Siberians as *inorodtsky* aliens. Later, the Soviets came to condemn native languages, outlaw shamanism, and forcibly settle all nomads.

The smooth military road is tarmac all the way via Kyzyl to the Mongolian border. It winds through extensive taiga of spruce and larch. At the lunch halt, bowls of red berries and jars of pickles are laid out on tables, and the vendor in long leather jacket and padded hat beckons to us. On the café terrace are two stuffed brown bears, arms outstretched like opera singers. From the smoke-filled kitchen, another woman serves us sweet tea and greasy pork on slivers of spruce. Army trucks grumble into the puddled car park. A raven croaks as we stroll back.

Climbing the pass through the dark forest, we come to the snow zone. Watery sunlight washes the blackened snow piled along the cleared road. Another raven caws, perched on top of a nearby burned spruce. A wide area is scorched, the stumps charcoal black. A prayer tree marks the border. Tied to the branches of the tree are hundreds of prayer flags, saturated silks of bright red and blue, green, yellow, and white, many faded and wind-frayed, their prayers dispersed. The raven ambles to another tree, and attaches itself. Another arrives, and the flags crackle with intent. Later we see a silver-tailed arctic fox. I jump out to track it along a ditch line, and a raven swoops from nowhere and chases the fox as it flees up scree and into the snow. At a roadblock, police with tall peaked caps keep the car waiting until our Tuvan drivers make a donation. Around poles no longer connected to carry electricity, a herd of hardy horses clusters, not looking at all like they would run their renowned eighty kilometers at a stretch. Then the road drops sharply into the capital on the southern shore of Siberia's greatest river, and we descend though coal smoke that pours from chimneys and seems to fill the valley.

Tuva is part of the Russian Federation. It is seventeen million hectares in size with a population of just three hundred thousand, a third of whom live here in Kyzyl. The territory has been inhabited for forty thousand years, home more recently to the famed Scythians, who from about three thousand years ago covered the land with gold-filled burial mounds, stone circles, and petroglyphs. Then came Hunnic, Turkic, and Mongol regimes, the Chinese Qing dynasty from 1758 to 1911, and Tuva declared independence as Tannu-Touva in 1921. In the acquisitive language of dominant states, it was integrated into the Soviet Union in 1944, making it the youngest region of the Russian territory. Far from the sea, the climate is continental extreme, annual temperatures sometimes swinging from $-40°C$ in winter to $+40°C$ in summer. Livelihoods center on the herding of livestock and four regular seasonal migrations to make best use of patchy grazing and water resources, on *temnejir* systems of sharing and cooperation, and on knowing nature and living with it. Wild animals and plants have always been a vital source of food, making Tuva an archetypal hunter-gatherer-herding culture.

That evening, Nicholas Colloff, Oxfam's country director for Russia, and I meet Dolaana Kadygo, and we eat in one of Kyzyl's tiny restaurants, the walls and tables covered with animal symbolism of recursive spiral antlers of deer and corkscrew-horned argali sheep. After good pasta, Nicholas and I repair to a public sauna up a back alley. There are lace curtains in the changing room, and windows of art deco glass that cast a neon blue on the plunge pool. No one else comes. The hotel backs onto the confluence of the two Yeniseys, a place of great shamanistic significance. Chekhov wrote in 1890: "I have never in my life seen a river more splendid than the Yenisey." It flows another twenty-two hundred miles to the Arctic Ocean from here. On the horizon are the Eastern Sayan Mountains that march six hundred miles northeast to Lake Baikal. In the sludgy water ice floes now grind and clash. On the shore, eight feet of ice is layered with winter's history of pollution. The river is gray under a front of dark cloud that advances from the west. In passing through, Colin Thubron reckoned Kyzyl a concrete blemish on the plain. At the ends of the grid of streets, you can see where the tarmac and housing give way abruptly to grassland.

I walk along the shore to a white stupa with golden spires and shining crown. Prayer flags snap in the gloaming. A concrete eagle gazes over the water toward the white mantra of bodhisattva on the hill, laid out by the Dalai Lama's team on his visit. I return for a beer in the neon bar. In my room is a picture of a tropical beach with waves and coconut palms. We couldn't be further from the sea, here at the heart of Asia.

—◦◦◦—

Tuvans are a people with a long stride, indicating to them freedom on the land, and so Dolaana takes us to visit the local shamans. They celebrate four treasures: beauty of the natural landscape, the reassuring presence of animals both domestic and wild, respect for family life, and an enduring humility before the spirit masters. Such themes resonate across many land-based cultures. According to the Vavilov Institute of General Genetics, Tuvans are more closely related to indigenous Native American peoples than any other groups outside North America. Their shamans use feathers of eagles in headdresses, and say that this practice was taken to the Americas by migratory peoples. The term *shaman* originates from the Evenk for *ones who know*, though in Tuva the specialists for healing were also called *xam* or *xaman*, now translated as shaman. Their charm-laden coats are multicolored, trailing with ropes and braids representing snakes. Bird symbols suggest flight, antlers the speed of deer to carry them to the land of the spirits.

Both Colin Thubron and Anna Reid were skeptical about the shamans of Tuva, calling them exploiters of local people. In Ted Levin's account of Tuvan throat singing, *Where Rivers and Mountains Sing*, one woman tells him, "there's a Tuvan saying: the poorer the people, the more shamans appear."[3] Like any profession, there are bad and good. But Thubron and Reid were not convinced. The Soviets did not stop at criticism: at the beginning of the 1930s in Tuva, there were 725 practicing shamans and 6,000 lamas at thirty-four Buddhist temples. By 1940, it is written that all were dead, the lamaseries rubble. But the Soviets were rarely that thorough: many may have just faded into the population. With the monks went centuries-long knowledge of Tibetan, Chinese, and Mongolian texts. The not-so-secret police took shamans in planes and pushed them out, saying, go on, prove you can fly. There had, at the time, also been Siberian plans for secession, a green and white flag briefly adopted, but this too was crushed. It is no surprise that the demise of the Soviet Union brought a brief violent reaction in Tuva in 1990, eighty-eight dead in a wave of hostility directed toward ordinary Russians.

Since the early 1990s, there has been much ethnic revival and political mobilization across Siberia. An awakening cultural renaissance led to the formation of RAIPON, the Russian Association of Indigenous Peoples of the North, who declared that "the rebirth of shamanism is a very important social and political development." At their 2011 Congress, they decided that "we, the indigenous people of the North, Siberia and Far East of the Russian Federation . . . know that . . . our way of life, based on time-honored experience of communal, social organization, has been created from original cultures and beliefs of our ancestors and is the one, true way of maintaining life and sustainable development." But when the earlier UN Declaration on the Rights of Indigenous People was signed by 143 countries in 2007, Australia, Canada, New Zealand, and the United States opposed the declaration, and Russia with ten others abstained. Today, there are some three hundred active male and female shamans in Tuva, and they are consulted for seasonal, everyday, and healing rituals.

"The main task of shamans," states straight-backed Dopchun-ool Kara-ool of the Adyg-Eeren bear society, "is to protect nature. We act for the mountains, rivers, taiga, and different landscapes of our homeland."

We have come to a perfectly normal neighborhood of Kyzyl. We think we're going just to talk and listen, but a ceremony will transport us away. The society was formed in 2001 by Kara-ool and three colleagues to work for the revival of Tuyvinian traditions and culture, and there are now forty shamans here. We are shown to a shadowy room with a small window where Kara-ool sits at a small desk. Murbat Victor Khovalygeyvitch, the silver-haired vice-chairman, stands alongside in tan jacket and roll-neck sweater. Six more fully masked shamans sit in a row, including Larissa Churum-oolowna and Orlanma Mongush. Larissa's father, grand-, and great-grandfathers were shamans, but she did not begin practicing until thirty-eight years of age. Orlanma worked in the police, hiding her shaman skills like so many others. Kara-ool has been practicing much longer, since 1961. His grandmother was a famed shamaness, and people came to visit in the depths of night. His grandfather was a Buddhist monk who studied in Tibet. It is a harsh thought:

lifetimes spent keeping knowledge from the ruling forces. The blue-green walls are backdrop for a menagerie: three bearskins pinned out, surprised skulls of ox and wild boar, eagles in flight, a bow with arrows, argali skulls, prayer flags, and many braided ropes and beads. A snake, a squirrel, a horn. Victor holds a drum as large as a shield, the north-south crossbeams carved into helmeted heads, the membrane representing the border between worlds. A small wooden table in the far corner is crammed with figurines and cards with signs. The room is silent. There is no sign of any other world, yet my mind is wondering what moderns would make of this.

Then a mobile phone rings, and Larissa steps out. No one blinks.

Kara-ool explains.

"To become a shaman, you have to know the voices of nature and the language of spirits."

"This is a time of bad fortune," he also observes; the world's recession has brought unemployment here too. "We work with old and young people, visit hospitals and prisons, purify special places."

The society does not receive financial help from the state, but public support for what they do runs deep.

"Our goal is the renaissance of a traditional culture," states Victor.

Kara-ool then sits back, and adds, "We are modern people, using mass media and the Internet."

They tell of the global movement of the Drum of Peace, expected here the following month. They wish to build a new center, attract tourists. A core principle of animism is that places of worship are everywhere in nature, in animals and hillsides, in trees and rock formations. Other shamans now shuffle in wearing their heavy purple costumes with brass necklaces and mirrors, feathers on hats, tinkling bells, and long braids tied with the pelts of small animals. The others stand, and two white scarves of silk are given to each of us by a handsome shaman with deep wrinkles and skull, claws and bones on her headdress. These *chalama* symbolize the white path and the proper way to live, and are an offering to the spirits too.

We sit outside in the warm sunlight, teacups spread out on low tables. Across the earthy yard is a cone of wood and branches on a ring of stones, topped by a circular symbol with cross-ties of cloth. The shamans stand at a distance, all now wearing animal masks. At each corner of the yard are poles topped with skulls and hanging with the pelts of wild sheep and bears. In this ordinary neighborhood of Kyzyl, like any other, the old world has its day. A shaman blows on a horn, and the fire is set in the sticks, and as crackling flames consume all, so our lives come to a quiet halt. A handful of aromatic plants are lit too, and the smoke brought around our feet and then our heads. The drumming and singing has begun. The sun shines hard, glittering off the brass and silver and whirling drums. Now there are combined high voices and low chants, the soundscape of rhythmic beating, reflecting the deer-steed's beating heart, smoke from the flickering flames, and many dogs barking. The spirits are invited by the drumming and fire, and I feel we have walked through a wall into slow time. I dream in daylight. Peace comes. The fire consumes yet more, and smoke swirls around the yard, in and out of dancing figures.

Much time passes. Then the drumming abruptly stops, the air congeals, and time restarts. The spirits have departed. The bear is a strong animal, dangerous, not mentioned by name in the world of the north, and the Adyg society has a powerful reputation. Wearing the silk *chalamas*, we leave on our own paths, blue smoke rising still, and head to the federal employment agency to talk about plans to support small businesses. Remote is bad when it comes to markets, trade, support from central government, but it can be good too. You look inward for solutions first.

<hr>

At dawn, I walk the wet streets, past blocks of flats with enclosed balconies, in their shadows older houses, single story with ornate wooden windows painted blue or green, water dripping from the slatted wooden roofs. I pass the prison, walls topped with barbed wire, through a park wet with puddles and onto the bridge. There are four grand marble horses with bowed heads, each with differing gaits, guarding the river crossing of the Ulug Xem, the great river Yenisey. I lean over to watch someone scramble in office shoes over the polluted ice. The rim of mountains is hidden in gray mist. Water drips from every surface, and from every chimney, domestic or minor industrial, black smoke soots the city. Back in the empty main square, where the Dalai Lama spoke in 1991, the crowds packed and anxious for word from the outside world, a Lenin statue waves his right hand toward a parked silver four-by-four, a giant prayer wheel beyond.

The long polished table reflects light from Lenin Square, now known as Nomad Square. We had climbed concrete stairs to meet the first vice-chair of government, the deputy prime minister, and Sergey Innocentyevich Ten begins by observing that the "nomadic way of Tuvans will be eternal. It will never disappear. It will always be a part of our spirit." On his mirror-polished desk are red files awaiting attention, and two flags, the yellow and powder blue of Tuva and the red, white, and blue of Russia. Beyond his windows are the wet square and the mountains beyond. He intends the railway to be built to link north to the Trans-Siberian Railway in Krasnoyarsk so that they can open mines and export coal and aluminum. There are plans to start building soon, but perhaps there always are. It would bring in tourists with money, help other exports too.

"We believe in balance," he offers, "the traditional ways of life and the needs of modern development. Even if we only exploit 10 percent of our reserves of minerals, it will be enough for our happiness."

Good point. The Tuvans have put a semicolon after the progress myth; they'd like the best of the modern, on their terms.

The economic problem facing Tuva is this: how to build a partly modern economy out of a discredited centralized system without losing the distinct culture based on the land. Hard, too, to protect rare wildlife and habitats, and do this in the face of the threats of climate change. One great advantage, almost unique save for devolved Nunavut and Greenland, is that the indigenous people of this republic are in the majority: they hold political power. If any government can match these competing demands—nature, heritage, and culture lined up against the invasion of the consumption-driven modern world—then perhaps it can be done here. Yet at a timber yard overlooked by half-completed brick buildings, the exasperated owner, Vladimir Set, sits by his wooden chess set and complains at how difficult it is to turn these people into a workforce. All in black, leather jacket too, he leans over to shuffle papers on his polished desk. On the wall behind is that photo of the topless Russian president standing in the Yenisey waters with fishing rod and military hat. By the sawmill is a straight-backed statue of Lenin.

"The nomadic mentality is hard to change," he despairs. Which may be no bad thing.

The director of the Institute of Humanities confirms this. Net curtains billow on a now warm spring wind, the sounds of occasional cars passing. A large photo of the Dalai Lama is on the top shelf, and on the wall are pictures from Sergei Badrovi's *Mongol*, starring Japanese actor Tadanobu Asano as the great Khan, later known as Genghis Khan. All the thousand extras were Tuvans. There has been, K. A. Bicheldy remarks, a renaissance of traditional ways of life since the end of Soviet time. The static collective farms are all closed, and modern animal breeds gone.

"The crisis happening in the world has given us hope. It will force us to look at new ways of living that build on traditional ways of life. Look at those horsemen," he points, all in full dress with swords. "There's a light in their eyes."

In the small museum and out in the yard are elegant petroglyphs pecked on stellae and chunks of gray granite. Deer with antlers swept back in graceful waves echo their swayed backs and curved necks. As we leave, I notice on his desk a backward clock, running anticlockwise.[4]

Up on the hill is the agricultural university. We sit in a classroom decorated with paintings of camels, yaks, reindeer, horses, lit by rows of harsh fluorescent lights. The tense dean in bright green shirt introduces us, then scuttles away. Every other member of the faculty is female, as are all the students. They sit at desk and smile. We talk from a top table set with smart blue cloth and crystal glasses. Even in here, mobiles are constantly bleeping with arriving texts. Unusually for an agricultural institution, their concern is mainly with animals, and there is much experience here, if it could get to the people. There is some small-scale vegetable cultivation in Tuva, and some barley grown, though yields are low: crops require irrigation to survive. Milk is used to make twenty-nine different products, including yogurt, cheese, both alcoholic and nonalcoholic drinks, and additives for other foods. In the long corridor, I peer at curled monochrome photos of herders with long pipes, wigwams of reindeer skins and birch bark, and hillsides dense with blurred reindeer. A wrinkled man is frying fish in a metal bowl of bubbling fat.

Outside I walk around the campus, past long concrete blocks of student accommodation, trees no taller than spindly saplings, an experimental plot laid out with grass varieties. In the far distance, the circle of mountains topped with snow gleams in the late afternoon sun. At the football pitch, railway sleepers brought from far are piled up as terracing. Beyond are multistory buildings with windows only at the top, either unfinished or all-too-entirely abandoned to the steppe. Nearer town are chimneys, conveyor belts angled up to silos, rusted and all crumbling. Against the dusky sky is another chimney belching dark black smoke. Down here, the earlier warmth of the day bleeds away.

On the western edge of town, we find the offices of the Ministry of Natural Resources, in among abandoned silos, brick chimneys, and rusting machines sprouting from plots scattered with litter and debris. On the wall of Vladislav Kanzay's office is a pike's head and gaping jaws the size of a small shark, and pictures of snow leopard and argali. A windowsill is cluttered with teacups and vodka glasses around a small bust of Lenin. A plan for the trip south to Erzin on the Mongolian border is laid and agreed. Slava's great grandfather used to spend his winters in Tuva, and summers 150 kilometers beyond the border inside Mongolia. We are heading for a vast inland basin, where rain from millions of square kilometers drains to lentic wetlands. The Uvs Nuur Basin Biosphere Reserve alone is 640 by 160 kilometers in size, comprising wetlands, sand massifs, dry steppe, rocky mountains, high forest, and alpine meadows. The region also contains the highest concentration of burial mounds in Asia, and has the headwaters of both the Yenisey and Ob Rivers.

We walk back through town, through estates of long blocks with ill-fitting windows, where fires burn and groups of children wrapped in pink and blue huddle, and then pass a T-34 tank on a plinth, gleaming in the last of the light but scrawled with white graffiti, and back along the river, blue at this end of town. And now the cumulonimbus layer clears to leave mottled cirrus to the west, and the sky blazes pink, and the river itself lights up with sky, and evening strollers lean on railings to watch the night fall. A raven perches on a floe jostling downriver. Across the river, factories on the northern bank still pour black smoke. We stop at the globe that marks the center of Asia.

Richard Feynman made Tuva famous by never coming here. He was captivated by the heroic diamond and triangular stamps, one depicting a camel racing a train. Before he died in 1988, Feynman developed a jokey obsession with Tuva because of its utter inaccessibility. At the time, the Cold War severely restricted knowledge in ways difficult today to imagine. In Ralph Leighton's account *Tuva or Bust!* are meetings in Moscow and Sweden with anthropologist Sevyan Vainshtein, author of *Nomads of South Siberia*. Leighton's book contains a photograph of Vainshtein and his wife Alla at this very monument.[5]

——　——

We traveled south through swirling snowstorms to Erzin by the Mongolian border, where the land opens up yet more and you can see many tens of kilometers in every direction to rims of mountains. The dusty road south to the border park passes granite outcrops and the scattered rusting agricultural machinery of state farms decomposing slowly in the grass. Windows are empty, roofs long gone, no more than temporary efforts to control this land. Yet Scythian burial mounds stud the steppe. Their one-thousand-year warrior civilization lasted from the eighth century BC to the second century AD. Herodotus wrote about them, as they came west to ancient Greece, some liking it enough to settle in Thrace. The Scythians developed advanced metallurgy, a distinct animal style for their art, notably depicting eagles, deer, rams, leopards, wild boar, wolves, and many horses, and invented bronze molds to produce socketed arrowheads, the short recurved bow, and cavalry horseback warring itself. They also left some forty thousand kurgan tombs ten to fifty feet in height, their pyramids of the steppes.

Until recently, the most famous complex was at Pazyryk, where the Altai Ice Princess was discovered. Water had seeped into the tomb, then frozen, and perfectly preserved her body. Her skin had been covered in tattoos, and removed at death and hung by the body. But then Arzhan 1 and 2 were discovered in the Tuvan foothills of the Sayan Mountains. The 300-foot-diameter Arzhan 1 was opened in the 1970s, and the 250-foot Arzhan 2 in 1998. The latter contained an intact royal grave, with a forty-five-year-old king and thirty-five-year-old queen alongside ninety-three hundred objects, of which more than half were gold. In all there were twenty-six bodies of people and fourteen of horses, sacrificed soldiers and servants to join the royals. Presumably the queen, too, had to die to join the king. All this remarkable gold is now in the Scythian Room of the National Museum, opening just months before we came.[6]

We climb a scree slope and then up an outcrop of granite crusty with yellow lichen, and now hundreds of Scythian kurgans are chains of islands in the sea of sandy grass. Perimeter rings of half-buried stones, and then standing stones of white limestone. Many were raided from the sixteenth century onward by teams of *buguroushchili* treasure seekers; some may remain untouched. In this high desert, we can see in the distance a smudge, a sheen, of an ice-blue lake. Before it are clustered dots of black and brown horses. Once there would have been saiga antelope, with their oversize and flexible noses to warm air in winter and filter out the dust in summer. All were shot in the 1950s by Soviet officials on the grounds that they were competitors of domestic livestock. There are now plans to reintroduce them. Here too are populations of rare snow leopard, argali wild sheep, great bustard, and wild reindeer. We won't see a snow leopard, but then neither did Peter Matthiessen in the Himalayas, and he didn't mind. In Mongolia far to the south, the vivid snows are bright on crumpled mountains.

"Look up sometimes," smiles Slava, our other interpreter. "It can be dangerous here." It could be space rocket debris, as boosters after launch in Kazakhstan are programmed to fall along the border regions of Altai, Khakassia, and Tuva. Some damage settlements, others cause grassland fires. Today the sky is vast and ringing with silence.

On the way to the lake, we stop at a blue truck beached by the roadside. Two men have the whole engine laid out on wooden platforms. The sun beats down on them, on the glistening black oil on their arms, on the front wing pushed to one side. At Lake Tore-Khol, we arrive at the cusp of winter and spring. A sprinkling of iridescent snow covers the ice, but two meters have melted at the shore, and the water is utterly clear. We seem too close to the cirrus that are stretched across a radiant cornflower sky. Patches of phragmites reeds flank Tore-Khol, frost crystals on the stalks and leaves. The air is quite still, up here at twelve hundred meters altitude. Mergansers gabble across the water. An egret flops by the shore. A raven, shockingly black against blue and white, cries as it flies across the shore and then is gone into the steppe, leaving a crashing, embracing silence. Melting ice then cracks, and a wader burbles. But there is no movement of air. I hear a bubbling laugh from the small yurt. It was a bitter night in the tiny rooms attached to the town's administrative center, but now it's warm enough to melt ice. A gull squeals at an echelon of whistling geese.

I find a platform used by pike fishermen. Half a dozen Egyptian geese wander the shore. The three poles for drying nets cast half shadows; on the platform are the rimed scales of fish. The light has the quality of moonlight—the sun is bright, and yet the shadows are not dark for there is so much reflected light filling the air from snow and cloud. In the glare, I shade my eyes. The water is full of filaments of ice. Smoke curls from the felt-and-lattice yurt on the sandy shore, solar panel on the roof.

"Come and eat," calls Dolaana across the beach.

I walk back and see that pike steaks are frying in oil over the hissing stove. A large loaf is chopped into pieces, and fills a cardboard box.

"The best pike in Russia," declares stocky fisherman Aldyn-Ool. The fish came out of the lake this morning, and the flesh crumbles as we eat, sitting on the multicolored carpet, oil soaked up by old newspapers.

Altai osman fish are endemic to these lentic lakes of the central Asian internal basin, where there is no outlet to the sea. But osman are now under threat from voracious pike. These *shortan* were deliberately introduced in the 1970s by the Soviets, and have since so expanded in numbers that osman need protection. Individual pike can reach twenty kilograms, like the one on Slava's wall. A quota of twenty-five tonnes per year has been set to encourage removal of pike, particularly by ice fishing in winter. In the time of storms, remembers Aldyn-Ool, waves could throw banks of osman onto the shore. Never now. If he could find a small line of credit, he'd buy equipment for smoking and processing pike, and a fridge. He'd catch more, sell more. We sit back, sun streaming through the smoke as it rises to the roof vent.

Back in Erzin, we stop at the regional compound of the Ministry of Natural Resources, where a red and white tablecloth has been laid with cold meats and cheeses, chunks of bread, and sugary rolls. Slava Kanzay is in dryland camouflage suit, with Russian eagle crest on his sleeve, just over five-feet-and-a-bit tall. He serves the crisp vodka, and we toast many deserving causes. I walk to the edge of town, and watch the sun blaze above the jumble of houses and electricity poles like so many lances of a gathered horde, none exactly vertical. Now the sky takes fire, pink and orange above the purple shadows. Clouds close in, lights brighten from homes, and the last of the sun glints from the golden roof of the Buddhist temple. Tonight, we sleep again in the three-story administrative block, in the flat for visitors. It's a long walk in the night to the toilet, down flights of stairs and across the car park to the pair of long-drops. Prop the back door open like this, say our hosts, or you'll be stuck outside all night.

———

It is evident that Tuva has been shaped by millennia of nomadic land management. There is a strong tradition of respect for natural places: each has an *ee* spirit guardian. Beauty to Tuvans is a landscape that is both wild and domestic. The winter camps can be dusty and dirty, but in spring and summer, the sheep and goats are bright on the green steppe. Beauty is also rocks, water, the few trees, birds calling, grass rippling to the horizon, an eagle or falcon, circling and calling. In summer, the grassland is covered with flowers, and the livestock are fatter too. A traditional Tuvan greeting is *are your livestock healthy; are they well?* There is great pleasure in livestock that are clean and fat. Vainshtein described Tuva as "a paradigm of central and North Asian pastoral economies." Not surprisingly the early visitors adopted lazy stereotypes. The English explorer Alexander Carruthers came to Tuva in 1910–11, taking five weeks to cross the Sayan Mountains, the taiga forest a torment of mosquitoes. The sunny grasslands seemed like paradise, but still he thought the herders and lamas loafed around too much. The economy needed modernizing, and he recommended Russia take Tuva rather than let it go to Mongolia. Russia agreed.

The Soviet period then saw decades of effort to reshape the land. Management was switched to static collective farms that imported livestock breeds unable to cope with the brutal extremes of the Tuvan climate. In a land defined by its grass, farms imported their feed from elsewhere in the USSR. Large-scale crop cultivation was similarly externally subsidized, with huge wheat and barley farms supported by costly irrigation. The Soviet view was exemplified by historian L. P. Potapov, who wrote in 1969 that local people were still engaged in "technically backward nomadic pastoralism." Soviet pride in Tuva centered on the transformation of a "once backward nation," with mineral, metal, and asbestos mines, female doctors and journalists, numerous factories, and a strong education system that had eliminated illiteracy: in 1924, official records sneered that only 106 people out of a national population of 52,000 could read and write. Modernization has brought many benefits to Tuva, but has left many institutions maladapted to the challenges of establishing alternative patterns of economic growth. Neither modern breeds nor crops survived the collapse of the Soviet Union. Tougher traditional breeds were reintroduced, and cattle numbers have since doubled.

Altair lives in Erzin and drives us from the wide streets to his *kyshtag* winter camp situated in the lee of a hill. He's wearing green camouflage jacket and striped woolen hat, Dolaana with her red and blue felt hat with long earflaps. For seven months, they have to obtain their water directly from snow. The Tuvans, also known at various times in history as Soyat, Mady, Uryanghai, Todjins, and Tuvinians, long ago evolved a strong social system of mutual help called *temnejir* that manages the collective use of lands, collaboration between *aal* family groups, shared hunting, and help with hay and crop harvests. Most *aals* move four times per year. *Chazag* spring, *chailag* summer, and *küzeg* autumn camps are always by a river. Winter dwelling is the longest, typically September-October to April-May, and thus sites often have permanent storage buildings alongside latticed yurts, together with indoor animal byres by corrals. Summer camps are held in different places year by year in order to protect grazing. Contemporary migration patterns typically mean moves of some 30–60 kilometers per year, though some livestock herders still move longer distances, perhaps 100–130 kilometers from the river to forest taiga.

When I asked, one family smiled and said, "We are always happy when moving."

During the summer pause between sheep shearing and grass cutting, many highly anticipated festivals are held, with competitions for food, wrestling, archery, and long-distance horse racing. Festivals are further statements of identity: in Soviet times, they were forbidden, as was Tuvan national costume.

At the camp, the single canvas yurt looks modest in the wide steppe, but when I dip beneath the low entrance, a warm world opens up. The central metal stove sits on a wooden plinth, and the cylindrical chimney leads to hole in the roof that lets in suffuse light. The pleated roof of blue leads to a wooden lattice that makes up the walls, hanging with embroidered textiles. We sit on red rugs, and talk about the lives of nomads. This yurt, like every other, is packed up with ease. Outside, lambs bleat. In here, I learn a horse-racing game using the knuckles of sheep. Before long, the carpet is covered with lines of bones. Dolaana's ring glints as she places them in a spiral by the stove. We walk out to the neighboring byre, improbably white lambs wandering aimlessly. Some have black noses, stripes on their necks, black tails, black heads; a few are jet black all over. They are awaiting their mothers. There is not a tree in sight, yet spruce make up the byre fence posts and lattice. The indoor housing for the animals is roofed and the walls thick. Snow leopards may be rare, and protected, but they will break in to take sheep and goats. The mayor and his wife lean on the spruce fence, watching the animals. He wears a warm jacket and black flat cap, she a glossy red coat lined with fur. We all stand around the byre.

The animals bring everyone together, content by the rough fence. Time passes.

Altair takes a fat-tailed ewe with black eye patches and yellow plastic ear-tag, and a shepherd reaches inside wool to pinch the aorta, and that is that. As the carcass is being prepared in the late afternoon sunlight, the blood ladled out of the body cavity into a metal bowl, I climb a hill sheltering the winter camp and look down on the yurt and animal byre all alone on the steppe. Over the brow of low hill a few dots appear, and then a white stream of returning ewes. And the lambs go wild. The ewes charge on spindly legs toward the byre. The lambs crowd up to the fence, and the land is filled with collective joy. All are calling, bleats, squeaks, warbling cries, *murrs* and whispers. Each individual speaks differently. For fifteen minutes the mothers crowd outside the fence, and the youngsters jostle into the wall of sound. I look to the distance, and over the rise now comes the shepherd on his shaggy brown horse, walking slowly, its large head dipping. He nods. Says nothing, ties up the horse. Walks slowly, unhooks the great spruce gate.

And pandemonium. The mothers charge in, the latecomers still out on the steppe now rattling along. The two worlds of sound clash, intermingle, pair up, and walk back out. Within moments a contented soundscape emerges. I sit and watch a single dark lamb, just a few hours old, crying as it stumbles out, bleating, searching. It is alone. All have gone from the fold. The recombined herd drifts to the pastures for a couple more hours' grazing before dusk. Two lambs race each other, back and forth, and the tiny one joins them, stiff-legged. The sun is dropping behind the hill to my west, and I look down again on yurt, byre, water tank, and blue tractor. The shepherd stands stiffly in the mythic light of the steppe.[7]

By now the sheep is being prepared for dinner, all fleece and mutton. The shepherds' hands are splashed red to their wrists. A blue bucket and silver dish contain organs and offal. Wood smoke drifts from the yurt's chimney, white cumuli over distant hills. There is nothing else but grass and sky. Ahead I see south to Mongolia. The far horizon is rimmed with mountains peaked like beaten egg white. Herders have come to winter camps like this for thousands of years. Tonight the sheep will be boiled, tomorrow they will pack up the yurt and move to the spring camp. Just as they have always done, except now there are vans and trucks to help. Now the wind is cold, swept over hundreds of kilometers with little interruption, and stiff-limbed I walk down the slope. I pick up a horse's jawbone, and it breaks open to reveal the catacombs of tissue between inner and outer walls. In the yurt, the liver is cooked first, and then back cuts, and all laid out on a low blue table, china cups for tea. Steam billows from the pan. In a cot, a baby in padded jacket sleeps on his back. We eat with sharp knives, tearing the meat. A shepherd saves the shoulder blades: they are for divination, put in the embers of a fire to reveal maps of animal locations. We talk of the beauty of this land, of traditions and children, and of throat-singing.

This is Tuva's other specialty. Known as *khöömei*, it is unique to Tuva and emerges from the land itself. Its under- and over-tones reflect sounds that derive from centuries of living on windblown grasslands, in taiga forests, alongside burbling rivers, birdsong, and livestock. The music, says Ted Levin, is a sonic mirror of the natural world. Some of the longest Tuvan epic songs contain half a million lines of verse; the Iliad has sixteen thousand lines, the Mahabharata two hundred thousand. Yurts are perfect settings for stories. Their natural materials allow in sounds of wind and animals—the very soundscape that creates song and story. Later, in the National Museum, beneath that vault full of Scythian gold, we are treated to a recitation by Chirgilchin, one of the country's famed quartets. Igor, Mongün-ool, and Aldar play a two-stringed *igil* and three-stringed *doshpulur*, the *byzaanchy* with bow pulled across horsehair strings; all instruments are made by singer Aldar. Percussion is added by Aidysmaa as she chops together a pair of *duyuglur* horse hooves with *shyngyrush* bells. Their songs are of nature, life and land. We had spent time with camel herders, horse men and women, sheep and goat herders, cattlemen. And here was it all, captured in haunting music.[8]

Before nightfall, I climb another hill in time to see the ewes and lambs returning in a meandering caravan, back to the safety of the island byre small on the vast steppe. As I watch, a falcon swings around the sky, halfway between the land and clouds.

Altair strolls up, sits beside me, and says "We are grateful for our isolation."

We return to town and its lovely administration block, and a celebration with vodka and brandy before the thin heat of the day has fled to the starry sky. Despite my thermals, I again shiver through the whole night under the single blanket.

As Tuva navigates its third decade, changes can be expected. Across Siberia, a priority will be to build new resilience into culture and economy. In a recent report, the federal agency Rosshydromet concluded that climate change has already had a greater effect in Russia than in other parts of the world. They are consistent with the findings of the IPCC's Fourth and Fifth Assessments of 2007 and 2013. What has happened already in Siberia is bad enough: an increase in average temperatures over thirty years of 1.33°C, greater than global averages, with the largest increases in minimum and maximum daily temperatures occurring in the cold season; and a decrease in the number of frosty days. Over the same period, annual precipitation increased by 7.2 millimeters per decade, resulting in more river runoff. The number of days with snow depth of greater than 20 millimeters has increased by six to ten days per decade. Yet up in the Arctic, the extent of snow ice has declined by 9 percent per decade since 1980.

The forecast is not good for Tuva and surrounding regions. Additional precipitation in Siberia will be in the solid phase, increasing snow depth and resulting in more melt in spring with consequential flooding. Vegetation zones will shift northward, and car transportation along frozen *zimpik* roads and solid rivers will become tricky. The incidence of infectious and parasitic diseases of humans and animals will grow, particularly of tick-borne encephalitis, Lyme disease, hemorrhagic fever, and malaria. Long periods of dry and hot weather will increase the incidence of forest fires. It is a tradition to set grassland fires to encourage new growth, to kill ticks, and to destroy grass seeds with twisting awns that bury themselves into sheep and goats.

All will have adverse effects on Tuva. Deeper snow in winter affects livestock viability and increases the pressure on herding families; parasitic diseases will affect livestock; spring flooding may influence choices of spring campsites; and shifting vegetation zones may mean migration patterns have to change. Nonetheless, there is cause for hope. Tuva is one of the few parts of the world that explicitly supports nomadic herding at policy level, and shamanism and Buddhism flourish again. On the other hand, factories have closed, rural electricity supplies are in disrepair, and there is much unemployment in the city and rural towns.

The eight businesswomen at Erzin market are grumpy. They did not want to be called away. Five appear in their twenties, and all stand with arms crossed, or sit leaning back with suspicion. We need small loans, they say. Enough to import goods from Mongolia. The shopping center was set up five years ago by the mayor's administration to stimulate small businesses. Now there are twenty-five stalls, mainly selling clothes and other consumer goods imported from Mongolia and China. There are a couple for food, and one for solar panels. None of the businesswomen received credit from the banks, even though all tried. It came from relatives, by sales of family livestock, or from husbands working in the civil service.

"It is hard," says one woman from across the vast distance between them and us. "We cannot borrow money from the bank because we are not permanently employed with a salary."

If they had credit, they said they would open more stalls, increase the range of goods, open food stores, and buy and sell jewelry. They also said they would employ more local men as *camels* to carry goods from Mongolia to Erzin. But the banks are no help: they prefer to make fewer large loans rather than many small ones. Microcredit is Nicholas's expertise, and successful schemes have been set up in western Russia. But this is going to be hard. Out on the periphery, there are both advantages and disadvantages.

Many family-based ideas exist for small businesses, but it can take time to obtain permissions. Perhaps felt from wool and leather from skins: both are now discarded, as there is no small-scale equipment available. The Soviet era was large and factory based. A constraint on many rural families is the lack of electricity. This was supplied to camps and collective farms in the Soviet era. Now the options are local generation by diesel generators or solar panels. This could allow adoption of electric shears, machines for mowing grass and cleaning out manures, lighting to ward off predators, and pumps for well water. Sometime later, I receive an e-mail from Dolaana.

"I'm doing well," she says. "I own a small canteen. Everything is quite good."

—◦◦◦◦—

A rime of ice had formed on the inside of the block's windows. In the car park, we skitter on the frozen puddles, and make our way through the wide streets to Altair's house. If you grew up here, and moved to a crammed industrial city, it must be profoundly disturbing. The streets are earthen, and fifty meters wide; mountains rim the horizon. The lace tablecloth is laid with cheeses, potato-and-mutton soup, pickled tomatoes and beets, salami meats, and chunks of bread. This has been a long winter of deep snows, strong winds, hard surfaces that prevented animals digging to the grass below. We feel lucky to be near the stove, with warm broth and hot tea.

On the road to more herders, there is nothing vertical above grasses, snow patches, inky black clouds, the road marked with white lines. At a junction is a stop sign: the road is empty for dozens of miles. A village of low white houses with dark roofs appears under a mountain of black rock rising above the snowfields. There's another cluster of leaning electricity poles and aerials. Ahead, the snow falls heavily, and the windscreen wipers snap from side to side and we peer out at more road signs with sole exclamation marks, at the ghosts of cattle in the blizzard, nosing at feed. At one camp, children with felt hats run among Angora goats with colored ribbons tied to their horns for identification. At another, the winter quarters are built from logs. From the windows, we see burial mounds on the plain that will fast disappear when the spring grass grows.

At a sacred mountain, we sit in tiny camp quarters to eat. Heat radiates from the stove, and steam bubbles from the pan. Everyone stays fully wrapped, loosening only an outer jacket or tossing a hat on the bed. From the byre, paths lead across the steppe, away from the mountain, marked by a winter's worth of animal droppings. A shepherd unties his horse from a wooden wall where a bloody hide is pinned out with nails, his eyes drawn to distant peaks eighty kilometers away. At the yurt of a Bactrian camel herder, a purple carcass hangs from the blue lattice by his bed. By the red plastic clock hang two rib-cages. The herder's hands are blackened, his face leathery, smoke from his cigarette curling with the sweet spruce from the stove. The white-faced camels have foppish fringes, and are shedding their thick tawny coats, humps slumped; the knock-kneed youngsters are white with long spindly legs. As I climb a nearby hill, heavy dark cumulus rush over and the camp disappears in shadow and then snow falls.

Temnejir is the reciprocity that forms the cultural strength of nomadic life. One relative may look after school-age children in a village, while a herding parent will look after the other family's animals. Cultural continuity for future generations is going to be key. *Temnejir* also means that sons and daughters come to livestock camps during vacations to help with grass cutting and hay making. "It's their duty," observed one sheepherder. Children from the city often spend the three months of summer in the country, and it is not unusual for school to start with many children still away. Where children in many parts of the world are becoming increasingly disconnected from nature, this is not true in Tuva. They are said to be able to forget the trappings of modern life in the country, though many families now have solar panels on their yurts to run a television or DVD player.

At the mouth of the canyon leading up into sacred Kezhege mountain, Slava Kanzai piles offerings on a stack of kindling. He looks up, and we move closer. He lights them with the clink of his metal cigarette lighter, and wispy smoke drifts toward the pole tied with prayer satins of blue, red, yellow, and white. After a time, when the spirit of the mountain is content, we walk up into the pink sandstone canyon sculpted by water and wind. A central well opens up, flags tied to every bush. It is good luck to leave something that relates to a wish, and there are baby dolls, children's toys, model houses and cars, and plastic animals placed on every surface. Here more flags are tied to bushes and fingers of rock.

A narrow fault leads to the roof of this world, and yet the steps are slick with several inches of ice. We can just about go up, but I am fearful about the return. At the top, I crawl out to an outcrop that overlooks the crater. And smile. Behind, the land slopes gently away to the valley floor. The song of insects is deafening, grasshoppers and the buzzing of bees. But when I sit down, all fall intensely silent. Yellow lichen leaks down the far wall, and a carving on a vertical face seems far from anybody's reach. I sit wrapped in the hushed quiet, and absorb into this place, melting away, as if closed off from the rest of the world, entering another.

As we walk away to the nearby river, not a tree in sight, leaving the insects to the mountain, an arctic halo forms around the sun, echo of stones that encircle those many Scythians. We all stare irresponsibly, astonished at this sign in the ice crystals of altostratus.

Later we stop again to watch a white cumulus cloud cast its shadow on a distant hill. Between the quivering grass and the sky, a small falcon circles, shrill music over a land of grass.

5

SNOW
Karelia, Finland

150° West of Date Line

Deep in taiga forest, lights gleam a welcome from the factory door. Seine netters wrapped in many layers crowd around the kitchen table, clutching strong coffee laced with vodka. Sweet biscuits just carried over from Russia are broken and shared. When the clear spirit bottle is empty, all click into intense activity. Torpedoes and chain saws are loaded onto snowmobile sleds alongside nets and plastic tubs large enough for half a tonne of fish. In the sensate surroundings, the few instructions are just whispered. Everyone knows his job. There is icy silence from the trees, then roar of snowmobile engines, lights streaming into the darkness. We hold tight on a towed sled as it bounces on the frozen lake.

At a certain *apaya*, the chosen fishing area, we stop and a long-bladed chain saw roars into life. Snow is scraped away, and the saw bites into the ice. A rectangular hole is cut, and dark water bubbles up into the harsh light of head-torches and headlights. Frozen machinery is unwrapped from cracking tarpaulins. It is well before any sign of dawn, and we will settle here for another eight or nine hours. There are no stars, no lights from the distant shore. Massive nylon nets are fed into the hole, and the robot torpedoes are slipped into the deep to guide the net outward and then slowly away for half a kilometer. In the old days, the seines were linen or cotton, tied with moose sinews or more recently manila ropes, weighted with stones wrapped in woven birch bark, and pulled by horses. From beneath us now comes the grumbling of motors, and under the ice we can see ghastly lights down in that icy underworld.

There is no marking of dawn. It just gradually stops being dark, and a neon blue light rises from the snow. Now the nets are under, and everyone stamps his feet. Esa Rahunen turns off his head-torch and pours cups of sweet tea and laces them with minty vodka. It keeps us alive as the wind now tears across the open landscape.

"This is a new *apaja*," points Esa. "We call it K1, because it's hard to pull," he laughs, harder than K2.

It is also beside the place where Risto Ketolainen's father lost a sled through thin ice in the late 1970s. One day the sled might snag the nets. I am glad of my borrowed hat of arctic fox fur, yet the hardy fishermen leave off gloves for extended periods. They hardly seem touched by winter's grasp, but you see the effects on their craggy faces. Joking and laughing, they face another day of cold and hope. But more of acceptance: if there are vendace, the main whitefish of these freshwater lakes, they will take them back; if they decide not to come, then there will be another day. Constant acts of patience mean survival out on the ice. Out here, the elemental land quiets all minds. But then thoughts creep in, and I'm wondering how everyone is, back home. Then I am hauled back by the wind and driving snow.

I had come almost directly to the North. The car to the airport was delayed by traffic chaos in our own snows, and I almost missed the flight. Then a calm taxi steered through the deeper snows of Helsinki where, it seemed to me, the roads are sensibly not gritted and salted. The driver's father is from Liverpool, but he'd never been to England. On a long platform, I stamp my feet, and then climb aboard the hissing train for the journey to the town by the Russian border. After some hours, I move from the bright metal and plastic of the carriages to the curtained restaurant car, down-lighters with a warm glow above the polished wooden tables. And then we're running late too. The only other people in the car are female commuters, chewing sandwiches and texting home. Outside the snow lies thickly. A train with dozens of flatbed trailers piled high and chained with trunks of pine and spruce glides by, snow peppered on the long timbers.

The near-empty train pulls into Joensuu at midnight, the town established by a Russian czar in 1848, and at last I am clambering down to an icy track through swirling snow. Tero Mustonen is elected leader of his village of Selkie as well as founder of the northern Snowchange Cooperative, and I climb into his winter car for the thirty-kilometer ride further toward the border. More calm driving on snow, soft tires, bit of slewing here and there.[1]

Nighttime arrivals are always heavy with mystery, and I can see the two-hundred-year-old farm buildings of solid pine set around a large courtyard under a deep layer of silent snow. All around is a curtain of pine and silver birch, encrusted white too. Inside a large stone stove warms the main room; across the yard is the sauna hut. Cold ghosts of farmers and fishermen stalk the dark dairy, stables, boathouse, granary. A moose skin hangs on the barn wall. At 3 a.m. we are up again to drive south to Puruvesi to meet the ice fishermen.

Now we watch and join an ancient practice. Says Tero, these seine fishermen are the "last tradition-bearers of a practice that has been going on for ten thousand years." Olli Klemola is a visitor too today, an elder in the Snowchange Co-op, and a winter seiner too. His long wiry beard frames a thin face with blue eyes behind oval glasses. Snow has settled on his green jacket and hood, his beard already icy. He has been fishing for fifty years over in the west at Pälkäne, but observes that fishing is only one part of his lifetime study of how to be with nature. It's been sad over this time, he observes, a downward loss of knowledge and traditions, damage wrought by the time of machines. He learned with his father, and tried anything himself too, innovating on the ice.

"When you have a certain knowledge of nature, you have awareness, and then you start to see," translates Tero.

"Now society says we must talk more, yet how beautiful is the system when you are alone in it." Olli tells of catching burbot at certain times of winter. You walk quietly out on the ice, lie down, wait as you absorb into the water and ice and air.

Then smack.

You hit the surface with a hammer in a particular way. The fish beneath is stunned, and you just make a hole and pick it out. He says this is the way: to be eye to eye with the fish.

Yet today there is more of a rush. He's not blaming the other fishermen. That's just what happens now. How do you know where the fish are in your lakes, I ask?

"It is an inborn feeling. I know where the fish are." He is famous for this, adds Tero. If you have good relations with the lake, you will have good contact, and know where the fish are.

"My mind is very clear," Olli adds. "I don't have outside pressures, I am just being inside nature. You can ruin a pull if you are not respectful."

Later, after a sauna, I ask if there is a way to transmit this knowledge, and he crosses his arms and legs.

"You can transfer this deep knowledge by asking someone you are with some questions, to see if they have noticed certain things. Over time you can ask more questions, but you cannot tell them. Just observe their growth." There is something unsaid we only approach, about deep aspects of being that are not public knowledge, about how to be with the spirit of the fish in a lake.

Out on the ice, Olli says, "What I told about fishing applies for the rest of nature, birds and animals too. This takes a lifetime of practice."

He picks up a finger-size salmonid, an *Osmerus* smelt, flipped up by the chain saw and nets. It is smaller than a vendace, and has a long cartilaginous spike on the tongue. Eat it, he offers. I take off my glove, and place it in my mouth. It's oily and crunchy. The fisherman's oath, turns Olli to the others. I didn't realize it was some kind of test.

Now it's time to create the pulling hole, half a kilometer away. On the way, the snowmobiles and sleds bog down in sludgy ice and surface water.

"It's too warm," shouts Esa, waving his arms.

Too much slushy snow has fallen this winter on the lake, pushing down with all that weight, forcing water up through cracked leads. Esa stands on the snowmobile, spins around, and looks both near and far. This slush brings more than a hint of fear. Last week, it was almost as warm as freezing point. Now it's back in the mid-teens below. At the new ice hole, everyone looks carefully at the cleared ice. Too many air bubbles to be strong, they conclude; too many warm periods this whole winter. Then in the dingy penumbra of dawn, snow starts to fall, and we quickly become distant figures in a gray land. Nothing defines where sky and land meet, only leaning figures pulling at snowmobiles. Snow pelts into our faces, covers everything in minutes with more gray. It was to be a day sunless and moonless, quenched of any kind of shadow, the lake dark and teeming below.

Now tarps are pinned to poles for protection from the driving gale, a new island camp emerging around the hole, metal-tipped *tuura* for ice-breaking and shovels upright, plastic boxes awaiting fish. Then the bubbling torpedoes arrive with the leading edge of the net, and now the serious business begins. For a couple of hours, Esa, Risto, and Victor will pull steadily. Not too fast, for the fish, if they are there, will sense the nets and flee. Not too slowly, or they will not be enclosed. It is hard work. I pull for a while, but will need the practice of weeks to be even half proficient. The net is fed directly onto a sled, where it promptly freezes solid. The snow sleets in, whipped around us, beating at faces and jackets and oilskin trousers. But still there is laughter, joking. This thing that happens every day when conditions are right. Backs bend, and still the net comes. I walk away a hundred meters, the camp receding, then more. The orange oilskins are the only bright color in this wide land. Under the ice, the seine net closes in, wrapping up, they expect, the fish.

And then I see them. Beautiful. Glittering like so much treasure from the deep. They are crowded in the blue net, leaping, flipping. From the inky water, the shoal of vendace is brought into the air. It is a kind of miracle, that these fish have given themselves up. Now a half tonne is gently scooped up, bucket by bucket load, and the plastic tubs steadily fill. Another harvest is almost complete, and black-eyed, black-backed, the silver fish flip and twist. Before long they are frozen stiff in the lake water that clings to them. Scattered individuals remain on the ice, in the lake water in the hole. A cloudy slime from the fish betrays their recent presence. It seems sad, wasteful, to leave several dozens of individuals, but spending the time to gather every single one will only add marginally to the harvest volume. The fishermen prefer to leave them for the ravens. Now they flip the rectangle of cut ice from under the ice sheet to refill the hole.

I have become cold to the bone by the time we leave, and now the wind angles into us as the snowmobiles slew across the snow and ice and slushy zones. We race to the factory to get the fish sorted, packed, and off to market that very day. But on the way, the lead snowmobile clips a bank of ice and tips over, and I leap away to avoid being crushed. The sled with half a tonne of fish totters, hesitates, and rights itself. We stand around looking at each other, breathing deeply, and now a slower haul across all the damper snow. After the fishing, the work is not done. Everyone helps at the conveyor belt, sorting fish into size classes. Some frozen vendace are packed into ten-kilogram polystyrene boxes, others vacuum wrapped. Local people waiting at the factory door are given bags of fish for nothing, others pay a few euros. Tero will carry some back to his village to give to friends. These vendace help to make community.

—⸺⸺—

We stay the night in Esa's wooden cabin by the lake. Before the sauna and evening meal, I walk the shore as the light bleeds from the sky and leaves a gray rolling cap over silent white lands of birch and pine. There are cabins in the meadows, by the shore, in the forest. Finland has seventy thousand islands and fifty-six thousand lakes, and they say the half million Finns with holiday homes spend eighty to a hundred days in them each year. People here are used to spending a lot of time outdoors, away from it all. Or rather, in it all. A Hansel and Gretel house behind dark trees is immaculately painted, but dark and foreboding. A black dog runs from another porch directly at me, angry and barking, but stops at my shout, then surges forward again. I manage to walk on, wondering if we only became scared of wolves after we bred dogs to be on guard and thus be ready to attack other humans. Maybe we caught the wolf-hating from our domestic dogs.

The sauna offers deep heat and the sweetness of birch leaves. But it comes with a test: now for the lake. Near the house or cabin, no one minds popping out completely undressed. But out on the ice, with long hours far from heat, you would not take any such risks. To be respectful is to understand how dangerous is the land. Like mad hermits, we scoot from the sauna to the shore where a wooden cap keeps open a square of water. I push past the ice by phragmites reeds, where a muskrat is said to come up to breathe. I climb in, and dip my head under the surface, and break back up, sucking in air, giddy with cold. Down by this ice, there is no summer hell of blackflies. We head back to the sauna, and then have late dinner at Esa and Vuokko's, talking about families, children, grandchildren. Esa plays his guitar for a few moments, long hair flowing now, the ponytail of work loosened. He's excited by the prospect of seeing old heroes—the English rockers Deep Purple are coming to Joensuu in the summer. But when autumn has come at home, and a mob of swallows is chittering and swerving around my garden, an e-mail comes back from Selkie.

They canceled at the last minute, writes Tero.

Esa is spokesman for the traditional fisherman hereabouts; he too knows where are the fish. The previous year, we had headed south to the Saimaa lake system to meet Esa to learn about the many lake landscapes, about dreaming up the fish, and about the expanding trajectory of climate change. A hard glittering sunlight shone across the open lakes at that time; in the forests the shadows were deep and still. We met at his garage where an engine lay in pieces, and repaired to his kitchen for coffee and whiskey. It will be cold out on the huge lakes of ice. When he looks, though, he sees stories, memories and fish. And five landscapes.

To succeed, you need to know the lake bed, the water column and its layers and currents, the undersurface of lake ice, the ice itself with its leads and treacherous secrets, and finally the air above carrying winds and weather. Across Puruvesi, Esa has 135 *apaja*, and on the table he lays out the family's secret maps, passed carefully across generations. Each *apaja* is now marked by GPS coordinates, each has layered stories. It is landscapes that contain dream and *tietäjä* seer knowledge. Such spiritual knowledge is not shared. It is ancient, rightly closed to outsiders.

This collective ice-fishing is a tradition once run by whole communities with horses and sheer muscle power. These fishermen remember when the seines were pulled by skittering horses on the ice. Forty-meter poles were used to guide the seines under the ice. In 1969, the first snowmobiles were introduced, a decade later mobile diesel engines to pull the nets, and in the 1990s GPS and underwater robots to guide torpedoes for the first time. It's a fine mix of the traditional and the modern. The problem, though, is numbers of practitioners. The region had fifty teams in the 1950s; by the 1980s it had fallen to twelve; now Esa's single cooperative has only eleven members. Seining crews are now male, though in the past women worked on the ice too. Today they are mainly involved in sorting and preparing the fish after harvest. These fishing practices have shaped and influenced this place over millennia. And to the advantage of fish and people. It is disturbing that we might be looking at the end of something so ancient.

Each morning, Esa decides which site will be the best to fish. He keeps a diary so that he can check what he did and how much was caught in previous years. But he also checks the winds, weather, and more importantly dreams. He describes how his father used to dream where the fish would be, and go there. He leaves the details of this procedure open.

"Just let the land speak to you," explains Tero later.

The other threat to these traditions is climate change. The fishing season has been from November to April for as long as anyone can remember. But they are losing up to a month at either end. Warm winds from the south are the problem, bringing fronts and warm air bad for proper ice formation. A little bit of cold is not good enough. They may need to adopt new methods, but will need different nets, boats, and above all will rapidly have to acquire and apply the necessary knowledge.

We walked from the cooperative's small factory onto the great lake under a light of breathtaking intensity and sky of shattering endless blue. On the horizon was a line of trees, and the light came from every direction. It was as if we were inside a white sun. Standing in the long light and deep cold, it was easy to appreciate that all journeys, all pilgrimages even, that make places sacred are in part internal travel, a reconnoiter inward, as Rob Macfarlane observes in *The Old Ways*. Snowmobile tracks curved out from the shore, cutting the sparkling sheen of snow. In the distance, we saw a black dot appear. The wind whipped granules of snow into a pulsing layer. Our long shadows stretched far across the tracks. And there, a red fox's tracks too. We stooped to look. The dot was joined by another, but neither seemed to be getting nearer. At the last they resolved into snowmobiles, and then we heard the high-pitched buzz. The first arrived with a pile of frozen nylon nets, the second with a plastic tub containing just two hundred kilograms of vendace. Both men's faces were beetroot red. No hat or goggles, but it was minus twenty-five out there. I had every kind of layer, yet know it is much colder on a rapidly moving vehicle.

The tub was hauled into the packing shed. Inside the catch glittered. We were drinking coffee and talking about the cooperative, which has received EU, government, and local support, when a commotion broke out. An MP who's head of the government's fishing and hunting committee had turned up unannounced with entourage. He was shown around, nods and listens, then at the kitchen table eagerly told stories about wolves. Round them up and shoot the lot, Tero translated. A danger to us all. He recalled how he regularly teases one of the green MPs. Wolves are a danger to people. And nature lovers, no time at all for them either, he laughed. A big problem is that some of these wolves may be technically Russian, sneaking across the border to steal prey on this side. Across the table, the fishermen looked at each other, raising eyebrows in the tiniest of twitches. On the wall was a montage by one of the fishermen's grandchildren, nineteen multicolored fish being enclosed by a net. They let him talk as they sat captured at the table in the kitchen, sipping the by-now bitter coffee.

The oldest net in the world is from Karelia, stitched perhaps ten thousand years ago. Along with other archaeological, linguistic, and genetic evidence, this shows that there has been continuous occupation since the end of the last ice age. The traditions of Karelia are ancient, but they were elevated into myth when a young district doctor sat under a pine tree with a seine fisherman, Juhana Kainulainen, also a hunter, healer, and *tietäjä* spirit man. Elias Lönnrot was dictated 2,341 lines of oral poetry by Kainulainen in the midsummer of 1828, and wove these into *The Kalevala*, an epic that came to shape regional and national identities. It also provided many ideas for a certain J. R. R. Tolkien.

The great pine still stands alone on a rise in the Hummovaara meadow, taller by a half than any nearby. To the west the winter sun is pinned to distant trees, and the pine is fiery pink. We tramp through deep snow in our own mini-epic, the cold deep, and the silence apparently endless. We stand by this ancient tree, relic of the primitive taiga, perhaps four hundred years old, and pay our respects to Kainulainen. His oral history led to *The Kalevala*, and Matti Kuusi has noted that a poem of this sort, derived from folk stories, is similar to the strata of a burial mound full of the artifacts of generations. It was common in the nineteenth century for poets and bards across Karelia to have individual repertoires of five to ten thousand lines. Men on fishing trips could sing all night without repeating the same song. It is clear that *The Kalevala* as written by Lönnrot is only part of the real collective epic.²

Väinämöinen is the central character: the setting a heroic world of some previous dark ages in which the worldview is animist, distinctly not the Lutheran or Orthodox imposed by the invasive Swedes and Russians over the previous centuries. Of Väinämöinen, the everlasting singer, the story says: "He lingered there many years, continued living / On the island with no words / On the mainland with no trees." He catches a revered pike, and observes "the catcher's hands the sweetest / the hunter's fingers the holiest."

"I wonder what these pike-teeth, this wide jawbone—could become, were they in a smith's workshop," wonders Väinö, and he makes a *kantele*, a stringed instrument of fish fins and bones. The pike-bone *kantele* is played by old Väinö: "there was none in the forest / running on four legs / or hopping on foot / that did not come to listen." Squirrels, stoats, elk and lynx, wolf and bear ran long distances, scrambling up a spruce, swung on a pine, to listen and marvel. "There was no creature / not in the water either / that did not come to listen." The pike and water dogs, salmon, whitefish, roach, perch, pollans, and other fish too, listen to Väinö's tale, take note of the music. Väinö "played for one day / played for two / and there no one / no animal, who did not fall to weeping / whose heart did not melt."

Tero and I are knee-deep in snow as dusk now races across the land, and clap our hands in chestnut mittens of reindeer skin. The great dome of Arctic sky seems to be held in place by this tree of fissured bark and drooping branches heavy with snow. Here in Kesälahti it is known as Lönnrot's pine, which is a bit of a cheek as it had been for generations the sacrificial tree of the hunters, gatherers, and singers of the Kainulainen family. Now a weariness comes with the half light, and soon the path of the birds, Linnunrata, the Milky Way, will appear in the heavens. The waxing crescent of moon is slim in the darkening sky, grading to cobalt and purple, and the tree is now a silhouette, more powerful it seems, as the dark arrives. We had gone to the pine.

That night we are possessed by a crazy whim. Shall we climb up the roof to reach the sky? As midnight approached, we clambered on the roof of Tero's farmhouse. It's getting on for minus thirty degrees. Up one vertical ladder, and then I halt. There's a terrifying transfer to be made across and then up the snow-covered roof. Finally we sit at the peak. Heart thumping, then slowly calmed and uplifted. The jeweled necklace of our own galaxy is brightly distant. The Milky Way was the tree to the heavens for shamans. We see the upper world, imagine the underworld. I wonder how we will get down. Some say you can see futures in the stars. There are no northern lights, but the sky seems both very near and far as it rotates around

Polaris. The cult of the Great Bear is widespread in the Northern Hemisphere. The Arctic, after all, was named after the Greek *arktos*, bear.

In all directions down here, we can see nothing human. Just trees and snow in the starlight. Karelians say it doesn't seem right to be able to see your neighbor. Finland is a big land for five million people, many now in cities. From the forest comes a dry piercing crash as a tree shatters like frozen pottery. The shot echoes across the meadows and forests. This is a sign, like many if you look and listen closely, that the world is changing. When the weather warms suddenly, melting ice collects around the trunks and branches of trees, refreezes, and then at night squeezes the life out of the tree with a shattering blow.

According to Finnish tradition trees are held to be animate and their spirits strong. Before cutting, it was always a tradition to bang on the trunk with the handle of an axe to warn the spirit to leave. Many are sacred, like Kainulainen's pine; others signifiers of messages. Another tradition was to cut branches in a particular pattern so that as the tree grew, the gaps would always remain. Some were memorials to the ancestors and the dead. But as with anything important in people's lives, trees have long been a focus for political and religious clashes. When the Lutheran mission pushed its way east from Sweden to meet the Orthodox Russians advancing toward the west, sacred trees were formally called *suspicious trees*. Edicts were issued by both church and state to destroy all of them. In Lapland, the Lutherans also burned Sámi shamans at the stake. The aim: to break this animist nonsense, to make people of the forests and lakes see sense and become proper Christians. This was why Lönnrot ended up etched on the heart of every Finn: he was the first to write down the oral traditions of centuries to stop them from being forgotten.

The southern boreal taiga of forests and lakes was under sustainable use, with pristine patches to the middle of the twentieth century, with the main lifeways being small-scale agriculture, hunting, and fishing. Settled agriculture was adopted only five hundred years or so ago. Hunting, fishing, and swidden clearings in the forest formed the land-use patterns. Families moved to harvest seasonal resources: from farm hut to hunting and trapping places, to fishing hut by a lake, and then in the autumn people gathered mushrooms and berries. All the land was known and claimed, and there was no word for wild, though someone coming from outside might have thought they looked upon many empty wildernesses. This was not settled farming, nor was it classic nomadic. It was hybrid foraging, hunting, fishing, and farming, in which knowledge and practice were interwoven. The Sámi people who today live in Lapland used to live in Karelia too, remembered in some place names of the region.

In the kitchen, Tero declares, "People living in Savo-Karelia have witnessed both colonial onslaught and full-blown modernity that have caused critical impacts on our landscape, tradition, and spiritual practices."

"However, we are still here." His wife Kaisu looks up, and smiles.

But today, the tree problem remains. All the forests outside formal national parks are termed economic forests. They grow to be cut, state the authorities. The modern management method of choice is clear-felling. Efficient and brutal, it sweeps history away, leaving nothing but land ready for replanting. Soon the old-growth forests will be gone forever: only 4 percent remain. Forest size used to be determined by how long it took to walk through them. Many forests are now called *ten-minute forests*, and the forest companies are succeeding where religious edicts did not. But now comes worse. An innovation: the new capability to rip out all the stumps too, as these are being burned to create bioenergy. The huge machinery and soil disruption results in destruction of sites. The result: pollution and runoff into the once pure lake systems.

Sweden established the forest industry in the late 1600s to meet the demand for tar from pine. Forest use for timber and the fur trade continued, but it was not until after the Three Wars of 1939–44 against Germany in Lapland that clear-felling was invented. The state forestry agency was established with a military command structure that persists to today. If you own a forest, it will be clear-felled one day. In the past twenty years, so many roads have been built that no forest is further than three kilometers from a point of extraction. The Puruvesi lakes have so far avoided the pollution from the paper and pulp industry, but this may not last.

Outside forces are also waiting for the vendace cooperative to fail. Trawlers could be licensed instead, and the lake efficiently swept clean of fish in the summer months. There are Saimaa ringed seals here too, endemic to this inland freshwater system. They migrate like salmon, treating the whole system as if it were a sea. The fishermen never report sightings, though, as they fear declaration of a conservation zone, which could lead to their own exclusion. North of Joensuu were the spawning grounds of the migratory freshwater salmon, but these are now blocked by several hydro plants. The salmon also undertake a two- to three-year migration around the lake system, but cannot get past the plants to the old spawning grounds. Now they are electric-shocked and milked in a hatchery. How will new generations of fish find their way back, you wonder? There is still a domestic tussle to be had.

One afternoon as Finland's two million saunas are being fired up for weekend ceremonies, we beat the bounds of a local forest in search of moose. In dense groves the sunlight never reaches the ground. We tramp through heavy drifts, up rises and down slopes, the fresh snow squeaking beneath our boots. Otherwise, deep silence: not a bird or animal moves. We see chains of hare prints, moose hollows, and many jinking rodent tracks, half hidden under overnight snow. We scramble down paths toward lakes and swidden meadows, where the snow glitters like mica against the low sun, the snow rippled like sand on a beach, tree shadows stretching far. Our footfalls crump thought the hard surface into the soft snow beneath. We reflect on the lucky lynx. They have come to like climate change in spring. The winter-camouflaged hares become cruelly apparent when the snows melt early.

We walk up a hill to look east toward the Russian Republic of Karelia. The boreal belt extends all the way to Siberia. Next year, this forest will be gone. Majestic giant trees, sunlight on their tops, so bright your eyes hurt. Bark of saplings chewed, stripped, more signs of moose. And beyond, a great boreal territory, stretching seven to eight time zones to the Pacific. The wind from the east freezes my face, ice forming on my hat and hair. Another rifle shot crashes from the cold forest. We do not know it yet, but the forest department will come shortly with no consultation. In they will lumber, and trash the memories and ghosts of local people and animals. They haul out the timber and scar the soils, leaving towering piles of branches. Tero sends me pictures by e-mail. I could not believe the methodical damage.

Tero and I reflect on a conference we had both attended at the famed museum by Central Park in New York. He had gone with his friend, Vyacheslav Shadrin from Siberian Kolyma, and they pressed for permission to see artifacts *recovered* during the Jesup Expedition into the North Pacific led by famed anthropologist Franz Boas. In a vast underground hangar, they are taken to shelves containing birch-bark maps and shaman drums. It's too much magic, and Slava nearly faints. The spirits are angry, he whispers. The maps are the only examples surviving, yet here they are in one of the world's most famous cities. But the museum will not return them. In the farmyard we stop to look at Tero's own collection of birch-bark artifacts from the farm: fishing weights, baskets, knapsacks, butter churns, spinning wheel and leather grouse decoys. Birch has many other uses: the sap for drink; gnarls for ladles; bark for utensils, decorations, canoes, medicine, glue, and fire starters; branches for whisks; and the wood for skis, axe handles, sleighs, and firewood. The sun has gone but strangely the sky seems to come alight with pinks and magnesium white. We return to the dark farmhouse where Kaisu has lit the roaring stove and sits reading by candlelight. In *tuonela*, the underground home for the dead, everyone sleeps forever. On the shelf at home is now one of those finely woven birch-bark net weights.

—⬩⬩⬩—

The next morning on the later trip, Tero, Olli, and I join Markku Tervonen and Asko Karjalainen. It was after the night in the bunkhouse by the lake, the wind tugging and beating at the windows, where we had basked in the sauna to recover core heat, and then thrown it all away by scampering down the path to the lake and climbing down the ladder into the black underwater. After all this, we will be on the ice again in the darkness so complete that it is again difficult to imagine dawn will ever come.

We leave after coffee and vodka again, cigarette clamped to Markku's mouth, his face creased and beaten by years of extreme weather. He wears a small blue hat with earflaps, but no cover for face or neck. Asko, by contrast, has a great black fur hat almost as wide as his shoulders. His face is just as weathered as Markku's. Like each pair, their *nuotta* technique is different. The net is coiled on a ten-foot drum leaking rust on a sled of its own. And at this *apaja* there is more slush than snow. In the earliest blue light, I later see every footstep soon fills with water. This morning it is wetter and colder, slightly clearer, for we can see the line of trees on the horizon. The frozen nets are pulled off the drum, snapping the lake's silence, splashing into the hole and disappearing again into the underworld. A half kilometer away, a diesel engine is started, and it will pull the net steadily for six more hours.

Markku is the dreamer of the pair: "Ninety percent of the landscape is in my mind," he says, narrowing his eyes.

His family has been fishing the same *apaja* for four hundred years. Today's is called *The Ice Road*. Sometimes he dreams the site, the unconscious mind processing all that is known and received. This will be a good catch, he predicts. Today a keen wind exposes weaknesses, and I quickly become cold. The landscape is dark above and light below. The air becomes more and more blue, as if the color itself was thickening, as Yuri Rytkheu has written of Siberia. Slow time, feeding of the nets into the hole, then the wait as the clumping diesel engine draws in the lines. I began to shiver in the long wait, and stamp off into the distance to generate internal heat. My camera comes to a halt, and I fumble out the battery to warm it against my skin. The raw wind continues. Asko waves, and magically takes out a dozen sausages, placing them on a blackened metal grille. He snaps a cigarette lighter and his blowtorch roars into action. The bubbling sausages scorch black under the charcoal sky, and we grin as we absorb the heat.

These men are here every day in winter, on the snow, above the depths, in the winds that blow down from the Arctic or across from Siberia. There is much waiting. Letting time pass, taking this life step by step. Five hours later, Tero and I lie on the ice and peer down into the lake. Then a dream in the depths, a hint of glittering, then darkness, then more silver tickertape, and up come fish, steadily hauled in. Then I see remarkable shadows of fish cast on the thermocline. Ghosts awaiting the catch. Where can the light be coming from to cast such shadows upward, I wonder? River of silver and amethyst from the underworld, and now up here and freezing solid. Soon the tubs are brimful, and the net is cranked back onto the drum. Scattered on the ice and water are dead fish. Again the only birds we see all day are two patient ravens appearing as the catch is pulled from the slushy waters.

Markku is wistful this February morning.

"We will be the last," he says. "Where are the young people, how will they know what to do?"

Out here on the lake, all of us are old, toward the ends of careers.

This has become Tero's task, though, for he and Snowchange organize seine net trips in both winter and summer for local schoolchildren. Could they be romanced into saving the fishing? First the knowledge, then the pride, then maybe the continuity. With emotional warmth, children could be given awareness of the traditions in Puruvesi and the role of seining in the life of their ancestors. Yet in the past five years, the weather has become noticeably unstable. It can now shift in one day from minus twenty-five to plus temperatures. Markku adds that winds have increased too, and with the instability of the ice, safety has become a greater concern, especially to their wives. The fishermen will be forced to adapt. Steel-reinforced boats will be used until December to continue open-water seining. *Apaja* sites are having to be discussed and exchanged. Perhaps tourism is an option too. These seiners choose to be out on the ice in largely extreme conditions when in theory they could have a job elsewhere. This shows there is something else that survives of great importance.

"This is a strong lesson," observes Tero.

<hr />

You should bring nothing when you enter the land. Just watch and listen. Early one morning at Selkie, we slip down through forests to Ylinen lake, a place name referring to the upper world. Again silence expands from the beginning to the end of human affairs. No wind, just the creak of boots on the snow. The gentle pattering of snow on my jacket. We walk out onto the ice under glowering clouds as if we are inside them, carrying ropes, shovel, hooks to pull the nets, and the *tuura*. This is important business for Tero. But like most people on the land, he loves to tease too.

Will there be a welcome? The nets have been left hanging under the ice. We shovel away the snow accumulated over the old hole, and then pierce it with the *tuura*. These are prized tools, metal and wood a meter and a half long, and wider toward the center to absorb the shock from the ice. Each year, someone loses one into the deeps, even though you make sure, doubly sure, it is looped around your wrist. The old fishermen knew ways of recovery from lake beds by making many holes and lowering strings and pulleys to snag them.

Nearby is an important island where the Selkie villagers gather at the time of spawning vendace. It contains many stories and memories, many of which can only be briefly spoken about, not really discussed. Like the bear, whose name is never mentioned, or indeed whose presence in mind is avoided as there are ways that mind and land intersect, and it is well to respect them. Myth has it that chunky-paw, apple of the forest, grandfather, was banished from the upper to the middle world, and if it chooses to reveal itself, this is an important moment. In the past, birch-bark masks were always worn out of respect by bear hunters during the dances and ceremonies.

We pull the first net, and the second. Both empty. Bare fingers are needed to tie and untie the nets set under the ice. We are both numb before long. The third, by the far shore, has a pike. We are pulling the net of filament, black on snow, black water, and the pike appears, teeth tangled in the filigree. We have been graced with a welcome. A twenty-inch female with roe, who would have spawned as the ice melted. The pike is at the center of creation myths. Eagle was looking for somewhere to lay her eggs in the water world, and she lands on the back of a great pike, who later feels the eggs warming her back. She tips them off to eat, but eagle fights back, and the white of the eggs became the moon, the yolks the sun, and the rest the stars and snow. Now blood spatters this pristine snow scarlet, the guts and head left on a mound of snow for the raven that waits.

Another winter, we caught burbot and trout in the same nets. The wind was bitter, and we quickly grew cold. Like the freshwater cod, burbot need skinning before cooking. Tero slices his thumb, and blood runs bright alongside the nylon red of the net line. With the guidance of Olli, Tero had this year set a traditional wooden fish trap under the ice, an elaborate structure of V-shaped channels and diversions leading to a hooped storage area. We pull up the hoops, but there are no fish. This is another skill that requires transfer. I draw water from the well, shovel snow, and carry wood. Time passes. This year, the snow has drifted to the tops of the barns. The pine planks are rimed with frost and powdered snow. The paths across the yard need clearing every day, for soon they fill with snow and disappear.

We walk to where we had searched for that moose. All that remains are some severed stumps and a single standing dead tree. Ashes do not go back to primary forest. Lives of animals ignored, memories burned in the rush for wood. It was a place where villagers came to collect berries and mushrooms to celebrate autumn. Now it will take a hundred years to recover. The land bled so freely, wrote Farley Mowat of the Barrens in central Arctic Canada. At the front end of the process, the destruction of forests, habitats, and lifeways; at the back end, now climate change. Yet at the same time, these deep traditions are absolute and eternal, as Hugh Brody has observed of the North. From the hill, the sun sets over Joensuu to the west in a blaze of evening light. A giant spiral of smoke rises from a factory fire. Then orange fades to blue, and long farmhouses of the village catch the final light. In the clearing, the tiny Orthodox church has a cross on a dome, the wooden bell-tower ornately carved. The sliver of moon rises in the darkened sky to the east. The sky hardens to black, and the stars light this chilled land. Step by step and pull by pull, we had marked some of the territory.[3]

We smoke the pike under the gnarled apple tree, bowed with snow. Put her in a small box with chips of alder and two sugar cubes, and placed the box over a birch bark fire. Smoke rises from the farmhouse, the first hint of clear sky beyond the layer of cumulonimbus as the light fades in the west. The smoke whirls around us and the swayback barn, both gray-brown in this white land. The fire flames bright, orange and red flames consuming the metal box. The waiting wood is the color of brass. We stand and watch the fire, welcome the heat.

Another branch snaps in the forest and falls with a thump. Otherwise only crackling of flames. No sounds of moose or sleeping bear, or creeping lynx or hiding beaver or otter. Then a tawny owl hoots, twice, opening a wide space on the land. Blue and great tits flock around the feeders, balls of feathers. After half an hour, I taste the pike. The flakes of tender white flesh are sweet and smoky. We leave the rest to cool for dinner long after the light has fled the land. We sit at the long table in the farmhouse, dark pine timbers aged by hundreds of winters. Warm tea, the water pulled earlier from the well across the yard. Modern dilemma: to check texts or not. Minds cannot be troubled here. After the ceremony of smoking the fish, we sit to eat the cold and blackened crumbling flesh. Tero declines. He's never been able to eat fish. Kaisu has also prepared a dish of moose.

We clink vodka glasses. Save for the crackle from the fire, the room is content, silent.

6

SWAMP
Okavango, Botswana

158° West of Date Line

A wall of sound surrounds the vast inland swamp. The sun bled from the sky and darkness rose up to the dome of stars. Now the frogs were in full song. The tent is pitched in a liminal zone between dry and wet Africa. Ahead are twelve thousand square kilometers of delta, extensive stands of papyrus, common reed, bulrush, and miscanthus grass. Behind is the dry savanna of buffalo grasses, aromatic sage, golden mopane trees, and great herds of wandering antelope or elephant. In the cold hours comes a ripping of grass, and the flashlight reflects back pallid yellow eyes of a stilled hippo. It grumbles, and turns away. Later still, there is much hooting and calling, and the *phoosh* of more hippos. All nights are long and noisy.

At home, it was watering twice a day that kept the garden alive during the drought. In the hot wind, a frog leapt through the undergrowth, and bees swarmed around the lavender. A green and orange hawk moth flew in through the windows flung wide. A distant child chuckled, and a squirrel by the steps suddenly twisted and flung itself into the air, and there by the fragrant thyme was a fat grass snake, silvery in the damp. Po Chu-i wrote "a day will no doubt come when dust flies at the bottom of seas."[1] The grass was indeed all to dust, but animals had come to the water. On the night air, the scent of honeysuckle wrapped around the silent darting of bats.

The Okavango wetland begins in the mountains of southern Angola, and flows south through Namibia's Caprivi Strip along the panhandle before six great tributaries fan out to the southwest. Rain falls in January and February in the Angolan highlands, travels twelve hundred kilometers to Okavango, then advances over the delta over the next four months, the flood peaking in July–August in Botswana's dry winter, turning the sand to grass and reeds. Most of the water will run into groundwater and desert, 180 kilometers away at the Maun boundaries. It is a landscape in constant change: waters running and receding seasonally, islands made by termites, channels opened by hippos and elephants, sedimentation, accretion, erosion. Nutrient levels are low, the waters crystal clear. More than nine billion cubic meters pass through in an average year, and though the annual variation in both inflow and rainfall is huge—one year can see double or half the previous—measurements show a decline during the past two decades. Long-term climate studies suggest a pattern over three millennia of forty dry and then forty wet years. The Okavango is now in a drier phase, but no one is quite sure if this is just normal variation.

From above, as the plane wobbled and leapt on hard invisible thermals, coming eventually low to the dusty runway scattered with elephant dung, the swamp of rippling grasses and blue water sparkling in the sunshine is clearly marked with rills and paths, all routes of mysterious animal logic. White salt pans blaze in the middle of circular islands of dead trees and tall termite mounds. The herbivorous architects of these swamps are both small and large. It is easy to imagine the effects of the numerous hippos and elephants, crashing open channels through grasses and reeds, churning riverbeds, stamping out pathways, toppling trees. But there's more biomass out here as termites than in all other herbivores put together. Without them, there would be no islands.

One island type begins with a *Macrotermes* termite mound, and takes a hundred years to become covered with trona salt deposits, clearly visible from the air. The insects fly in to begin their work on a dry patch. As the mound emerges, birds have somewhere to perch, and they deposit tree seeds. As trees grow, leaf transpiration draws water up and inward, leaving salts behind as the island dries and rises. The center becomes super-saline, and now the colonist trees die. Date palms go first, then the broad-leaved trees, until only salt-tolerant fan palms and spiky sporobolus grasses remain. Linear islands, by contrast, form as papyrus mats build up along channels, creating raised peat beds. Roots capture sediments, encourage growth, and as the banks and channel floor rise, so water flow falls. But when a hippo or elephant breaks through the papyrus, the water rushes away to the lower surrounding habitats. Subsequent fire leaves nutrient-rich ash to line the islands, and these sweet floodplains come to support grasses, shrubs, and trees. No islands are high: there is a variation in height of less than two meters across the whole delta's twelve thousand square kilometers.

In this swamp that ebbs and flows like an ocean swell, there are odd contrasts in perspective. In a boat, at water level, you can see yards at a time. Then among the reeds emerge clumps of trees on nascent islands, or the land opens up to wide glittering lagoons. The sun beats on the salty flats during the day, but a quiet serenity descends when the sun dips low, doubling its light with fiery reflections off the still water, a cool furnace at the day's end. Senegal coucals hoot across the marsh, and now the frogs are trilling too.

At dawn in the still gray air, a blackened kettle boils on a flickering fire. The wood glows, light flickering on the underside of trees, water slipping silently past. The guides squat and warm their hands, murmuring hope. It was a noisy night, hooting and calling, near and far. Now it has grown silent. The kettle boils and issues steam. The reeds and feathery papyrus emerge from the gloom, sandy green. Clumps of two or three mopane trees, sometimes five or six, mark growing islands. I stand beneath a wrinkled morula whose yellow fruits are gathered for an alcoholic drink. Somewhat reassuringly, we were not the first: these ferment on the ground too, and are a favorite of elephants and monkeys. The wind blows up, and a cascade of dry leaves flutters down from the trees. White butterflies swirl too, and press on.

As we leave, wavelets clip the boat. The wind drives across the open lagoon, and now the bow slaps loudly, spraying water into the air. But soon the sun is above the reeds, thick with a tangled mist of spiderwebs, and provides warmth that some days never becomes enough. We stop on a grassy atoll where a *mokoro* canoe is moored, but it is too windy to board. Inland are clumps of date palm, ivory palm jackalberry, and acacia knobthorn. A chestnut-red lechwe antelope watches, its lyre horns still, and all around are the great churned footprints of elephants, huge dishes by our tiny feet. Even though the most populous large mammal in the delta, the lechwe is rare to see, its elongated hooves allowing rapid movement into flooded areas. By a patch of white and brown trona, we find three green-and-gray-speckled eggs of a blacksmith plover, all alone on a patch of grass with no nest. The parent birds watch us from a distance, hopping up into the air.

—◦◦◦◦◦◦—

Johanne Nxereku is of these swamps, shaven-headed with dark goatee, and navigates the boat quietly through the vast swamp of miscanthus, phragmites reeds, and clumps of papyrus sedge. He's from Jau on the northwest of the delta, from a farming and fishing community. There are five main ethnic groups in the Okavango: the Hambukushu, Dceriku, and Vayeya, and the two Bushmen groups, Bugakhwe and Ilanikhwe. There are some three thousand subsistence fishers around the delta, using baskets, traps, rods and lines, and net enclosures. The local livelihoods are mixtures of millet and sorghum cropping, fishing, hunting, and collection of wild plants, and livestock. Off-take is low, and they represent little threat to the overall ecosystem, though this has not always been the view. Fish stocks, though, are relatively small compared with other African wetlands, though this marsh is the fishers' larder. They supplement diets with water-lily roots, the outer skin removed, put in the pot with meat or fish. You can buy them at any market. Other wild foods include water figs, fruits of many trees, including morula and jackalberry, and fish, locusts, and cicadas. And termites too. Johanne smiles and explains: termites look at you; you cannot crush their heads. Even after frying, they still stare accusingly.

Once we could have traveled by wooden *mokoro*, hewn from a single piece of *Kigelia*, the sausage tree. Builders would dig deep underground for the place where the main root of the tree comes to a point—this will be the bow of the canoe.

After cutting the tree would come three to four months of work, scouring it out, and intermittently leaving in water to prevent cracking. In the roof of the dining hall hang two such *mokoros*, lacquered and patinated but fissured, their years of advancing through reeds over. Fiberglass has come, as it has to many boatbuilders. The poles used have a distinctive V-end to stop them from sticking in the mud, flipping in the fisherman. It's dangerous enough territory without having the wrong tools.

Nearly 40 percent of Botswana's land is designated as protected areas, a remarkable mix of national parks, game reserves, and wildlife management areas. This is the Moremi Game Reserve, created in 1963 by moving most of the Okavango communities out. Joe Mbaiwa of the University of Botswana has interviewed elders who remember huts being burned and household goods being loaded onto trucks for relocation outside the reserve.[2] This area around Xakanaxa and on Chief's Island used to be the hunting and gathering grounds of the Basarwa, now stationed at Khwai village to the north. A number of studies have shown that wildlife use was sustainable at the time. Yet like almost half the protected areas worldwide, nature preservation was assumed to be delivered by removing local people.[3] In this way, hunters were turned into poachers, gatherers into thieves. Worldwide, central governments have found it easy to assume that wildlife and rural people cannot coexist in the same area.

Exclusions are not new to southern Africa. Laurens van der Post in his 1958 *The Lost World of the Kalahari* searched for the "lost" Bushmen, and came to realize they were not Bushmen only of the Kalahari Desert and of the deepest Okavango.[4] These were simply the places where they survived longest, having contracted away from everywhere else. The first Europeans landed on the Cape in 1652, and relentlessly pursued the Bushmen. They were framed as survivors of the stone age, which does not help to convince moderns that they, too, could have a place in the world. They were inferior, many said, and thus impeded the progress of the superior. "He would not learn," van der Post was told of the Bushmen. "He just wouldn't be tamed."[5]

A decade later, Marshall Sahlins used the evocative phrase *the original affluent society* to describe hunter-gatherers in a novel way. They generally want not, and thus lack not. Their affluence derives from needs and wants being readily satisfied. They work relatively few hours per day, in contrast to farmers and moderns, and seem content. Individuals walk far, and still do, up to twenty-four hundred kilometers a year. They are not troubled by all the things they do not have. But still this has not convinced the settled. Botswana, for all its diamond wealth and political stability, still can do no better than Canada, Australia, Russia, or the United States when it comes to relations with its own indigenous minorities. The San Bushmen were made famous by van der Post, long supported by Survival International, featured in many a documentary about hunting prowess, yet the national narrative remains one of belief that they would be best suited by joining the modern world. The great spaces of the Kalahari seem not to be big enough for a small people to hunt and gather, living as they have always done.

The Basarwa San have been subject to a more recent and bitter conflict over relocation from the Central Kalahari Game Reserve. Government wanted the reserve for wildlife, perhaps for mining too. The people wanted to stay. Government closed local services and capped wells at the village of Xade, and established a new settlement to the west of the reserve at New Xade. People were moved in 1997 and 2002. Still government was firm: this was about "bringing the standards of living of the Basarwa up to the level obtaining in the rest of the country."

The case came to court in 2004. Two years passed, marked by 4,500 pages of legal documents, 134 days in court, and 750 pages of final arguments from each side. Two of the three judges ruled that the residents had lawfully occupied the land, and were unlawfully deprived of it. Those named in the case could return, but only them. Government was not obliged to restore services. Yet the hard positions of both sides were never fully based on evidence. The CKGR is large; the numbers of Basarwa San small; even mines would not take up much land. But animals do need protecting from some hunters. The dispute was really centered on the idea of how people should live, which was certainly not, as one government official put it, "chasing wild animals barefooted." George Silberbauer, Bushmen survey officer in the 1950s and 1960s, made clear in his court evidence that the main objective of establishing the reserve in 1961 was "to protect the food supplies of the existing Bushmen against conventional hunters."[6]

Silberbauer lived with the G/wi San in the CKGR for a decade, dry and cold in winter, a furnace in summer. In *Hunter and Habitat*, he describes the G/wi universe as having three tiers, but with no overarching authority. All creatures have equal rights to existence, and there is no concept of human primacy. At the same time, when misfortune occurs, it is not necessarily because of agency. Things happen, not always with reason, and thus blame is irrelevant.

The G/wi put great emphasis on congenial company, wrote Silberbauer. They express regret when people are not present, when company is missing, and emphasize friendliness, generosity, wisdom, calmness, and good humor. They have respect for animals, but fear lions, leopards, and hyenas, as they can kill. When something can kill you, your conservation ethic is different. Many Bushmen, though not the G/wi, had large menageries of mythical beasts, shadows in the landscape that help explain surprises and uncertainties. Silberbauer lists sixty-five species of useful plants from the desert, used for foods, traps, quivers, fast and slow burn firewood, salads, arrows, glue, bindings, axe handles, fluid sources, poisons, and many medicines. This is not unusual: you have to know plants and animals of the desert to survive. And the location of water too. Sip wells are highly valued: insert a long hollow stick or grass tube deep into hot sands, and suck the water out.

Back at the swamp, there have been important efforts to develop community-based wildlife management, notably for the community of mainly Basarwa Bushmen at Khwai on the northern edge of Moremi. They have been given two controlled hunting areas, coded locally as NG18 and 19, in which they can sell tourist hunting and safari services. Khwai Development Trust is a local institution formed in 2000 to operate wildlife management. They sell their annual quotas to safari operators and hunters. But now comes a new dilemma: becoming reliant on tourists is risky when there is a global recession with no obvious end.

—◦◦◦◦◦—

We travel north, deep into the delta, far from Chief's Island. The permanent swamp of water lilies, water chestnut, reeds and papyrus seems to have no end. The islands here are mostly deep in the reeds, impossible to reach, then we turn up an elephant channel to moor at Ivory Palm Island. A mature patch of dryland where trees are dying. A troop of vervet monkeys scuttles into the sage and fever-tree scrub, squabbling and shouting, and we are left alone with dense birdsong. The ground is a blinding white, crunchy underfoot, like snow on a cold night. Bleached trees stand like so much driftwood sculpture. We climb a collapsed termite mound, and there's a view for dozens of square miles around. The highest point built by the smallest architects. Then, on the far shore, three elephants are sauntering on a ridge, heading for the channel. They stop, waving trunks and catching scent on the wind. Stock still they pause; we too wait.

They resume tearing off leaves, pulling up grass, reshaping the landscape as they move, and then disappear into the reeds. For a moment there is tension. If they decide to come to this island, we need to be anywhere but here. But then splashes, and we see them swimming away. Johanne says that last week, was it Thursday or Friday, an elephant killed a guide on a *mokoro* nearby. It swam after him. He couldn't pole the canoe fast enough, and he was killed. But the tourist in the boat was spared. We sip coffee in the sunshine. An azure sky, white ground, yellow reeds, and patches of deep-green papyrus. We look up, and see they are still swimming upriver.

This may be an inland swamp, the greatest wetland in Africa, but it has not managed to escape invasion by an alien South American weed. *Salvinia* kariba weed was first found in the Zambezi River fifty years ago. It is a native of Brazil, and forms dense mats of up to a meter in depth. The fern is also an ideal breeding ground for mosquitoes, as well as blocking navigation and natural light. Then twenty years ago, scientists found a weevil, *Cyrtobagus salvinae*, in Australia, both adults and larvae actively feeding on salvinia. Participation of the local guides was a second stroke of brilliance. Tanks have been placed out front, full of salvinia and swarming with weevils. The guides collect the weevils or take infected salvinia, and carry them on all their trips. They reinfect wherever they see fresh green ferns. Whole lagoons clear in two to three years in this way. But given the size of the swamp, it's going to be a job that never ends.

We drift up to two maribou storks on a nest over a water fig, two meters from the water but for all the world like they were in the crown of a great forest. A spray of guano is white against the dark green of the fig. We find a huge hammerkop nest wedged in the branches of a jackalberry marsh tree. The nests are abandoned each year, and invaded by snakes. Johanne's parents told him and other children never to climb those trees: the folk story is that the misshapen birds catch snakes and carry them to their nests to protect their eggs.

All this water, but no one swims. At least not intentionally. Unlike most of Africa, bilharzia is not a problem in these slowly moving waters, though you can catch the parasite from the embrace of a leech. It is the crocodile to fear. One came into Xakanaxa camp and tried to grab a visitor. Another snatched a worker from his tent, pulled him toward the river, and only the actions of colleagues heaving an outboard motor persuaded it to let him free. Some years ago, another visitor was killed when swimming out front. Such stories of the dangers of wildlife are told everywhere with some relish. They help to define a place, like all legends designed to limit behavior. A cobra bit an old man on his hand, and he died after a couple of visits to Maun's distant hospital. A hyena took a child from a tent at the camp along the waterfront. I recall all too well an early childhood experience of walking into our bathroom and coming face to face with a spitting cobra, reared up. But there the memory stops. Hippos, though, are the worst, always bad-tempered. You cannot outrun a charging two-ton hippo at thirty miles per hour, but you can hide. Dive into bushes and keep quiet, is the stark advice. Or better still, just don't wander around at night.

I suspect the focus on these ancient causes of death is simply because they, with infectious diseases, are the main sources of illness and death. Cancers, cars, cardiac disease, and obesity are modern society's narratives. We escape the infectious diseases and dangerous animals, thinking this is progress, and walk into another set of causes of ill-health. Here the animal dangers are shared among visitors with an old frisson and fear. Here is the presence of real animals that can kill. In other places, there is fear of water babies, mermaids, fairies, wildmen. Whether these beings exist is not really the point. If we tell their stories, creating codes that transcribe behavior, then it can be no bad thing. In 1987, Henry Sharp wrote of the apparently irrational behavior of the Chipewyan people of the Canadian Northwest. Their universe is populated by many giant creatures that both shape the environment, whether lakes, rivers, or forests, and influence behavior. The giant otter is deeply feared: it knows what is in a person's thoughts, and thus provokes honesty and respect. It wreaks dreadful deathly revenge too, when someone breaks the codes.[7]

At dinner, collective discussions circle close to controversy. We sit at the long table fashioned from reclaimed railway sleepers. Above are the two hanging *mokoros*. The Flemish dentist and his wife have been everywhere, taking many long holidays, say there is no problem in Belgium at all: it is just the lazy, grabbing French in the south. The Texans from Austin like hurricanes as they bring them only rain: they're happy now, they've done Africa. The Australians are confident about their choices: their daughters are both travel agents. Our Botswanan hosts smile and eat slowly. They've heard it all before. The conversation reverts to the wildlife celebrities. For some, the day is a disappointment if untouched by the spectacular or the predatory. Lion, leopard, wild dog, not really elephant—too common. Giraffe, perhaps. But chacma baboons and impala feeding together, vervet monkeys leaping or swaying from a branch, the jumbled chatter of glossy red-billed buffalo weavers, or the shocking red beak of a tall saddle-billed stork—none of these are of more than passing interest. No one comments on the many impala. Yet if we saw one such herd of deer at home, we'd all be captivated and telling the tale. Any form of ecotourism is built on high expectations of visitors. Guides need not to just know, they must be magicians too.

A poor leopard is hunted over two days. At night, we hear its gruff vibrant cough, and by light see the tracks leading to a depression of wet grass and a single tree on which three expectant vultures are perched, silently waiting. No wonder big cats are hard to see. We had been trumped: out in the quiet wide lagoon, the call crackled on the radio about the leopard. We should go back, Johanne half asks. No, no, I want to say, let's stay here on the water. But our Italian friend has never seen one, and really cannot resist the pull. We return, and race from the camp to find the tree with a young tsessebe antelope cradled in its branches. Vehicles circle through the grass when we should be on the road, and then reluctantly the haunted leopard rises up, looks at us, and slinks away. The mottled cat is the same color as the grasses and their shadows, and within ten meters it is gone, reabsorbed. We breathe again. It is a sight to behold, this wild cat at such close proximity. The mayhem will be forgotten, the outcome only what visitors expect.

—◦◦◦◦◦—

Again the winter air is cold, and an easterly wind drives across the flats and through the woodlands. A pale sun seems to have no effect in this early hour. We stand wrapped in blankets, but my hands shake so much it is hard to keep the coffee in the cup. The tropics bring no guarantee of warmth. The fish in one clearing of mopane were still themselves in deep shadow, fearful of the two upright African fish eagles, eyes dark on white necks and heads, yellow beaks bright, dark talons attached to the limbs of a dead tree. Snowy white statues against blue sky. We linger in the flats with the blanched mopane, beaten to the ground by elephants, in the distance the white phragmites reeds buffeted in a golden aura of low sunshine. The wind pours across the land, and we craved warmth or the shelter of the swamps. Across a track, a sole hyena lopes, and then comes a silver jackal. Both drawn by another's kill, somewhere out in the yellow grass.

On some game drives, we see nothing and everything. Just mopane stripped of bark, bleeding red sap. And limpid pools, circles of ripples. Pale dry gasslands churned by the scuffing feet of elephants in search of moist roots. Tall gray termite mounds, more dead mopane, pushed to the ground, acacias surviving. Montsho the guide has been driving these swamp edge-lands for thirty years. We assure him we are entirely content. At one point, my eyes close and in a half dream I feel animals off to my left. I look up and there is a family of giraffe among a stand of acacia. Then, on the road, the rare prints of rhino, absent in the Moremi until 2001 because of poaching.

We stop out on Paradise Flats, named for its parkland, fading to wetland swamp. Two stilt-legged blacksmith's plovers *tink-tink* metallic alarm calls, then leap up with broken-wing distractions. We stand by termite mounds and drink glasses of cold white wine as the sun slips into the trees. To the west, bright Jupiter follows the sun, and beneath will be the Tsodilo Hills, the Slippery Hills, sacred mountains for very old and great spirits of the Bushmen. The cave and rock paintings there are made by the spirits. When van der Post went, their cameras and film jammed, the vehicles breaking down with regularity too. They should have asked permission first, they were told.

The evening light shines through the fur of a pack of vervet monkeys, tiny youngsters tumbling and swinging from branches, chattering, twisting, laughing, falling again, and climbing up. The adults sit patiently watching. Nearby, under a swamp ebony, the jackalberry, is that group of baboons and elegant impala, feeding on the fallen fleshy fruit. Jackalberries typically provide protection for termites around their roots; the termites in turn provide aerated soils into which moisture can penetrate. The fruit can be ground into flour, or fermented to produce beer and brandy. There are many wondrous termite mounds, these model cities rising up to three meters in height, below which lies a nest full of brood galleries, fungus combs, and food stores. In the queen's cell, up to thirty thousand eggs are laid per day. Warm air rises up the central chimney into thin-walled ventilation tubes. As the air cools far from the ground, it falls through separate chambers. Cooling veins are further kept damp by worker termites.

The mopane form a cathedral here, light and airy, no shade in the heat of the day as the butterfly-shaped leaflets fold together to save water. Van der Post wrote, "I knew of no tree which parallels so deeply of the nature of Africa. . . . All the year round they are green, red and gold." It's a heavy wood, termite-resistant, and so favored for housing and fences, and at one time railway sleepers too. It's also the food source of the emperor moth, *Imbrasia*, whose fat caterpillars are gathered for roasting as mopane worms, and a psyllid that produces a sweet waxy covering favored by both humans and baboons. Where there have been elephants, the trees bleed sap, and the air is filled with the scent of turpentine from crushed leaves. We come upon a family group tearing leaves from trees, ripping grass, stamping up roots of tussocks, all with imperious brows, brittle ivory and the deepest of wrinkles on charcoal skin. In another knoll, a group of young bulls push over a tree with a crash, and begin stripping it of bark. They are the constant reshapers of this landscape, hinting of danger with growls and kicks. Few visitors bother with the marsh. They are after iconic animals rather than landscape. We decide to go back on the water.

Out in the marsh again, we float, drift, are in the place fully, rather than trying to rush to another. Sunlight flashes on the water, reeds bend in the wind. On the wide lagoon, the smooth effortless passage over the water contrasts with the bumping of the jeep on land. Water spiders skitter on calm protected reaches. The water is blue, the grasses lush green, waterside meadows grazed short each night by hippos.

We see a shaggy sitatunga from a distance, out on an island, and feel touched. We have a book, and do take pleasure in ticking off those we have seen. In the thatch of a hut, I find a straw-colored Peters's epauletted fruit bat, roosting, white spots in front and behind its ears. I stand and admire. Then a stonechat clinging to a yellow reed, and two gray lories wheezing from a water fig. An African darter races over the water and then is under. A jacana dances on the surface of water lilies. Beneath we can see water lettuce trailing broad leaves, bent to the southwest direction of water travel. We hear the nearby *phoosh* of hippo, and then turn toward a pod in Xakanaxa lagoon, wavelets slapping their intent stares. We turn back. There is no arguing. If their ears start fluttering, they are readying for attack.

The bullfrogs and toads are calling. A sign that summer will start, says Lettie Letsole, owner of the camp, as we stand by the crackling evening fire on the deck over the water. The dry grasses that flare in the low sun are dark. A large bat flits by. The wind swirls through the trees. Back at the tent, the candle by the open window is worn down, wax splattered to leeward. A shooting star flashes across the unpolluted sky, chasing the new moon.

—————

Before dawn comes the *pee-oo* of the African fish eagle. All night, the purr of a Scops owl filled the silence. A fire now burns at the center of the forest camp, shadows flickering over the tents. The sky lightens as we stamp our feet, and the sun draws up through the leafless trees. Chacma baboons creep up on the kitchen tent for a raid. Grumbling, they return to a monkey orange tree, grabbing up fruits from the ground. Now a vervet scampers across the camp, long tail trailing in the sand. We had followed the water flow northwest from the Okavango to join the Chobe River, on its own twisting way to the Zambezi just beyond Kassane. South was the Kalahari, and we passed over a landscape dotted with trees equidistant, just like bushes in other deserts, gaps around every individual. The plane thumped on hard thermals.

That night, a distant bush fire threw up a towering anvil cloud of smoke and ash, the sky itself blazing orange, and two male lions walked by our sides. We had watched one for some time, lying in the bush, waiting for some sign, it seemed. Periodically, it lifted its head, and yawned. But then a distant growl, and in an instant it was up and walking. It strolled up the dusty track, and stood by our open vehicle, completely ignoring the prey that sat spellbound. A meter away. Tan with russet mane, mouth white beneath intense face. We held tight. The other arrived, and the lions simply walked along the road, deliberately toward the sunset. They sat together and howled at the bush. A grunt first, followed by a deep, full, grumbling roar. Across the bush, every animal now knew what was happening. The announcements were broadcast far. One finished roaring, a chilling sound that scraped at our very bones, and then the other started up. The dusk dropped away, and dark advanced out of the shadows. The two lions faded into the dark, and were gone from view. Tonight, they will walk far, as they beat the bounds of their territories.

I found my hand ached, and there was a deep splinter in my thumb.

Chobe National Park was once home to Bushmen, and David Livingstone passed through in November 1853 on his way to name Victoria Falls. He was thinking of development when he wrote "should the country ever become civilised, the Chobe would be a convenient natural canal." It became a game reserve in 1961, a national park in 1968, and is now home to huge herds of elephants, legendary across the continent. It is a mix of lush vegetation on the river plain, mixed broadleaf woodlands, and dense forests of cathedral mopane. Across the river is the Caprivi Strip of Namibia, the long finger of land separating Angola from Botswana. Some say more than 450 species of bird have been recorded in this park. The 10,500 square kilometers of Chobe has some of the largest concentrations of game animals on the whole continent. Where to start? At the water, of course.

Vast numbers of animals come to the river and its wide meadows every dawn and dusk. There are at least fifty thousand elephants, maybe one hundred thousand, in Chobe. Their numbers here greatly expanded in the past twenty years. They are Kalahari elephants, the largest in size of subpopulations, and characterized by short tusks. They are spectacularly migratory, spending the dry season at Chobe and Liganti Rivers, and then heading far south when the rains come. Culls have been considered, but this is controversial. Elephants swim across channels to lush islands in the middle of the river, trunks held high like snorkels. Others line the riverbank to drink. A mother with two tiny infants nervously pulls them under her legs. Twins are very rare; perhaps one is an orphan. In the bush, the herds move with deliberate and consistent pace, rear legs slightly bandy. But in sight of the glittering light on the blue water they scuff up their own dust storms as they rush the final hundred meters or so. On this side of the river is national park, on the Namibian side villages. Cattle are their herbivores, and fishermen in *mokoros* stay close to the far bank, setting nets, standing and observing. But where the river is narrower near Kassane, it is possible to see that farming has kept that side greener. There are more palms, more trees, more understory. On this side, all is eaten by elephants. The land is as it is because of choices made about its management. What we think and do matters for both wildlife and people.

On the high southern bank of the Chobe, we come upon the ruins of Serondela settlement. Vines have strangled walls, and this place is being reabsorbed into the bush. When Chobe was declared a national park, all settlers were asked to leave. These are the foundations of waterfront houses knocked down when the park was established. A single house stands, home to William "Pop" Lamont, born in Scotland in 1884, sometime farmer, miner, and tourist officer in South Africa, then retired to Serondela in 1950. At that time, it was a waterfront community by dense woodlands of mahogany and teak, overlooking Livingstone's canal. Lamont refused to leave when the park authorities sought to evict him. Standoffs with shotguns persuaded them to let him stay, though not without cost. He shot an elephant stealing from his kitchen window, and as punishment the authorities left the corpse to rot by the house. He died in 1974 at age ninety, and is buried between the house and riverbank by a stand of teak. Today there are still traces of the nearby former timber extraction business, rail lines, concrete standing, buildings eroding to dust. To the south are rocky hills where there are many cave paintings, signs of original habitation by the San. Their names are forgotten.

Another evening, we stand on the wide riverbank. The sun is dropping fast into a distant South Atlantic, and the land is salmon pink. Before us is an explosion of dust. Clouds fill the air above the waterside grassland. Six wild dogs have poured upon an impala, snarling and squabbling. The white tails of the dogs flash above the mad scramble, and in two minutes it is ripped apart and gone. Nothing remains but a few scraps of skin. This is disappearance, not just death, and it takes the breath away. The blotchy wild dogs walk slowly away. In van der Post's day, it was routine for hunters to shoot wild dogs, as they were held to be in some way unethical hunters.

We take a boat upriver, and lose count of the birds: egrets, spoonbills, storks; a sky-blue billed prancing jacana; a squacco heron spears a huge fish, and takes several minutes to flip and swallow it. On an island, armored Nile crocodiles lie by the water, and hippos burn in the sun. Elephants and sprawling herds of buffalo have crossed too. A single warthog trots along the shore, tail held high. A herd of zebra kick up dust that envelopes them all.

As the boat surges over the glassy water, wire-tailed swallows with orange caps and snow-white bodies dip in front to catch insects put up by the bow waves. They swoop and stall in the glittering light, then are away again.

Back at home, swallows will be anxiously chittering on the wires, readying for their own dreamline journeys.

7

MARSH-FARM

East Anglia, England

179° West of Date Line

The sun has climbed out of the sea, and washed the marsh with a summer glow. On my way, pairs of pigeons gathered night warmth from the tarmac of back roads, horse chestnut trees already skeletal. A sharp diagonal line of cloud marked the front pressing up from the southwest. I had driven into clear air, but rain is predicted. I park by a gate where a shire horse with giant feet gazes over, black mane flopped over its sparkling eyes. Billy Frosdick pulls in and waves, many decades a man of these marshes, and we drive to Stone Road to walk a green track across the marshes from the inland village of Halvergate to the coast. This was rural villagers' main path to the bustling port of Yarmouth and its shops and markets, also more routinely to the candlelit marshland pubs lapped by the ebb and flow of estuary and river.

These hundred square miles are the largest fresh marshes in the UK, and like all low-lying places appear as if in a bowl. Dry land hovers on the rim, itself only at sea level in places. To the west are the highland villages, across Breydon Water is the castle on a high hill of a dozen meters, and then the ribbon of Yarmouth itself to the northeast. The horizontals are broken only by trees around the old marshmen's cottages and farms, and by scattered drainage mills. Halvergate marsh was long underwater, part of the estuary in Roman times when the sea ran to Norwich. Since then, walls were raised and the land drained for grazing marsh. In the 1980s it was the first Environmentally Sensitive Area in the whole European Union for which farmers were to receive payments for their active management. As we walk, the marshes are acid green, Fleet Dyke and the side dykes glittering blue, the pastures roaming with cattle and sheep. The grass is damp from the previous day's torrential thunderstorms. It is swarming with young froglets.

Twenty or so unique drainage mills are stationed across these marshes, all designed to move water off. They have layers of multiple identities, taking names from keepers or marshmen, then acquiring others. They fell into sudden disuse when a pump was installed at Breydon seawall with such power it could suck water off many miles of land. The regular rounds of repair would have ceased, the wooden sails gradually rotting and eventually wind-torn to pieces. Mostly, all that remains are tapering brick mill houses, boarded up, perches for seabirds and hawks. We walk past new sluice gates and old cattle pens fenced off and brimful of nettles. At Mutton Mill, named after its final keeper, Fred Mutton, the two remaining sails are locked at northeast and southwest, and a single cormorant perches at the top. The brick is tarred black, the white cap and fantail bright under the last of the sunshine. Great blocks of oak lie in the reeds, abandoned after recent restoration efforts.

Billy's sleek black Labrador, Fleet, is at heel, resisting the temptations of rabbits and even the sheep. Billy smiles, and allows him a swim by Howard's drainage mill, the dog surging through the clear water, spinning water droplets into the sunlight on his return.

"These marshes have been my playground all my life," he declares, fifty years of walking, observing, fishing, shooting, building up a granular knowledge of all these wetlands.

Mother and father grew up in the Rows in Yarmouth, the narrow streets of the fishing town that took eight thousand bombs in the war to confer on it the most blitzed coastal settlement in Britain. Long before, its prosperity came with the herring, and went with them too. Nearly a billion fish landed in a single year a century ago, the harbor choked with drifters. Scottish girls came south on their own migrations to gut and speet the herren', but now barely a boat fishes from the harbor. Billy's family moved to Cobholm before the war, squeezed between estuary and river at the south of town. He knew the Platt brothers who set up the gun club, evolving later into the wildfowlers club. Without such organization, he reflects, they would have lost the rights to shoot as conservation interests grew. He still has a wooden punt, but now that the public slipways have gone too, it's impossible to get it in the water.

"I can't be doing with plastic and metal," he says. "Timber is always alive." The loss of the boat shed is keenly felt by many—a boat in a shed is always moist and watertight.

We come to Marshman's Cottage submerged in a copse alongside only one of two crossings of Fleet Dyke. Life would have been hard out here. No electricity, water, or sewerage. A cool larder at the back of the house, food kept belowground, drinking water collected from the roof or from the dykes themselves. But marsh and estuary were source for many wild foods—birds, mammals, plants, and fish. To the southwest the clouds are stretched gray. The front advances. In dark winter, when the easterlies drive across the North Sea, it will feel like they come from Siberia. Three large chestnut horses, too, walk alongside us after we climb a gate, and in a pasture are shaggy cattle with horns, highland crosses, well adapted for this marsh life.

Billy points to a new problem: the water soldier, *Stratiotes*. No marsh seems able to avoid invasives. With sword-shaped and saw-edged leaves in a rosette, they clog up waterways, rising to the surface in summer to bring forth creamy flowers. A marshman's job for winter was to clear the dykes of reeds and other water plants to ensure steady flow. But those men are mostly extinct now. But Billy gazes at a narrow stretch of brown water, and reflects on the loss of bream and perch, and jack pike too, from the Fleet Dyke. Where did they go? he wonders aloud.

An odd problem for those wishing to continue traditional practices of shooting and fishing for food has been the emergence of conservation as a primary goal for land management. For some, shooting and fishing cannot be reconciled with protection, even though the places with the highest abundances of wildlife have also been where local people have gathered from the wild over centuries. Here marsh and meadow have been bought, and shooting prevented. Some local wardens have been good, acknowledges Billy, friendly, willing to listen and engage, perhaps because they understood the complexities of ecological management. Others, though, have been dogmatic. As in many other parts of the world, it seems a pity that a cleverer language cannot be found, one that binds common interests: conservation needs an ethic that puts people in the picture too. Eugene Anderson knew this, in *Ecologies of the Heart* writing, "the real problem is not managing the resource but managing the people."

We look up. On the far side is Berney Mill, the tallest in Norfolk at twenty-one meters. Built in 1870 to grind cement clinker, it later morphed into a drainage mill. There was once a hamlet of grimy cottages by the Berney Arms, points Billy, but they were abandoned and pulled down. The pub can still only be reached by foot or water. Like many places on the coast, near rivers or estuaries, those close on the map can be ten or twenty miles away by path or road. On this side too, we find signs of former habitation. Near High's drainage mill, also known as Gilbert's or Lubbock's, is a triangle of grass between three dykes, and bleached tree trunks and branches are piled on rubble of brick and tile. The mill man's cottage was once here. Nettles grow where was the house, and there are twisted hawthorns in the old garden. High's is also tarred and long-since encrusted with orange lichen. It is weatherproofed with an aluminum cap, and this and the ground are splattered with the guano of many cormorants. The cast-iron scoop-wheel is rustless, though the giant oak axle lies split and rotten. We try to get inside, but the door is nailed shut. The old tradition was to set the sails upright on these mills when the customs and excise men from Yarmouth were on their way to intercept smugglers. As we walk on, a snipe flights out of rushes, and rises into the wind, dipping and racing across the marshes. Each step taken toward the estuary, and the level of the land slowly rises, the banks of the Fleet becoming steeper.

Near Marsh Farm is Howard's Mill, partially restored. I say to Billy, I could take one of these, imagining sitting at an upper window, writing. The farmhouse is surrounded by a dense copse of oak, ash, and apple. A line of blackthorn promises sloes for gin on a cold winter's night. This was a hippy commune, once, but it too is being restored with thatched roof and new windows. Across the dyke, though, is a cottage converted to ranch-style settlement. All the trees have been stripped out, horse paddocks laid out with purple plastic jumps. A flatbed truck is parked on the drive, and the green road has been scattered with rubble to ease access. We are curious about the steep-roofed building. A stable, or something altogether more secretive? The windows are barred. No one is about.

Onward we press. The path is again alive with yellow and black froglets as we head toward Breydon Pump, and across the railway line are graceful swallows swooping over the deep water of the dyke. They are nesting beyond the grill that is designed to capture floating plant material before it enters the pump workings. The swallows fold their wings at the last moment and cleave into the shadows beyond the metal strips. Returning from the inside, it appears they hardly hesitate, flashing out now empty-beaked, ready for another hunt. They have flown so far, each year navigating from southern Africa, to nest here. Under concrete, above marsh water, safe behind a five-meter sunlit portcullis.

We step up onto the river wall. And here is the famed estuary of tidal Breydon Water, five kilometers long by one and a half wide, waves slapping the shore and driven harder by the strengthening sou'westerly. Billy and I stand and watch, saturating ourselves with a small space in this crowded world. Over there is Gariannonum, the Roman fort now called Burgh Castle, where three long walls of knapped flint and layers of red Roman tile are still standing on the ninety-acre site. The sun disappears, and to the south the mills are gone behind a bank of gray mist and approaching rain. These river walls have been raised and strengthened by concrete matting, smoothed too, making walking easier.

Billy huffs. "See, you can walk up here in a pair of slippers."

On the inside the land drops sharply away, far below the salty water on the outside. In 1953, sea and river walls were massively breached up and down this coast during that dreadful last night of January. The sea poured into the marshes. Billy remembers lingering on the bridge at Yarmouth watching timber jostling upriver, thinking with a friend they could come back for some the next day. Then soon realized their predicament: the great tide had crashed through the town itself. They scarpered all the way home. The winter water kept coming and would end up being four feet deep as they, like so many others, retreated upstairs for the dark and terrifying night.[1]

The rain now pelts across the water, and herring gulls lift motionless above us. We are alone. This used to be a peopled wall, with many houseboats perched on ronds of wooden pilings. Writer Arthur Patterson's was at Stone Point, and I have a picture of him on his punt with sail raised, the houseboat just beyond. Billy himself had a houseboat called *Pintail*, and others along the shore were named *Lapwing*, *Wigeon*, *Curlew*, and other birds of the estuary too. But they came under repeated vandal attack, and one by one were burned or robbed. One old boy, a river watcher, had a caravan on the inside, had to surround it with so much barbed wire and fencing that he just gave it all up. Today it is just a pasture grazed by bleating sheep. Billy's was burned one summer's day ten years ago. Perhaps this land could not survive with the town so close. Remote enough for vandals not to be caught, but not far enough to prevent them from coming. The wall was a liminal zone between town and estuary, and largely untouched marsh.

On the inside is Lockgate drainage mill, also known as Banham's Black Mill, four stories of redbrick tarred black. The farm was demolished thirty years ago, but the mill itself burned in 2001. From out on the marsh, Billy saw the smoke, and called in the fire service, but no engines could find their way in time. You have to know your way across the marshes and its lanes. Fire had become the invaders' tool of destruction.

We repair to a tiny restaurant on one of Yarmouth's bustling Rows, barely an arm's width across.

"The usual, but two," he asks, and soon shepherd's pies with veg appear. We are wet, but soon warm inside. Condensation smothers the windows, and every table is taken. Billy is one of the few who remain from the lives recorded so distinctly by Arthur Patterson and later James Wentworth Day.

"When I was a bor," he reflects, "Breydon was where we got most of our food." But there are no youngsters out there today, no professional people left either. The oily smelt has died out, the eels virtually disappeared, the herring out on the salt gone too.

"We used many eel pots in those days," he says, "with melch from the herren' as bait." Traditions have been nibbled away. For the wildfowlers, Billy hired four hundred acres on Halvergate near Fleet Dyke. When the geese come over in winter, the sight is breathtaking, he declares.

"Now, a lot of the time, I just stand there and marvel." Outside the rain falls heavily, and the day has switched seasons since that clear summer dawn.

In 1910, William Dutt walked the Suffolk and Norfolk coast and described Breydon as an "ooze-bordered expanse of tidal waters, where the Breydonners of smelt-fishers, eel-pickers and punt-gunners made their living, and lived in houseboats." He also thought the area "primitive and almost primeval."[2] Wetlands seem outside of civilization, which is perhaps why so many have sought to tame them and rid them of their people. Some of the best accounts of rural life in England turning on the point where the traditional and the modern collide come from this region: Ronald Blythe's *Akenfield*, Julian Tennyson's *Suffolk Scene*, James Wentworth Day's *Marshland* and *Coastal Adventure*, and Mary Chamberlain's *Fenwomen*. They describe lives close to the land, and the dense social networks that kept families and communities together. They also document the growing disconnections as new work patterns took people away from nature.

But there was a hard edge in the isolation. Women married young, had large families, and engaged in a daily struggle to survive. Their jobs were potato harvesting, flower cutting, stone picking, or in the long hours of local service, which was never the soft option. Fens and marshes are also where monsters lived, where breedlings and mermaids called and captured, and where legends of Grendel and Jack O'Lanterns emerged. Many are the myths of black dogs moving through the shifting, forbidding places, on the edge of the imagination, past the ruins of farmhouses and drainage mills, dripping fear.

The most famed photographer of the life of the marshmen and women of Norfolk was a New Englander. Cousin of Ralph Waldo, P. H. Emerson came to Southwold in 1883 on holiday, and took his first cruise on the Norfolk Broads two years later. His plate camera was to record powerful images of peasant subjects in their landscapes, thus celebrating the harsh lives of Broadsmen, longshoremen, wherrymen, fishermen, osiers, millers, blacksmiths, brick makers, lily gatherers, eel pickers, basket makers, poachers, and ferrymen. This greatly annoyed the rural elites. He had put the rural poor center stage, but there was a hidden story.[3] Emerson was less sympathetic than his photographs imply. In early books he attacked local landlords, and defended workers' rights, but then came to advocate the retention of rural hierarchies, writing that he just wanted to improve "the peasants' lot." He came to see them as specimens of a passive class. He did not support the agricultural labor unions, many of which had emerged from the Methodists who did not believe that the existing social order was preordained. His pictures were *types*, and meant to represent a kind of fixed perfection that would never change.

Arthur Henry Patterson was born in 1857, a year after Emerson, and wrote *Wildfowlers and Poachers* in 1929, six years before his death.[4] He was the youngest of nine children, also raised on a Yarmouth Row. He was more understanding than Emerson, his almost exact contemporary, living among his subjects, drinking with them in pubs, traveling together across the marshes and estuary. Patterson intimately describes the lives of forty to fifty Breydonner families who made their entire livings from the estuary and marshes. They clustered around the Bowling Green and Lord Nelson pubs where the Yare and Bure Rivers meet, where now are abandoned grain silos, and in the medieval cottages of the Rows. The inshore and deepwater fishermen looked outward to sea, the Breydonian fishers and hunters inward, and lived as eel babbers, shrimpers, wildfowlers, smelters, and oystermen.

Livelihoods ebbed with the seasons, and the flowing rhythms of days were determined by the tides. His rabble were all known by nicknames: Pintail Thomas, Short'un Page, Old Stork Thacker, and Silk, Punt, Admiral, Peg-Leg, Spunyarn, and Cadger. The estuary meant freedom, but also uncertainty and possibility. No one exactly told the hunters and gatherers what to do, though all did live by local norms and rules. Men became angry when someone broke the rules, especially if they came from the outside. Governance seemed to work. Patterson described cold, biting winters, when birds would be snared by the ice and snipped off at their legs, when ice floes would jostle down the rivers and snow covered all the marshes for weeks. Above all, it was stories that stuck people together. Stories told by women while they braided and mended nets, tales told by men of the life on the marshes, sharing knowledge of behavior and distribution of birds and fish, of techniques and experiments, though always a little reticent when it came to detail of successes.

What have you got? someone might call from the quay.

"Nothin' bor, nothin' much—only a few titty totty ones."

Everyone had a comprehensive knowledge of birds: there were kitties (black-headed gulls), harnsers (gulls), greenies (greenshanks), and arcty terns, all eaten. The rank shellduck, though, was never put in the oven. Rarities were valued, as they could be sold to collectors, and Patterson records spoonbills, glossy ibis (called the black curlew), avocets, ospreys, buzzards, and white-tailed eagles. Over this century, some disappeared; others are returning, the avocets and buzzards. Wildfowling has managed to survive, evolving from that era of professional wild-fowlers and punt gunners to one where wildfowlers today shoot mainly to be out on the land. Now wildfowlers have purchased Bridgemarsh Island, parts of Hamford Water and on the Alde Estuary, and land here on Halvergate marshes.

"I wouldn't change any of it," Billy states, though he's seen smelting die out, eels fall away, old marshmen go, and drainage mills fall still. He still shoots, particularly geese in winter.

"I daresay you need to be there in the dark," he says.

⸺⊶⊷⸺

The boarded pub stands dark on a wide bend in the river, the car park potholed and empty too. Along the eight-mile Acle Straight with its single jink in the middle, early cars overtake madly to arrive at the coast a few seconds early. Last month it was closed all morning after a fatal five o'clock crash. Some have called for the ditches by the road to be removed, others for substantial widening. I stand in the grip of the keen December wind and pour a coffee, and can't help wondering what is the rush, why those few seconds matter. I look up as Dick Platt pulls in, Norfolk boy who's spent thirty years as an oil man overseas, and we drive along to Kerrison's Level to meet Tom Bindley. We wait until dawn lines the horizon above Yarmouth, and then set out across these dark levels, ahead a single pin of light from a lonely farm. This winter, the marshes are the wettest they've been for years. The harvest across the region was late, blackened wheat still standing into October. At the gateways to fields, the drenched ground has been churned into clutching mud banks by cattle and sheep.

Yarmouth is a chain of sparkling pearls too far for us to hear the grumbling of the yeasty sea and crash of waves. We walk over the railway line, taking care, for the joints on the tracks have been removed and trains no longer announce their arrival with a clickety-clack: they creep up, whisper by. We splash and slip toward Howard's drainage mill, and High's; in the distance will be Berney Arms, Stone's, Mutton's, Langley Detached, Lockgate. Mills in the witchery of shadows, as Patterson wrote. The lights of cars recede, and as we proceed deeper into the muddy marsh we hear the pinks out on Halvergate marshes. They never used to come this far, but because of the positive actions of farmers across Norfolk, these pink-footed geese have been drawn further south to spend their winters. I once spent a similarly biting morning on a friend's farm, and our very breath was sucked away as we watched sixteen thousand of them fly in echelons from the coastal marshes to feed on sugar-beet tops, whiffling at the last to turn the field a bubbling blue-gray.

Today, we are in the wild and by the modern in these dark lands. In here are remnants of ways of living that emerged from the very land and its proximal water. Take any ditch, and you could navigate to a larger feeder, meet up with dykes and new cuts, find a sinuous river, and head north into the Norfolk Broads, landscape of swaying reeds and hundreds more square miles of sedgy wetlands. We see the blink of a light from Halvergate itself, raised up on the ten-meter contour. Billy's cottage is there, his bad back keeping him in this winter morning. But after an update by mobile, he will come out with three dogs to help search for a pink.

The sky grows mauve, and the land emerges first as strips of sky. The easterly wind drives unhindered over this open land, turning our faces and hands raw. It already feels a good five degrees colder out here. It is, as Wentworth Day described, a "bold, cold land. A land of greens and browns. A land so lonely . . . where the wind cuts like a knife." In Wellington boots, my feet gradually freeze. Tom sets up by a gate, a post to hide behind. This is a hunt. If the pinks see anything unusual, they will veer away or lift just far enough. The guns have a range of only thirty to forty yards with steel shot, bismuth and tungsten being too expensive. Now green grass and tall ocher reeds emerge, a single blackthorn, drainage mills, the dykes and fleets now fully reflecting the low steely sky. The light coalesces into grayness. It cools the heart. We still stand stock still and wait. The pinks begin to lift in skeins of several hundred, flowing across the space between sky and land. Some head south, others west.

None come toward us. Still we wait.

Then a group of fifty or so fly directly toward our gate blind. Tom raises his gun, pointing vertically to the sky. A double *crump-crump* echoes across the land. The final pink is clipped and drifts downward a hundred meters or so away.

Tom walks off, trudging through puddles and grass, and disappears. Like all hunting, there is much waiting, intense periods of observation and readiness, then the long walk out to find the bird. The geese continue to fly this way, now lower as there is no gun present, it seems. I watch them carefully, and listen to their neighborly chatter. I stamp up to generate some warmth. And then walk back north to join Dick. Tom has called Billy, and he arrives with wool hat pulled down tight, rolling across the land like a sailor, his dogs rushing off to quarter the land.

We talk of the life of this land, how it can continue. It'll be difficult, they say. Yet this is a simple land on which each day is different. A wide expanse of green grass, vast gray sky, a line of a dyke, a copse, a gate. The men walking back, dogs flowing around their legs like fluid themselves. The brick drainage mill with white cap. The magic of the first moon of November has already brought woodcocks, flighting low across the sea and arriving so very tired, resting up in the marram grass and sand hills along the coast. Now that the country has woken, the traffic is nose to tail, and we have to wait long for the modern world to part. What do these drivers think when they see us, two with guns, and three dogs appear from the cold wet darkness? They are commuting to work; our work is done. The bird is for the oven.

We head to the outskirts of town where the Bowling Green pub stood, and attend the café of a modern supermarket. For here awaits a hunter's breakfast of sausage, bacon, beans, tomato, potatoes, and much coffee. We sit at a small table and look at the map, talking more of wildfowling on these marshes and the salty estuary of Breydon. This subculture exists through historical tradition and common identity. These hunters shoot to eat, and to narrate the land with stories. Above all, to feel a part of their own history and culture.

Can the wild save us, really, from ourselves?

The last nomads of eastern England are mostly settled now. They traveled when there was space in the land for a caravan, when much labor was needed on farms, their ways of life also emergent from the land. But now physical and cultural space has shrunk back, and they have been tied to specific places year round. They faithfully live in caravan trailers, but most are no longer mobile. Their diaspora started from India a thousand years ago, when some thought their origins had to be Egypt. Thus the Egyptians became gypsies. They too remain a culture slightly apart, and like nomadic or formerly nomadic people across the world are subject to much misunderstanding. Hugh Brody observed that the invention of agriculture resulted in individual agrarian families being settled while their farming cultures pushed out across frontiers; yet individual nomadic families remained mobile within fixed boundaries. The tensions between gypsies and the settled *gadjes* or *gaujos* remain. If this world is to survive the converging aspirations of so many to live high-consumption lifestyles, then there will surely have to be better understandings of those who wish to live differently.[5]

Essex is one of the better county authorities for accepting its obligations. There are official sites for caravans, each with a washhouse and kitchen. Some are behind pull-offs on busy roads, others on the edge of industrial parks, a few down quiet rural lanes. I spend nearly a year seeking links, building trust, before I can make field visits. At Brick House Lane, I meet Syd and Elvie Smith, both in their seventies, and who have been here for twenty-four years. On this day of August sunshine, the faded orange and rose curtains inside their Atlas Fanfare caravan are drawn, and the heater is on. Mirrors and glass cabinets full of Crown Derby porcelain line the walls, making the van look larger. Elvie is wrapped in a fawn tartan blanket, feeling her age. Her hair is braided, and she wears a heavy gold chain around her neck. With no bank accounts, gypsies need valuables in wearable and mobile form. She was born in a wagon up in Harlow, she says, and they've been together for fifty-four years now. They've lived through the transition too, from the days of constant mobility to settlement. Across continental Europe, such sedentarization is called the Great Halt, which many still see as a kind of cultural surrender.

"They say the good ol' days," observes Syd, "but they were hard work too."

They knew their farmers personally, and had a regular route around the region. There was sugar beet hoeing in the spring, tough work if the ground was dry. Then pea picking and strawberries in summer, wheat and barley thrashing too; then to Kent for the hop harvest, and back for potatoes in the autumn. Winter work might be potato riddling, and then me and my dad, says Syd, would do ditching, hedging, and trimming. Trust was key. Farmers trusted them to work; they trusted farmers to provide for them a site to pull up, and drinking water for them and their horses. The fast mechanization of agriculture eroded those relationships, and thus was the beginning of the end for the *lungo drom,* the life on the long road.

It did not, though, change the nature of trust. There were never problems if they and local people were on first-name terms. They're all OK, they'd say. But many was the time they'd come back to the wagon and find a policeman saying they had to move on. It is some of those memories that make the settled life happier today.

"We were only looking for peace and quiet in the end," Syd reflects. They made use of many wild plants from the roadside. Dandelions and other flowers to make drinks; tiny young nettles were washed, boiled, and the water drunk. Good for the blood.

"They're a bit bitey," agrees Syd, "but not when they're washed, they aren't. I could walk along that hedge out there, and pick all my food. We used to get all our living out of the fields and hedgerows." We forgot all this, and then it seems came a revival, and we are rediscovering the pleasure and tastes of wild foods.

Family is important, and the internal links are stronger than in many non-gypsy communities. Six grandchildren, I think, we've got, Elvie screws up her face. With large extended families, it is almost too much to know everyone, to follow their changeable lives. But she saves all her £2 coins to give to the grandchildren when they come to visit. But her sugar diabetes and blindness in one eye keep her in most of the time, except they do go up to the cemetery in Colchester to see her daughter.

"As far as I go now. Since I lost my girl six years ago, I lost a bit of my mind."

"We can talk without *gadjes* knowing what we say," smiles Syd. They want to keep the Romany language going. A separate language is another way of sticking together, but raises suspicions too. Deliberate deception is a way of maintaining cultural boundaries. Language helps, but stories do too. Some people do not want others to know. In *Bury Me Standing*, Isabel Fonseca states that "Gypsies lie. They lie a lot. . . . Not to each other, but to *gadje*." Deception is considered a duty: "We don't want you to know," one said to her. The dilemma is that this allows myths to propagate without correction: all fairground children are abductees, goes one traveler myth.

I ask about the prejudice. It happens, shrugs Sid. At the school, their children were called half-breeds, but the head teacher did nothing.

"But there's good and bad everywhere," says Syd.

There are gypsies who leave rubbish by the roadside, don't follow the travelers' code.

One incident sticks in Elvie's mind. She was up at the cemetery putting flowers down for her girl, when a man came up to ask if he could buy some flowers for his father's grave. He'd missed the shop. She gave him some, and a week later he arrived at the same time and gave her two photo albums for her pictures. Syd then leans across and flutters his gnarled hands, blue eyes sparkling.

"I wish I could do that," he says, pointing at my notebook. Neither of them can read or write. I take a bright blue feather from the book, and give it to Syd.

"What we've told you is true," states Elvie, "nothing added." Syd comes outside to show me his fishpond shoaling with dozens of golden and yellow carp, and talks of baby rabbits kept as pets, tamed leverets living with the cats, their dogs that never barked but would come and tap him on his chest at night if something was awry outside. Being outdoors every day is part of his life.

"I can't get on with a house. It's like going to prison. The outdoors is home."

Ann Lee's husband is Elvie's cousin, and I meet her for the first time in northern Essex near the river that marks the border with Suffolk. Ridgewell is at a bend on a racy road, on an old corporation storage site, and I sit in the tiny site office with Patience Buckley, husband Davie, Ann and Steve Andrews from the county council. They talk too of former lives on the move, from Kent to the Fens near Cambridge. Summer farmwork, winter work that was mainly independent and flexible, trading, car dealing, horse trading, scrap metal, and driveways. Up to the famous horse fair in Cumbria, and Epsom too. Many gypsies still keep horses, turning them out on roadside verges or common land so they get used to motor traffic.

"You know why the black-and-white nags are best?" Pashey asks. I don't.

"It's so they're easy to identify when stolen." I nod.

Ann's husband can't read or write either, and used to navigate the land by pub signs. Other marks were left at crossroads: branches broken in a particular way, twigs bound with a red rag, useful plants grown and encouraged, looking like weeds to others. Places made sacred by intervention and signs.

Prejudice is a problem, but not as bad as it used to be, says Davie. Their local school is good, the police are better, you can go to the pub without being thrown out. You know why it persists? he raises his eyebrows. They think we don't pay income taxes or council tax. When they know you pay your dues, then it all changes. But there are complications. Many of the English gypsies don't get on at all with the Irish gypsies in the region. They can just go back home anytime, I am told, reflecting again, further complexities about the layering of identity.

"On our site," says Pashey proudly, "everyone knows everything!"

If you have a case of measles, by the morning everyone knows. In fact, the networks of family linkages across the county amount to a bush telegraph. Something happens on one site, and all know. There is no broadband, so no links to knowledge networks and social interactions that have rapidly become the norm elsewhere. I like this place, says Davie, because when the girls get married they'll get a site. The atmosphere is good, everyone helps the other out. Many gypsies who have opted for houses experience loneliness and social isolation. They miss the outdoor life, the sense of community, and the fact that people are always around.

There are other lost traditions, but some that hold children back. Wild foods, rabbits, jugged hare a traditional meal, peg making, cut flowers to earn a few bob. A measure of family respect is to call children the parents' names, so Patience's daughter becomes Pashey-girl, and she is Pashey-mother. But it was also the tradition that girls aged twelve or thirteen would stop going to school, and remain at home to look after the wagon or van. Boys would commonly leave unable to read or write; Ann says it's still common today. This is a dilemma, I suggest. If you want to keep a tight and continuing culture, it's important for the younger generation to maintain some, or all, of the previous norms and behaviors. If they grow up to be lawyers, then they probably won't want to live in a caravan. On the other hand, a few other skills and associated networks of influence could help gypsy culture protect itself. Outside a dog yaps in a stream of long anger. No one blinks.

On a wet summer's day, Ann shows me the site she runs. It's on the edge of Basildon, not so far from the famous Plotlands where Londoners escaped the slums of the East End to live on their own pieces of country freedom. A century ago, my grandmother was born in one called Raven's Rest. Now those plots are subsiding under woodlands, the garden plants running wild, apple and plum trees producing for no one. A land of ghosts, of escape and loss. Many left to live in houses when Basildon new town was created. Today, though, we're on the edge of an industrial park. The site used to sit alone in the middle of open space running alongside a river.

"We were stuck away from everyone," says Ann. But then factories marched in.[6]

Next door is a twenty-four-hour recycling plant and anaerobic digester. The workers thump footballs against the metal fence. Beyond is the roaring A127, another late invader. When it rains, the surface water pours off the road down to a small patch of grassland, and forces out the rats. They flow onto the site around the caravan bases. In all these ways, the mobile become settled, then become invaded themselves. Who would listen to complaints from gypsies anyway? The environmental health officers did come one night, but mysteriously the factory was dead quiet at the time.

Two of Ann's daughters, Lisa and Louise, are here too, and then we're joined by granddaughter Sherrie-girl. Ann has three mobile phones for work, but no one else has any credit on theirs. The talk flows like a river, streaming and intersecting, as it does in oral cultures. Liaison officer Steve is here, and he explains how little outsiders really know. They make casual assumptions. There are *keniks* who live in brick houses, some of whom don't want to be known as gypsies anymore. There are van dwellers on official sites, others on private legal sites, and those that attract the greatest negative publicity on illegal sites without planning permission. Thus gypsy is not a homogeneous term: it is applied to English Romany, Welsh, Irish, and Scottish travelers, to New Travelers and to fairground travelers. There are many terms used to describe difference: didicoys for half-halfs, the non-gypsy *gadje*, and of course the derogatory term derived from those who traded on the turnpikes. Ann says they fear the worst with the rise of the elected Far Right in East London councils neighboring Essex.

Yet there is fond talk of the annual summer migrations to Epsom and Appleby, and of the cultural links to horses. Families here keep horses on rented paddocks nearby. People travel first for the Derby and pull on for the week, then travel up north to Appleby for the greatest gathering of gypsies anywhere in the world, the fair running annually since 1685. Some ten thousand gypsies and travelers attend, and another twenty thousand visitors come the Sunday. In every pub and shop there are two queues, one for locals, one for gypsies. The locals smile—their rent is paid for the year. But when the foot-and-mouth disaster struck in 2001, the fair was canceled. A single horse was taken up to ensure continuity of tradition and rights.

But Lisa objects to the warm consensus. "I don't go, I don't like horses!"

People sing, tap dance, put on trotting races. Horses are ridden into the River Eden and washed before sales fetching up to £20,000 apiece, and sprawling audiences gather on the banks under overhanging lime trees. Each is a piebald mosaic of white and black, some spotted like ancient war steeds. It is also the greatest collection of traditional wagons, decorated vardos, brush wagons, Readings, and bowtops with green roofs and maroon and cream paintwork. Not many now follow the old tradition, had said Davie up at Ridgewell, where the men and boys never slept in the wagon, always outside and underneath. Yet such caravans have only been used by gypsies for about 150 years; before they slept in bender tents made from hazel and covered with canvas.

The conversation turns to Sherrie-girl, who's a local hero. She continued through school and college, became a teaching assistant, and works in the local secondary school. She was recently married at Brentwood registry office, a small affair.

"We didn't want it to end in a brawl," she says.

Big weddings often end in trouble, though marriage is for life, and divorce rates are very low. The father of the bride pays for the wedding; the father of the groom provides a new home. We walk over to her new van, where the steps are yet to be added. The interiors of caravans are pristinely tidy, yet the outside territory can appear much less well-looked-after. This again plays to stereotypes. Gypsies are equally puzzled by the *gadje* practice of keeping cats and dogs in a house, and cannot understand how elderly are put in care homes, and children in day care. Within minutes, Sherrie's mother comes over to see what the fuss is about, bringing a flock of younger brothers and sisters. Life expectancy among gypsies is ten years lower than the national average, mainly due to lack of access to health services. There remains much to do to meld the best of both worlds.

—————

Nothing much happened. It was a good evening.

We stood in the dark and waited for the ducks. They didn't come. We were in a black hole surrounded again by industrial society, and only we knew it. We had walked out onto the marsh as the sun dropped toward castellated Fobbing church, sensibly sited up on the thirty-meter contour. To the south are the remains of Shell Haven and Coryton village, now mainly an oil refinery and soon to become the largest container port in Britain. So that we can go on buying stuff. As the clouds rolled in, and the sun blazed off the giant oil storage tanks, Ryan Lynch and I climbed the old seawalls that jag across the freshwater grazing marsh, and walked out into this in-between land. We pass under electricity transmission cables that run from Tilbury power station into inner Essex, and then came into a hushed land.

At the fleet of open water surrounded on three sides by young willow, we stand in the flanking reeds, and watch the western sky behind us now flare orange. We let roots grow, as the light changes, drifts, darkens, falls away. The fleet fills up with sky as the land darkens. Lapwings wheeze out on the meadows, rooks *kraa*, a moorhen cackles. In the end, no ducks, no geese or wigeon or teal. The two shiny Labradors have no work after their earlier runs on the walls. Yesterday Ryan was successful, but today the birds decide not to come. Now in the dark, the neon haze of the refinery smudges the southern horizon by the Thames, and the gas chimney flares bright every few minutes with a vibrating whoosh that seems to suck the very oxygen from the marsh. Each flame sears an image on my retina. Up on the ridge of this bowl, two streams of white and red traffic intersect in silence. Rather than being between the spaces of the real world, we gradually get a new sense.

The description is the wrong way round. This is the real world, down here in the dark. Civilization flows around us like a river, and the two of us with these dogs wait for nothing much more to happen. We walk out slowly, across a marsh that was home to the shepherds who started the Peasants' Revolt in 1381. Not far from here lived the last wizard of Essex, Cunning Murrell, sleeping by day and walking at night as we are now. It's easy to imagine nighttime on the marshes in those times: no lighting from nearby settlements or vehicles, just the moon and stars, whistling wind, scudding clouds, animals tame and wild, ghosts and witches imagined in every shadow, and everyone fearing to go near the ruined castle over-looking the Thames.[7]

We join the stream of traffic and then swing around Vange marshes and back down onto Canvey Island. Ryan and I head for the Lobster Smack pub, settling in the glowing warmth. Herbert Tomkins sat here a century ago, and smoked a pipe by the spluttering fire. Then he could see over the seawall to the estuary of the Thames. Today the pub is dwarfed by high concrete walls. And a fine thing too, for a recent storm surge brought the river near to the very top of these castle walls. In 1953, fifty-eight people were drowned on this island when the earthen walls had collapsed and the sea had roared in and flooded houses. Ryan's grandfather was the first to raise the alarm. As river watcher, he was up on the wall at midnight by their home in the Sunken Marsh, and saw the terrifying expanse of silver water in the moonlight where there should have been islands and saltings over to Leigh. The cold North Sea breached the walls under the violent wind. No one here has forgotten that hellish night. The story has been passed on. But stories don't stop angry seas.

Before dawn, I leave the Oysterfleet Hotel and walk some of the sixteen miles of walls that now surround the island. The sky is clear, save for the ribs of dark cloud to the east. Ships thump upriver, lights gleaming. The eastern sky lightens, presses forward. The moon in the west is heading down. Now silhouetted seafront architecture appears, the saltwater bathing pools wrinkled by a breath of morning breeze, Labworth's art deco restaurant, groynes marching out to sea. *Danger, deep water*, says a rusting sign. Out at the far eastern end of the island a fisherman tramps across the mudflats to dig for bait. Curlew and godwit probe the muds too. The dark outline of the man stands still, bends to dig, stands again, and a flock of several hundred waders shivers and rises, then falls again to the muds. He walks back with spade over shoulder and bucket hanging from the shaft. The sun comes up like thunder, stretching con trails salmon pink, and leaving a line of cumulonimbus dark and brooding. From down on the beach, no houses can be seen. White graffiti proclaims *life is shit*, but further west I find the famous declaration relating to a discovery in the 1970s. A woman saw the Virgin Mary in her garden, and for years coach loads came to visit. On the outer wall is painted now in fading letters, *Canvey Island, England's Lourdes.*

——⫘⫘⫘——

There is a place, three small islands a thousand feet across linked by broken sea-walls, out on the salt marshes. A gimcrack lodge has accreted on the shore, ligger boards of flat timber are covered with chicken wire and lead to the tiny jetty. At low tide, an expanse of sleek muds separates the largest island from the mainland. Six hours later the tide will have risen more than four meters and lap at the lodge's footings. One September, I row across with bags of supplies and large bottles of drinking water.

Wind batters the lodge all day. The reeds sway and rush, and create that continuous whispering song of the marshes. Curlews out on the mudflats burble, an insistent piping. The egrets are at roost, cranky at the day's end. Earlier I had seen a flock of sixty; only twenty years ago there were none in England. As dusk fell, the orange lights of the coastal town beyond the hill rim the horizon to the east. But down here, in these twenty-five square miles of oozing, drizzly, effervescent muds, among the cord grass and sea lavender, sea blite and purslane, and rare stands of sea hog's fennel, all seems of another world, or perhaps the original. This is a characteristic of our wild places. You can feel far away, and yet there will be neon streetlights on the hill. The tide did come over the salting, and lap at the lodge. Then it fell, and the sheet of water was gone, revealing the drover's wet road down at the bottom of muds. The stepping-stones are deep in silt, suggestive of the old marshmen's horror of being stuck in the mire to watch the waters rise slowly. The crabs, they say, take your eyes first. This is another point of being alone on the land: stories seem the more vivid.

I slowly fix cheese sandwiches in the tiny kitchen. The lodge is three sections cobbled together, beginning as Fred's garage, then the conservatory added, and lastly the sitting room in the 1980s by a later warden. Wide windows and ceiling fan, a curved roof, flower-patterned sofas and curtains, aluminum windows with wide gaps, and shelves of fine nature books from the 1950s and 1960s. The wind is both outside and in, and the small windmill is spinning and charging up the batteries. Before the 1953 floods, this was land grazed by cattle and sheep, but the breached seawalls were not repaired, and the salt marsh returned. In 1979, the two hundred acres were donated to the wildlife trust as a reserve. I walk both the west and east islands, and these seawalls are a struggle. You make a path by walking, and no one has been this way for a long time. I twice pitch on my face after slipping in rabbit holes. The easiest walking is down on the saltings among the mauve haze of lavender. These salt marshes are dynamic habitats, where plants go in and out of the salty tide more than seven hundred times a year. These are natural rhythms that must be respected.

On one day of consistent rain, everything becomes damp. It falls all day, and the tide is even higher. I go out to check the boat from time to time, retying the mooring. It is cold for September. The wind has dropped off, but the rain stays beneath ashen skies. I drink a cup of hot soup, and stand and watch. The hours pass, but nothing stays the same.

"You can learn a lot in the country by sitting still and doing nothing," wrote Samuel Bensusan, laureate of the Essex marshes.[8] The wind veers, the rain eases, then pelts down again. The tides move ceaselessly, emptying and refilling the creeks. You can see how quickly your life becomes dominated by water. A really big tide would scare the living daylights. Material progress is not a good substitute for all this. The comments of long-gone visitors are revealing: *magic* is the most common word. The deep desire for the simple life. The escape. Nothing to do. It is like being on the beach—it legitimizes doing nothing. Somehow, people find it hard to do nothing at home, where other demands invade. Yet here deep in the marshes is that potential. It is being somewhere, not exactly doing nothing, that matters.

At the barn, a ghostly white owl eases out, wings cracking. It flies down the ride. I watch a curlew through the glasses, and a hawk arrows after it, closing fast, only in the end to veer away as the fleeing bird drops hard toward the mud. The sun sets over the western thickets of blackthorn, elm, and hawthorn on the other island, and lights the sky pink and orange. High cirrus corrugates the sky. Egrets lift from the slick mud, stationary in the wind. Darkness advances. I spend the evening writing. Alone in the natural world, time is less dense, less filled with information. I feel attentive, just in the presence of something very old.

Arthur Patterson was asked in later life, "What can we do with Breydon?" His response: "Let it alone."

8

COAST

Antrim Glens, Northern Ireland

186° West of Date Line

Once we walked the world, wearing paths into every land. Then came domesticated horses and reindeer, and soon after, five thousand years ago, the wheel took us faster and further. Paths became tracks and turnpikes, streets and roads, boulevards and lately motorways. The Romans made them straight, others followed old field boundaries or river courses. They were paved with stone and brick, tar and timber. Now there are seventy million kilometers of roads worldwide. All make one thing possible: places become permeable, allowing outsiders in and local people and resources out. They also open up coasts. One of the finest is in Northern Ireland, and I thought I should walk it. The road was an engineering triumph, built in the 1830s to link Protestant Larne to Catholic Cushendun. It winds around the feet of cliffs and across broad bays, a perfect fit for a land of black basalt, green grass, red sandstone, dazzling white limestone, and waters shimmering in the sunshine one day, and crashing angrily the gray next. The coastal villages had never been directly linked by land, and transport had always been by boat or way inland along the wet glens. Scotland by boat was nearer than Belfast.

The purpose of the Antrim Coast Road was political and economic, just like today's roads driven deep into rain forests. Following the Irish rebellion of 1798, London abolished the Irish parliament, and landlords and the military petitioned for a road, partly for trade but also to control dissenting voices. A Scottish engineer, William Bald, was appointed, his vision to lay a route at sea level. It opened in 1842, exposing the distinct cultures, customs, and Gaelic language of the glens to a rapidly industrializing national and global economy. Soon came the dreadful famine, when the whole population of Ireland fell from eight to five million, and much later the Troubles, when starkly different views brought decades of violence. The thirty-mile Antrim Coast Road is now a source of collective local pride.[1]

I crawled out the door at four on a late autumn morning to fly to Belfast, intending to walk that day. The airport was half empty, grills still hard down on coffee shops, eventually rattled open by cheerless workers. At the gate, passengers stared blankly but patiently, and then we crossed the dawn-washed tarmac to the plane. I wandered in the rental car toward the coast, trying to follow the map and drive. The land was green, the windscreen wipers snapping back and forth, working harder as I approached Larne. I picked through puddles to meet Liam Kelly at the visitors' center.

"It's good that you'll be walking," say the ladies at the center. "Not many do." And then I follow Liam northward up the coast. He warns, "Don't expect sun!"

I start walking at Cushendun, where the peaty river flows past a black goat on a polished plinth. It already seems a century away from airports and the tang of kerosene. In 2001 foot-and-mouth disease also leapt across the water to Ireland with dramatic impact: sporting fixtures and Sunday Masses canceled, and visitors arriving from Britain advised to wash clothes and bathe on arrival. Many livestock were culled, and a dreadful silence was cast on the land. From Cushendun used to be a regular livestock trade of black cattle and pigs to Scotland and returning with Highland ponies. Now the lone sculpture of the last goat stares inland from a limestone harbor flanked by a row of Cornish cottages designed by Clough Williams-Ellis, better known for Portmerion, made weirdly famous in *The Prisoner*. Beyond, the gray-green promontory of Tournamoney tips sharply into the flat calm sea. The road glistens in the drizzle, and there's the sweet smell of silage in the air. I am alone. In the rain.

From Torr Head north of Cushendun it's only a dozen watery miles to Scotland's Mull of Kintyre and isles of Arran and Islay. In this narrow stretch where the Atlantic collides with the Irish Sea there are said to be five hundred shipwrecks. Here the fresh water whispers over flat stones, and sentinel redshanks cry *teu-eu*. A blackbird chatters, and water drips and splashes, gathering into trickles that in turn pour toward the river. All else is still in this land of giants and fairies. The ice ages made the glens wide and deep, and raised beaches produced by geological-scale fluctuations in sea level left a perfect surface for the constructors. The nine glens in the coastal hinterland of valleys and undulating plateau-bog stretch from Glentaisie in the north to Glenarm in the south. Taisie, princess of Rathlin Island, to the glen of the army, the seat of the Earl of Antrim. And between are glens for dykes and hedges, plows and fields, little fords and rush lights, the slaughtered and dead, a brown peaty river, reeds and sedges. On this isolated coast, the Gaelic language survived intact with customs that defined the region. Foods were both wild and agricultural, singing and dancing common. A road surveyor observed in 1831 that the people "were very peaceable and well-conducted except when they were whiskey drinking."

I trace the River Dun up from Cushendun, past a stand of healthy horse chestnut all wrapped in fiery foliage. Such trees are becoming rare on the mainland, for the *Cameraria* leaf miner dispersed by traffic has been bringing on leaf death by midsummer since its arrival a decade ago. Far from main roads, though, trees can survive, as they do here. I climb the steep hill out of Knocknacarry past whin bushes sprinkled golden with flowers perfumed with coconut, once famine food, and turn toward Glencorp, glen of the dead, and Glendun, the brown glen. Looking back, the white and cream houses of Cushendun are lost in the layer of low stratus.

Iron gates at meadows strewn with fallen leaves hang between meter-wide gateposts with conical tops, symbols of luck and fertility that work like ancient standing stones. The front door to one farmhouse gray with slate roof and mottled plaster is on the first floor, up crumbling steps. The ground floor would be barn space for animals, it seems, but half the upper also has windows of wooden slats. Cloud descends further, and in the enclosed mist I pass a concrete social club of hard angular architecture. Cars are dripping wet, and look abandoned. *Main entrance*, points a sign at the solitary flagpole. *No trespassing* states another. But though the land seems deserted, occasional car drivers all wave and smile behind arcing windscreen wipers. I'll also realize something else. Everyone is proud of the beauty of the Coast Road, but like many old routes it's become more for driving than walking.

I cross the six-hundred-foot Cross Slieve Hill with its four ancient ring-fort raths, signs of ancient occupation, and pass down a narrow lane hedged with crimson wild fuchsia, flowers like fairy lanterns. Below is Cushendall. I stop where *caution!* has been sprayed on the drenched road. Rain squalls tear in from the sea. Down a mossy lane to the left is Layd church, where the legendary export John MacDonnell is buried. Born a little way on at Waterfoot in 1762, he set up as a doctor in Belfast, and every two weeks took a journey of some fifty miles by horse and coach back here. He wouldn't have minded a good road. MacDonnell eventually became Belfast's leading physician, establishing the first hospital for the city's poor, out of which would emerge the Medical School of Belfast in the 1820s. From the hill I see the plateau of Knockore jutting out to sea, and then the ceiling of cloud separates and sunlight falls on the sea beyond the head.

Now there's black cloud, gray promontory, silver sea, wet-black trees, green grass, and a hint of promise. Local poet Phyllis Cottrill wrote of the Coast Road, "There's always something around the corner, always sunshine on the road."

Darker clouds advance again. A sign on a dripping sycamore proclaims: *no shooting*. It's in a big meadow, but all the black-faced sheep are huddled together in the rain. Beneath a dead alder is a fallen concrete pillar crusty with lichens and spreading moss. Water patters from the corrugated asbestos roof of a lime-washed farmhouse on a slope, the rotten white frames of the downslope window a good foot lower than the windows on the upside of the front door. No smoke issues from the cold chimneys. The view is of the sheer volcanic plug of Teiveragh, on whose gorsey slopes are axe factories and chambered graves, and where stands a single fairy tree that no one would dare to cut down. The land is densely populated with mythic beings. One chambered grave is Ossian's, warrior-poet son of legendary Irish giant Finn McCool, who built a causeway to Fingal's Cave on Staffa to pick a fight with a Scottish giant. When huge Benandonner came striding across, McCool scooted home in horror, where his wife dressed him as a baby. It became Benandonner's turn to flee: the baby clothes made him think twice about adult giants on the Irish side. McCool tore up the causeway, leaving hexagonal basalt columns to form the Giant's Causeway, now a World Heritage Site. Finn lost Ossian in a tale of temptation. Ossian chose to live with Niamh, beauty of the underworld, but was drawn back to this rugged glen of little fords, Glenaan, but he fell from his horse, died, and lies here still. At least, this is one way to tell the story.

The masters of the nine glens are really the fairies. Belief in fairies was once widespread across Britain and Ireland, and they were variously known as elves, pixies, pucks, brownies, hobs, or commonly just the wee people. Some were mischievous and dangerous, others friendly. Their assumed presence caused people to behave properly toward them so as to avoid sanction.

"You don't want to upset them," says Liam later. His father, William, was born in Larne in 1918, and because it was also believed that fairies stole boys, his mother dressed him as a girl when young. Fairy music, though, the sweetest in the world, could lure anyone away. The local Antrim and Down fairy is a *groga*, two feet tall and strong, a willing helper of farmers at harvest and threshing. Moderns might smirk, but the point is not whether such beings are corporeal or not; it is that their imagined presence in the landscape codifies behaviors and ensures respect toward nature and its many unknowns.

Fear of punishment is a key part of the code. Much folklore is like this: it is either real people with special powers, such as cunning men, witches, and magicians, or mythical beings who imposed a particular kind of behavior, effected by stories of mermaids, dragons, fairies, and lantern men. Here it is good luck to take a spoonful of dew from a neighbor's field, but always bad to cut down a *skeagh*. Many are the local stories of disaster befalling those who cut fairy thorns. Such beliefs are, in many ways, similar to animist spiritualism in which nature is to be respected, never dominated.

I cross the River Dall and walk through the soaked streets, lined with hardware shops and empty hotel car parks, and toward the red sandstone prison tower erected in 1809. The bell was rung at 9 p.m.: all inside. A curfew to keep people off the streets. Later, in quieter times, Thackeray stayed here and praised in his *Irish Sketchbook* the boiled bacon and small beer to be found at the Cushendall Inn. He reckoned this region a miniature Switzerland, for its "cataracts, valleys, rushing streams and blue mountains." Later Cushendall became briefly famed as the first place up here to be lit by electricity when the generating station was built in 1923. Today the hurling pitches are sodden like rice fields, and next door is a tall palm tree in the grounds of doomed St. Aloysius's school with its magnificent bay views. Behind the wall of tall metal-framed windows stands a thin woman in white staring through the dense condensation. It may be she knows it'll soon be over.

By kelp beds in Red Bay, the ruined castle sprawls behind broken wire-fencing long since ineffective at stopping even the least curious of sheep. In these caves of red sandstone laid down when this was desert are stitched two stories. Ann Murray made one her home in the mid-nineteenth century, and to avoid punitive rules about alcohol cleverly sold water by the glass, giving away the whiskey for free. Up the cliff is another cave where bombers hunched, pressing a button to kill a policeman on the road right here. Some must have thought such atrocities achieved much, but all they did was kill people. I stop for some minutes at roughly the unmarked spot. Ahead the road swings sharply to the right, and disappears under the Red Arch, a parabola topped by layers of crumbling sandstone and tangled grasses. A path passes around the outside, and still the water gurgles off the land, over a brooding yard fringed with cranes and covered with hummocks of dark coal. The surface water runs black into Red Bay, and I walk on.

The land blooms into a sweeping bay. The settlement on the shore rims the broad sands, and ahead is the thousand-foot Garron plateau. Angled inland is the glen of the plow, the fertile glen. In Waterfoot, also known as Glenariff, is a vivid yellow mural on a gable wall depicting Laurel and Hardy smiling with a Guinness bottle, saying *that's another fine bar you've got me into*. This may have had success, for the wet street is empty of pedestrians, save for a group of workmen with blackened faces, discussing the finer details of their tarmacadam. They seem indifferent to the two rows of queuing cars. Still I walk. Beyond the houses, the town-land strips give way to booley pastures under the towering Lurigethan crags. In the glen behind Waterfoot is a seam of porcelainite, rock for curling stones, and thus famed all over.

A boarded and peeling building is decorated with faded photographs of waterfalls and the valley's past. McAllister's store is long abandoned, most of its pink paint flecked away and the exposed sullen concrete eroded by wind and more rain. A row of gray terraced houses, only the one painted, another with gaping upstairs window, ferns growing from sills, the front door and other windows boarded with peeling layers of plywood. An old tragedy, it seems, for along the roofline is a tangle of ivy. How long have the neighbors endured this blight, I wonder. Yet even as I write, the beach at Waterfoot was being quartered with ground radar and readied for digging machines. One of the country's disappeared may have been buried here in the early 1970s. On camera, an anxious family watches from the water's edge.

Such pain is echoed in a local saying: "There's no happiness without an inch of sorrow through it." It has become so different now. The Troubles as they were are nearly past. This is not to say that anguish does not cut deep or guilt persist, and indeed some still plot on. But many of the atrocities were committed by young men locked into patterns of conflict who when they reached middle age became haunted by their dreams. Many have given themselves up, seeking some kind of closure; others ended their lives. Others have become politicians.

So many buildings are abandoned and unrepaired. The glens once tamed by the road; the economy struggling today to escape the crushing history of the Troubles and now the credit crunch and recession. Strong communities, though, can get through this all, despite the pitted dichotomies of religious and political divide. This was a coast of shipping wreckage, the MV *Princess Victoria* the most recent disaster sixty years ago. South of Waterfoot stands a single white horse in a pasture of grass and rushes dotted with yellow ragwort. It turns and watches as I walk by, barely able to move its shaggy mane and sodden tail. On the shore, redshanks *flit-flit*, crying again. Curlews lift silently. Oystercatchers wander the shore. Inland comes the *seep-seep* of tits in the pines. The compact graveyard surrounded by a gray wall seems full with standard and Celtic crosses, stones with shiny patina, marble memorials, and words suggestive of long stories. Yew and blackthorn run alongside the inner boundary wall. John Masefield met his wife on this coast, and in his *Biography* poem wrote: "In the curlew-calling times of Irish dusk / Life became more splendid than its husk," and concluded, "the days that made us happy made us wise."

In the nineteenth century, the main exports from Larne were limestone and iron ore, and from agriculture potatoes, barley, oats, and livestock. Then people, too, after the famine. From the 1870s, a transatlantic service was begun from Larne, such was the demand from both emigrants and their relatives. Waterfoot then became the famed location for the *Feis na nGleann* or Gaelic Revival, begun in the 1880s. Concerns had been rising that this road had opened the door to rapid acculturation, and that local language, song, and dance needed protection. The revival led to the formation of a local committee with representatives from all nine glens. The first *feis* was held in 1904, supported by all religious and political groups. It persists to this day, held annually in high summer.

Now, looking back, the designs of stitched ladder-rack farm strips are clear, running from sea upslope until reaching stone walls across the hills. The booley common pastures formed the core of the Rundale system of farming, part private arable and part collective management of the commons for cattle and sheep. The booley, or bally, is a common name dotted across this land, the townland of the clachan village, and survived as a system of management in parts of Ireland to about the 1940s. The designation of the uplands as commons ensured that livestock could be shepherded collectively, and thus moved to the most productive parts of the grasslands and bogs as weather conditions and seasons continually shifted.

"Every acre's got a name," says Liam. There are sixty-three thousand town-lands with place names in all Ireland.

Today, the fields have all gone to grass. Once they were cultivated, and farmers used the locally invented slipes, wheelless slide cars, to work the steep slopes. A horse pulled a boxy car that carried manure, turf, hay, or crops with iron runners that slid along poles laid on the ground. The peat from the hills, or *up on the moss*, was long a vital resource for cooking and heating. It was cut, footed, and the trinkets hauled down when drained of water. A freshly cut turf of peat will weigh fifteen pounds, but only two when dry. Everyone savors the sweet reek of peat in winter.

At the south side of the bay is the old pier where a six-mile railway instead brought iron ore from surface mines also up on the glen. Another first: this Glenariff mineral railway was the earliest narrow-gauge line in Ireland, and seven hundred men were employed at the height of operations. But like so many extractive industries, it was fast overtaken, running only to the late 1880s. Milltown pier itself was washed away in a storm, and today a dozen cormorants perch on the remaining concrete blocks drying their wings. Water sucks and swirls around the base. Nearby are two limestone pillars that formed the rail bridge over the road, cool and damp to the touch. By a terrace of white miners' cottages, I find a patch of wheat on the sea side of the road, the ears green and looking like it should be June rather than November.

The road hugs the base of a basalt plateau that holds the largest blanket bog in Northern Ireland. This is a landscape good at absorbing rainfall. The view back north across Red Bay is of Cushendall and tall Teiveragh, Layd church and Cushendun Bay. Now the road narrows, with no footpath, and I'm forced to be traffic-aware, listening and watching. South under Galboly, I stop at a roadside memorial for a dead motorcyclist. Flags, colored sponsored shirts, and a pair of corduroy trousers are tied to fence and bushes; the number plate glued to a rock, and beneath a piece of exhaust. Another newly sacred place added to the land. There are limestone outcrops on the outside of the road, and where the marble rock has tumbled into the sea, the water takes on a tropically green luminescence. Rathlin Island appears from the gloom, and I can see that the dark clouds are at last showing signs of lifting. Over there are shearwaters, petrels, fulmars, rare choughs: eggs and young seabirds were long gathered for food, the barefooted men descending cliffs on hemp ropes.

And then the rain just stops.

But the wind leaps a notch. I feel a lift to my stride. Just before Garron Point is the infamously inscribed roadside stone. Lady Londonderry, Churchill's grandmother, lived up at Garron Tower, and placed here a memorial to the famine of 1846–47. She raised money from England, invested much in the local economy. But her choice of words was not subtle: the memorial contained phrases that give the impression that the famine was natural, and concluded imperially that this was an "imperishable memorial of Ireland's suffering and England's generosity." The brass plaque with the full inscription is up at the school now; the offending script on the stone long ago chipped away, erased in another battle of graffiti and identity. Today the granite slab is fringed with a wig of tangled ivy. A white line on the tarmac runs along its base, so close is it to the racing traffic.

As I track south, the tide ebbs, exposing a line of rounded stones of black basalt. The long sweep of road takes me slowly around the Garron plateau, and then directly south five miles to Carnlough. By a faded red phone box is a single-room telephone exchange. On the rocks of the beach is an upturned rowing boat, red too, split and patched and apparently without a future career. Among the pebble field are bright pieces of chalk and long stalks of kelp. Ahead the road is still wet. Beyond a grove of pines is an odd patch of phragmites reeds on the salty side. The light quickly flees, and soon seems to emanate from the road and cliffs, from the sea, from the whispering reeds, rather than from the sky. I pass the only house on this coast on the seaward side of the road, with paved yard and mobile home, learning later it's a focus of long-standing planning conflict. Today, the sea is benign, but high on the telegraph wires hang pieces of kelp and seaweed. This is the coast where the Atlantic argues with the Irish Sea, where currents rip and pull and local weather patterns batter the shore. Many dead walk the seabed.

The air darkens to heavy blue, and I trudge the final stretch from Hunter's Point to Carnlough in full dark. Ahead I see attractive lights, and the promise of food and warmth. The sea is almost flat calm now, and sheep have fallen silent for the night. Waterfalls from the tall cliffs are soundless. Cars flash by, and I pull myself close to the wall and watch their taillights disappearing south. My feet are sore as I walk through the streets of the metropolis that is Carnlough, a village of four-teen hundred people. Enough community to support two football teams, a vibrant rowing club, and darts, clay pigeon shooting, hurling, Gaelic football, and angling teams. In the morning sun, I'll see why. You couldn't fail to be inspired to action in this bay. But then later I'm reminded—on this Marine Road is where John Turnley, Larne Borough councillor, both protestant and nationalist, was murdered by the UDA. Three men were sentenced to life, but his Japanese wife and two children had been sentenced to a life of horror from being in the car too.

Just before the coaching inn, I pass under another sign of mined exports: the railway that carried limestone from a quarry in the hills for export from Carn-lough harbor. The Londonderry Arms is bright as I walk in. I realize I haven't spo-ken a word for fifteen miles. Shall I try to speak, I wonder, or go on in silence? Of course, I chat: everyone is welcoming, especially to a walker. I tramp up the stairs decorated with local paintings and newspaper clippings to the warm room. I open a window to let in the autumn sea air, and put up my feet.

Liam Kelly drives up from Larne. He's in gray jacket, black shirt, and red tie, thick white hair over a broad face with a permanent smile.

"How are you keeping this landscape a secret?"

"We're not," he says, opening his arms.

Over dinner in the elegant front room we talk of more stories of this coast. He is deputy lieutenant and justice of the peace and active member of the Folklore

Society, and narrates the coast as we take a glass or two. Harry Browne wrote in the 1960s of such an evening in his *The Nine Glens* poem: "And there when evening's light springs up / Along the village street / You'll hear the sound of happy songs / The lilt of dancing feet." The Larne and District Folklore Society was established in 1971 to ensure the community would remember a world that might disappear. John Clifford and Sam Cross formed a committee, and membership grew as people of the region came together to support the recording of oral history, memories and stories. Liam says he hopes it will go on another forty years, though today's members are fewer and older. He's still one of the youngest at sixty-three. Today's challenge, perhaps, is to ensure the young feel just as strongly about preserving those elements of past culture that can help shape future pathways toward contentment.[2]

—⬛⬛—

This coast was populated by hunter-gatherers from about 6000 BC, whose main foods were deer, pig, horse, wolf, fox, and shell and sea fish. The Celts then brought farming from central Europe by 600 BC. They were fair-haired, using lime wash to make their hair thicker, herbs to redden their cheeks, and berries to dye hair and eyebrows. Perhaps they foresaw the dangers of overeating: it was written that "they try not to become short and fat-bellied, and every young man who exceeds the standard length of girdle is fined." Later came Vikings, Normans, then the Scots and English.

Wild produce was important to all. Sundew from the bogs cured warts and corns, helped with sunburn. Rushes from bogs were gathered in bunches, the green skin peeled away, and the pith dipped in melted fat or lard: when lit, these rush lights gave off a steady flame. An old practice, as Moira O'Neill, famed poet of the glens, wrote: "Oh maybe it was yesterday, or fifty years ago! / Meself was risin' early on a day for cuttin' rushes." Seaweed fertilized the fields, was eaten as dulse, and burned in kilns for industrial feed. Kelp was collected in March to June, dried, and then put in troughs filled with whins for their high burn. For days, the air would fill with clouds of acrid white smoke. The hardened ash was used for soap, glass, bleach, dyes, salt, as an antiseptic, and for photography. Flax weaving was traditional to the region, and the salvaged tow from linen processing used to make doormats and dog beds. Willows and hazel were woven for baskets, donkey panniers, and sturdy creels.

People hunt, but today mainly to tell stories about the in-weaving of animals and people. They talk of birds, foxes, squirrels, and rabbits; of their own dogs' behaviors and that of others; of those who run hunts, and about types of guns and shot to use; of the land and its many particularities. Jaimie Dick of Queen's University and I are walking the lanes of County Down as another autumn sun rises from the sea to throw long shadows from bare trees. Jaimie is wearing collared shooting shirt and brown waxed jacket, gray-green flat cap, and olive boots with a flourish of bright feathers tied to the top. Patrician pheasants strut, and then scamper back into fields and woods where the drives are planned. A rime of frost covers the puddles at the churned entrance of a field. On the far side of an expanse of golden stubble several thousand squabbling starlings cover every branch of a dead ash swathed in ivy. Suddenly, a great crack shatters across the field, and we watch a branch slowly fall and thump on the bank below. The flock lifts, swirling like smoke, and pours across the field toward the sun.

We return to the farmyard, and everyone is wearing subtle variants of the uniform of green or tan jackets, flat caps or deerstalkers, plus-fours or slacks, green boots, also shooting shirts. Jaimie has added a yellow and brown cravat of silk. Spaniels skitter between groups, jumping, tails wagging, meeting old friends, never a bark though. Those with guns and beaters with sticks cluster to tell their recent stories too. And make predictions. There are nine drives, so who will get the best of them? A hunt is both social and ecological occasion. Everyone has granular knowledge of ecology and the farming practices. And of each other: they are in not so subtle competition.

We are south of the nine glens on the Ards Peninsula, a twenty-five-by-five-mile strip of coastal land that encloses Strangford Lough and its seething narrows. It's the largest inlet in the British Isles at some 150 square kilometers, with oyster beds, seal colonies, basking sharks, many migratory birds. Today's birds, though, are raised and released, and will test those with guns by their clattering flights. There's much planning and organization. In the barn, lots are drawn for where each person will stand, and then the groups disperse. It is cold; the sky cloudless; the sites a grassland by a wood of golden gorse and pine, a pond with rustling reeds, a grassy slope poached by cattle, another pond, a line of ash by the farmyard lane. At lunch, both guns and beaters crowd into the tall barn and sit at a long table.

The men sit, but the ladies serve. Do women shoot, I ask? They do like to occasionally. I chat with the Belfast boys. All big men, very big. Beating today, but they'll shoot on other days.

"What do you do?" asks Billy leaning forward, the others going quiet.

"I work at a university, like Jaimie," I say.

He leans back, uncrosses his arms. "Good, we like that." They all nod.

The lads are using today to train their dogs. But they're grumpy about an acquaintance who runs a syndicate yet treats it as his power game. Over this hot and liquid lunch, they hatch a plan. Then there are wicked stories of those who miss: one man who let off fifty shots on the last shoot and missed the lot. And whispered seethings about another who invents stories about his grand past. But the whole table ripples to silence when someone brings news from the sea. Woodcocks are flying in from the Continent and across England. The first full moon of November is past, and there are detailed observations to be shared now. Who has seen one, who has yet to; where are they heading; where will be the first shoot.

After lunch, the sun drops across the lough toward the Mountains of Mourne. There's distinctly more joking and laughing. A local landowner in cap and quilted jacket offers a silver flask with three compartments—one each for his homemade sloe whiskey, sloe gin, and sloe vodka. There is much admiration and nodding. They all taste very well. By a dense wood, pheasants and partridges are laid in a long line of braces, but most pay them little attention. They'll later be divided up in the yard, but this hunt is still less for the meat than the story. On a meadow overlooking the lough, birds sail down into a hail of shot, and the spaniels rush around on collection duty. But on the final peg, where the wind now bites from the water, an ultralight flies toward the field, veering sharply away when all the guns are suddenly swung upward. The whole field laughs.

Not all hunting is explicitly so social. Jaimie lamps at night for foxes and rabbits, but this still has a social function. A specific request from a landowner comes in to clear her land of rabbits. The hunt is then in a private and thus unique space. There is pleasure in having sole access to a piece of land, because you know no one else will have a story about it. It is an exclusive, and so creates status when told. Indeed, the collective element is really like this too. Everyone has unique positions and experiences. How one peg worked, or did not; how a left-right combo worked, or missed completely. In this way, stories emerge from our interactions with the land.

Jaimie and I rise on another day when the stars are glittering and the air chilling, and head for some inland fractal landscapes. By the gloaming of the winter dawn, we clatter onto the ferry to cross the one-kilometer narrows at the mouth of the lough between Portaferry and Strangford. The boat beats across the fierce current, and I stand outside to watch the wall of frothing white waves at the bar. There's been a ferry here for four hundred years to save a journey of nearly fifty miles. But you have to be very good to sail out across the bar; the standing wave can be several feet high. Toward the mouth is the red tower of the tidal power station. We stop at Oliver McCullough's house in the woods for a hunter's breakfast, and well fueled, all leave the coast to head inland for the westernmost county of Northern Ireland.

We are in search of those mystical woodcock. And we will have to walk the Fermanagh mile to find them.

Blanket bogs once covered a sixth of all Ireland; today perhaps only one in five remain in their natural state. They are environmental regulators, holding water and carbon, low levels of nutrients and high acidity, producing a unique flora. From a distance, the land is a mosaic of brown, green, and gold, rimmed with forests of planted conifers. When you walk into the land, it is so different. You will walk, the saying goes, three miles for one covered on the map. There are tussocks of grasses, reeds and sedges, soggy buttons of red sphagnum moss, deep crevasses of black, oozing peat, thickets of impenetrable brambles, and patches of dying silver birch. I walk on the tops, but slip and fall. I try staying in the valleys, but the water pours over the tops of my boots, and my trousers and socks are sopping wet and it feels like I am carrying half of Ireland's water with me. The cloying peat grips feet and I pitch forward, then sideways, then on my back. From a distance, this does not look like such a wet land. But up close, you learn a new respect for inhabitants.

I empty my mind, squint into the sun, and see the light glistening through the acid grasses. A golden land. I listen to the long-tailed tits, the blackbirds chirping alarm calls, and then discern the whirring beat of a woodcock. It jinks sideways. Slipping air, and cleverly puts a tree directly in line. We see another four as we tramp and the spaniel quarters, and I get shots away. But hit not one. In one horseshoe glade, I look up and watch one arch across the unlit spruce, rising to the sky of purple clouds and then fall quietly back into the shrubby vegetation. In the woodland, the ground is hard and mossy, the trees so dense that barely any light reaches the floor.

We walk out past a yellow giant clanking and roaring, chopping trees, buzzing off branches, and stacking them by a track. Up the hill, we meet Oliver by a forest track, and he has three birds. Our shirts are dripping wet from sweat, and we all change. Bare skin briefly meets raw winter afternoon. A lad walks up the road in blue school uniform. A grumbling lumber lorry appears, and tries to turn where the boy has walked. We pour warm soup, eat sandwiches, and share pieces of cold snipe and woodcock.

The sun drops over Ireland to the west.[3] It's just twenty miles or so to Sligo and Donegal on the coast; in the other direction, to the northeast, eighty to the Antrim coast. Dusk falls over another glade by a dark wood. At this time of day, the woodcocks flash along the rides. By now all is quiet, no other birds are singing. We split up. A couple of pigeons clap into an oak. I see nothing. Oliver is quiet too. Jamie's gun cracks twice, then again. Then a deep, penetrating darkness falls on the land, and the moon rises silver through the silent trees. And the land is as it ever was.

—◦◦◦—

Breakfast is good, and the sky better. Cobalt blue through the windows. Sunshine glitters on the wide puddles. The cloud has scattered, and there's a hint of rainbow over cream and brown McAuley's Hotel and the Glencoy Inn. The sun blazes above Straidkilly and Whitebay Point, and washes the Carnlough front with warm light. Along the promenade, watery sunlight casts long shadows from the two empty benches facing northwest to Scotland. If you can't see Scotland, it's raining, so the saying goes; if you can, it's about to rain. I head past a church with every window boarded, and then look back north to see the right end of a rainbow diving into the town from its arch over the hills. Beyond, the sun has caught the edge of a towering bank of retreating cloud, and it flares white. I wonder if Carnlough Bay can ever have looked better. It's the Bay of Naples, but without Vesuvius. In a meadow, a flock of curlews probe the pasture alongside small jackdaws. I wish they would just cry for the marshes, for those cold winter days of home. At the entrance to the field, more two-meter-wide cylindrical gateposts are topped with conical stone, like huge mushrooms. And then a rainstorm races across the bay, lashes down, and is gone. The sun shines again. It's going to be one of those days.

By the time I have walked to Straidkilly's slippery slopes, the whole arc of the rainbow is visible, spanning perfectly the whole bay. Around the point to the south, the air is brighter and welcoming. I walk on the glistening tarmac with a springy step. Among the rocks, a cormorant swims, its body entirely below the surface. The rain has blurred my map at its folds, colors eroded to leave a white papery subsoil. I am where the last two glens join the sea: Glencloy into Carnlough, the glen of the dykes and hedges, and Glenarm into Glenarm village. At the top is Slemish mountain, another volcanic mount famed now for booleys where a slave from Roman Britain was put to work as a shepherd by Melvic, and walked out six years later to become patron saint of all Ireland.

Clouds race across the fresh blue sky, and I walk along the shore into the warm sun. The tide gently laps at the sweeping wall of the bay. A promontory of blue lias clays regularly encroaches onto the road. They are chock full of fossils, but there's not the time to search. Down here, the road had to be widened out to sea. Up there, Straidkilly nature reserve contains some of the best woodland in Antrim, coppiced hazel and patches of ash and birch. Spring is said to be the best time, for the anemones, primroses, and bluebells, but all seems fine to me today.

But at Glenarm, the police station is protected by large metal gates and pillars with cameras pointing all directions. The river is dark and rippled, running straight by the castle walls. Salmon have returned here, swimming upriver in June to the eight-hundred-acre forest. In the new limestone harbor, a dozen yachts doze in the marina, and older derelict buildings are surrounded by fencing and granite blocks. A faded sign instructs, *No Fishing*. As I stand, an inky sheet of rain suddenly appears, and drives across the bay. The distant hills are bright and beckoning, but here the light is switched off and darkness brings pelting horizontal rain. At the far end of Glenarm under Lady's Hill is an abandoned lime works, the factory open to the road, empty save for two great metal pulleys. I slip into the dusty ruins of stone and patched tin, the floor, pipes, grills, stones, everything dusted thick with white lime. Another example of this liminal and changeable coast. This promontory is Cretaceous limestone, also good for fossils of ammonites, sea urchins, corals, and fish. The factory is being reabsorbed into the landscape, soon to become a fossil itself.

Mostly, the coast road is built on a raised platform at the base of the cliffs. The long swell of the sea is on my left side, just meters away. As I walk, I write. Not this book, but a previous one. I spend steps imagining different sections, new orders, alternate spines to chapters, creating backstories for characters. I notice that the sea is now crystal clear over the limestone. I will walk all day and again not speak a word out loud until arriving at the retreat, the hot spots on my feet by then blisters. Now below the limestone cliffs, a hundred meters of grass and bracken has opened up, and at Whitebay Point under the cliffs of Crockandillish three great weathered rocks lean in half an arch against the hillside of rock and bracken.

Through this Madman's Window watched a man for his drowned sweetheart, crazed and "gazing out to sea / waiting, waiting, waiting / For my girl to come back to me," wrote a later poet. Today a fishing smack with three white masts and simple wheelhouse quarters the calm waters. I sit awhile and watch, absorbing into the tussocky grass. From here you can see, too, the Maidens or Hulin Rocks, two islands with lighthouses, the east and west towers, first lit in 1824, combining with the rocks to take the shape of a battleship. As I walk, the ship mirage slowly morphs and separates.

Beyond Madman's, the coast to Drumnagreagh is rebathed in warm sunshine. Streaks of high cirrus remain, and the white stone shore sparkles between water and grass. White lines dash down the middle of the road, and cars, buses, and delivery lorries streak past. There are no other walkers. I can see why on this stretch. There is no escape. The road is flanked by walls on both sides. On the inside of a derelict pigsty, misspelled graffiti has been painted over with smears of white paint, but the original is still visible: *Andy is Gorgous*. On a grassy rise, a bungalow with one tiny window at one end and bay window at the other is boarded up. Behind, the hills rise sharply up to another craggy plateau. Much of this detail would be lost from a motorcar.

In a field on the inside of the road, a weathered door of wood is painted with more white lettering: *End Collusion*, and more that is confused, and finally *Our happy day have ended*. All the trees here are tall and spindly. And then appears another end-of-era sign for a hotel, struck through with two lines of tape scrawled over in faded pen with *closed*. Restaurant, bar food, carvery. All gone. But then four months later, before this winter is over, fire breaks out in the disused hotel and fifty firefighters have to run pulsing yellow hoses into the sea, and pump seawater to fight the flames. "Very rare," says the fire captain, "to use seawater in this way."

Marking small fields are more conical gateposts, and I come to the Halfway House Hotel, very much open and famed for the owner, a former world boxing champion. Ballygally lies ahead, and I decide to press on. But there is no shop. A developer bought it, knocked it down, didn't get planning permission for his grand scheme, and the site remains no more than abandoned rubble. There's nothing to eat. I should have stopped at the Halfway House. There's a pebble-dashed castle here too, more like a four-storied square house with round towers on each upper corner.

But it is all closed. And I am still hungry.

On the shore of Ballygally lived once Jean Park, now known in myth as Marina Jane, wife of a farmer who fished and was drawn to the sea. She had come, they say, as a baby found on a boat drifting in the bay containing a dead woman. During one of his trips, she dreamt his drowning, and raced to the beach to await his return. So much time was spent standing on the shore, looking to sea, that she was evicted from her farm. She built a house of beach stones, driftwood, and kelp, lived off limpets, came to be thought of as a witch. Her husband never returned, except as a ghost. It was drowning that took her back during a December storm in 1894. On a signboard by the shore is a black and white photograph of her crouched by the shelter, right hand pressed to her head, eyes wild and staring at the photographer. A pail for water is propped on rocks. Today, the sky has darkened, but the line of surf along the shore is a luminous white against the green sea. Kelp strips mark high water on the sandy beach. To the far south are hints of industrial Larne, a chimney billowing smoke, sunshine glinting on the factory perched on the hill. Much has changed.

In Drains Bay, where blackthorns have been replaced by bungalows, is the last arch of the coast road. Blackcove tunnel by the Devil's Churn is a semicircle and a squeeze for modern traffic. A dozen concrete steps lead down to basalt rocks covered with green sea lettuce. Rusting rails have leaked stains on the concrete. A piper is said to have drowned here: at certain tides his pipes can be heard from the gurgling and sucking sea. Beyond I can clearly see industrial Larne. From Larne Lough appears a blue and white ferry heading for Scotland, the low throb more felt than heard. Behind is the remote finger of Islandmagee, called by Ptolemy Isamnion Akron, and later used by the Vikings for a war cemetery, proving they lost as well as won.

The road now rises long into Larne, and I stop at the plaque placed by the Folklore Society to the Coast Road constructed by "The Men of the Glynnes" under Bald's direction. Larne was the lands of the legendary prince, Lathar, earlier called Portus Saxus by the Romans, the port of the standing stones. Harry Browne's poem "Coast Road" centers on the clash of the new and old: "The man that made the roadway / From Larne to Cushendall . . . / He broke the rock and boulder / He drove the pathway through / But—a fairy sat on his shoulder / And showed him the thing to do."

I turn left into the long drive of the castellated convent on the hill, where a retreat will be held on the topic of slow living. Apart from the nuns who live here, I am the only participant who did not come by car. But then again, I am the only one hobbling with blisters. The mackerel skies are blotchy with cirrus, and wind will come again. Sister Margaret Rose McSparran is standing at the door to greet me, even though I have not called ahead. This feels like it's been a pilgrimage, walking the coast road and arriving at the convent. But it's not about arriving somewhere, more just being on the journey. She was born at Cushendun, and when I had mentioned the plan to walk the road, she had e-mailed, "What a good idea! A more beautiful area you will not have encountered in all your travels. And look out for the goat."

I call Liam, and we go back up the road, stopping at St. MacNissi's college at Garron Tower, his old school, where once tropical monkeys were released. We stand beneath a giant double-trunked gum tree and look down upon the sprawling school buildings. Every day by bus Liam came here, homework written on the knee, or maybe time spent staring out of windows wiped clear of condensation. Now MacNissi's will be combined with St. Comgall's in Larne and St. Aloysius's in Cushendall to form St. Killian's College. Liam drops me at the hotel, and I pick up the rental car to drive the road just walked. It takes minutes: walking at the edge of the land and sea, when pulsing light and calling gulls meet, took days. At once the sea was turquoise, gray, steely, mercury; the settlements gathered at the base of slopes, later to twinkle their welcoming lights across the bays.

At the front at Larne, we look across the bands of limestone, sandstone, and the one bone bed, full of fossilized teeth of fish. Overlooking the ferry route around Islandmagee and into the lough stands the new stone memorial. Before I came to this coast, I had not realized that 1953 was so etched into everyone's memories as it is on our coast of East Anglia. There, we were flooded; here the ferry MV *Princess Victoria* was lost in sight of the coast in dreadful seas, and 133 drowned. No women or children survived; only 44 men. The names of all those lost that terrible day are etched on the marble.[4]

At the retreat, we listen to the battering wind, talking in the dining hall of ways to live that might be slow. We walk in the gardens, coats pulled tight, and all agree that the land has much to say. We need to create new rituals, just to get us all out on the land more often.

9

SNOW

Nitassinan, Labrador, Canada

240° West of Date Line

Inside the darkling depths of the sweat lodge, all are lit by the flush glow of super-heated stones. The whisper of steam combines with the wheeze of many gasping lungs. I lie down, and it is still fiercely hot. The sweet spruce boughs strewn on the floor lull us into a dreamworld. There could be fifteen people crowded in this tent wrapped by layers of canvas and plastic. Someone pours water on the stones, more steam surges up, and we are translocated deep into the heart of the primeval earth. Steam fills ears and eyes. All the while is the quiet murmur of Innu-aimun. For some this is a healing ceremony, a mix of confession and links to tradition; for others, not in this tent, it is something that should only happen in the country, not here in the village beside the treatment center on the main road.

Each time I wriggle outside, the summer light has dimmed yet further. We are hemmed by the boreal forest of black-and-white spruce, balsam fir, jack pine, white birch, and tamarack, trembling and balsam poplar. There is no real sense of passing time, it is just that the long northern evening gradually heads for night by gentle degrees. The outdoor fire crackles and leaps in sharper color, and replacement stones gather more heat. Outside, everyone steams. Some lie to recover, others draw on cigarettes. Once I stagger with dizziness, and fall, unable to wave off the mosquitoes.

At the end of three hours, we walk slowly back through the now twilit village of wooden houses.

Dominic Pokue has a house in Sheshatshiu, and lives in a canvas tent in the garden. We sprawl on the spruce in the warmth, while outside rain patters and inside is filled with the rich odor of resin and the Innu doughnuts cooked by Philomena, his wife of forty-three years. He's one of the region's many great hunters, not originally from Sheshatshiu but a Mushuauinnu from the tundra, the knowledge of the homeland of Nitassinan layered over decades. The hunters traveled great distances in their youth. Food was killed or caught on the way, caribou, porcupine, trout, and they carried flour, baking powder, sugar, tea, tobacco, and ammunition. But it is a big land, and sometimes there were no animals: his father once found two white men starved to death out at Kamestastin Lake. In hunger times, spruce boughs were boiled and the liquid drunk. When you arrived at camp so starved, you were forbidden from eating solid food, says Dominic. No bread or meat, just melted lard or flour mashed in a liquid. We pause, and eat our doughnuts.

Dominic calls on the time when hunters used spears and arrow points of stone or caribou bone. Then, they used to shoot the lead caribou, causing the rest to circle, thus allowing many more to be shot. But today, noisy snowmobiles have changed things. Skilled men could spear caribou from land or canoe, though the best were shamans, as they used dreams to call animals. They were the leaders of the people, singing with drums, dreaming up the animals. But dreams were also dangerous places: some Innu fought in dreams, people could be harmed or killed. The main function of the *matashan* sweat lodge was to deal with injuries and physical ailments such as flu or pulled muscles. It was also used after the killing of bears as protection. Bears are considered almost human, so killing and eating them brought the Innu scarily close to the arch taboo of cannibalism. As well as the sweat lodge, the shaking tent was used by shamans across all the northern areas of the world to communicate. The last event in Sheshatshiu was held in 1969 by *Uatshatshish* Sylvester Pokue just downstream from Muskrat Falls.

Every hunt is remembered in full. Each is unique and emotional, connecting people at each particular point of their lives to both place and the animals. All hunters can give detailed accounts of each of their hunts, even from fifty years before. In this way, memories are woven into the land. The next morning we arrive early to join Dominic and his daughter and son-in-law to check their nets on Grand Lake. The skiff roars under the North West River bridge, and ahead are forty miles of gray water. Waves slap, and at the shore are spruce and firs and fringing alder. The water is brown with leachates from the forest soils. Three nets are pulled, cold water splashing into the boat, and we gather a lake trout of about two feet in length. It lies on the deck, twitching. It is a long trip for one fish, but it's the connection to the way of life that is important. Also the food: Dominic's diet has never changed; he and his wife do not care for domesticated meat.

There have been three great European writers on the lives and land of the Innu: Norwegian Georg Henriksen, British Hugh Brody, and my colleague Colin Samson.[1] Henriksen's *I Dreamed the Animals* opens a window into ways of knowing about life and land that elude most moderns today. Technically, Kaniuekutat, or John Poker, spoke this book and Henriksen wrote it. What you think matters; how you dream influences animals and our own interactions with them. People operate in an intertwined natural world and spiritual realm in which survival was dependent on respect. They had no supreme position; did not control life, death, and birth like farmers do. Life on an unpredictable land also determined social and political relationships, and thus no permanent leadership class emerged. People shared food and resources within families, families shared with wider communities. Any form of anger was seen as dangerous, as no one wished to provoke animal spirits. Over millennia, the Innu developed a deep emotional attachment to a land cultivated by their social and hunting events.

Later that evening, Basile Penashue's father Nui said three black bears were wandering around, here on the beach, not so long ago. "What do you think of that?" he asks. It was strange, they did not seem to want to cause harm. No one had ever heard of black bears at this time, though they are common scavengers in spring and early summer before the berries are out. The dogs did not even bark at them. Was it a warning? Basile shrugs, says it could be so. He was recently driving home from Goose Bay late at night, and came upon an owl in the road, bright in the headlights, walking in circles.

Odd animal behavior is always instructive, but of what? When they arrived home, an ambulance was parked at the neighbor's house; a child had died.

The Innu are Algonquian people of the Labrador-Quebec peninsula. For at least eight thousand years, they and their ancestors ranged over an area the size of France. In their slow-growth boreal forests, taiga shield, and tundra of the interior they hunted caribou, including the vast George River herd, as well as bear, beaver, otter, marten, lynx, fox, ptarmigan, ducks, geese, several species of fish, and seals, walrus, and seabirds on the coast. First contact was with the Norse around AD 1000, then Basque whalers in the 1500s, and fur traders of the Hudson Bay Company in the 1700s. Though they remained deep in the country most of the year, the Innu began to come to trading posts to obtain sugar, tea, baking powder, flour, and tobacco in return for furs. They were famed for their hunting skills, but most explorers and commentators judged them as inferior to the white settlers, their hunting itself seen as an impediment to civilized living.

In the mid-twentieth century, the Indian Act was implemented in Quebec, and those Innu coming to trade at the various posts were registered and officially regarded as domiciled. Labrador and Newfoundland joined the Canadian federation in 1949, and provincial authorities initiated a peculiar assimilation campaign that resulted in the sedentarization of Innu families in the late 1950s at the village of Sheshatshiu, near the North West River trading post on Lake Melville, and at Utshimassits Davis Inlet on Iluikoyak Island in 1967. Davis Inlet was later abandoned following a further relocation of the Mushuau tundra Innu to Natuashish on the mainland in 2003. Today, there are some eighteen thousand Innu in Labrador and Quebec, of whom some twenty-one hundred live in these two Labrador villages.

Sedentarization successfully undermined the relationship of the Innu to their hunting culture. Children had to attend school, and so their families needed to be settled. Many children, though, were simply sent away to a variety of Indian residential schools of northern Canada. These were brutal places, supposed to civilize Indian children, who were not permitted to speak their own language. Under severe physical punishment regimes, roughly a quarter of the children died. As they were late to be sedentarized, the Innu missed the worst of the practice, and actively opposed the punishment regimes. Yet the last of these schools did not close until the 1970s. There are people alive today who led those schools, perhaps with children themselves.

Families also had to have a proper address to receive welfare payments. Above all, missionaries and priests made it clear that heaven was open only to people part of modern society. Politicians knew best. Walter Rockwood, director of the Division of Northern Labrador Affairs, said in 1957, "One fact seems clear—civilisation is on the northward march, and for the Eskimo and Indian there is no escape. . . . The only course now open, for there can be no turning back, is to fit him as soon as may be to take his full place as a citizen of our society." His views were not unique: he warned, "There is a danger that the Indians will become loafers whose only aim is to extract more and more handouts from government."

Today, the Innu are indeed settled, but not at home. They visit the country they call *nutshimit* when they can, but mostly they have been disconnected from a life and its sense of community that safely brought them across some four hundred generations. Today, alcoholism is widespread, childhood mortality high, life expectancy low, and type-2 diabetes affects many. Instead of active lifestyles eating country foods, dense in protein and light in fats, people have become mostly inactive and have taken on junk foods as a norm. Many now feel they have lost all hope.

Mary Adele is a thin elderly woman, and she gazes wistfully out a window.

"It feels lonely here, when you look outside at the sky and the trees. Even though we are here in the village, we feel lonely."

Her husband adds, "It was beautiful and happy before. Now I sit in this home, and I feel pain and feel sick. I feel very unhappy in the house."

When Mary and other Innu look at the country, they see places tied by stories to specific events, they see ancestors and animal spirits wandering the land, they see the past and present intimately linked. But when Rockwood's civilization marched, it chose to see the economic value of lumber, of reservoirs for hydroelectricity, of nickel in the rocks, and of the wildlife that needed protecting. No reliable source of wage labor has been found for the Innu, and most families have to survive on welfare payments. Most employed Innu work in the government-created institutions of the villages; only a handful work at Goose Bay or in Voisey's Bay mine near Davis Inlet. Hugh Brody described the pathology of similarly situated Aboriginal communities elsewhere in Canada: "Many northern reserves appear to be grim and even hateful little places, clusters of houses crowded together by planners in order to achieve economies of administration and services. . . . Such compression of a people distinctive for their free roamings through unbounded forest is bizarre and painful."

Farley Mowat was the first Canadian author to draw stark attention to the way people of the North were treated. In *People of the Deer*, he called the neglect, created dependencies, and outright destruction of the ways of living a *genocide of indigenous people*, and for this he was not forgiven by the mainstream. He first visited the Barrens in the mid-1930s, an area talked up by outsiders as empty and terrible. Said one, "I guess it was the emptiness that bothered me most. That barren and bloody space—it just goes on and on until it makes you want to cry, or scream—or cut your own damn throat." At no point did authorities consider letting the Barrens Inuit live on their land. All missionaries, police, traders, and policy makers believed they were doing good by bringing people into the modern world. They were saving souls. Yet when outsiders came into the country to set up mining camps or supply posts, they were taken care of by what they saw as stone-age Eskimos.

"The Inuit had an option," wrote Mowat; "they could have turned them out to fend for themselves." They did not. Yet even then, missionaries were ungrateful. One, a Fr. Biliard, wrote home, "They do not have a pleasant appearance and at times even repulsive. . . . They sorely need the missionary to drive away the dark clouds of paganism and show them the way to Heaven."

"In the old days," says Katnen Pastitchi today in Sheshatshiu, "people did not find it difficult. We never used to be tired. We were strong and happy." There were no snowmobiles, but pulling sledges did not feel like hard work. It was just part of life. Men were the hunters, and women in charge of the camps. Both were equals, both with their own sphere of activity and decision making. Katnen learned all she knows from her grandmother, and today still makes clothing from caribou hide. She laments the loss of a way of life. These human communities and forest ecosystems have coevolved since the last ice age. What we see now is an emergent property of human intentionality, not an idle wilderness. Federal authorities, though, still see going to the country as something akin to a recreational summer camp.

We waited on the buffeted beach all day. Seen from the sunlit shore, the whitecaps do not look so bad, and we are keen to start. But when Shushep Mark says we can go, sometime after five o'clock, the boat crashes and shudders, smashing down on the waves, me hanging onto the side in freefall every few seconds. Shushep is in control, erect at the stern, staring forward in the glorious evening light. I spend too much of the journey wishing we'd arrive. Beyond the mouth of the Kenamu River, beneath the Mealy Mountains, we pitch the square tent on a foreshore strewn with bleached driftwood. We collect spruce boughs, pile wood, set a fire. Shushep and young Shustin Rich, also known as Sebastien, return from the nets with a salmon and two trout, and on a flat table of wood, bright pink steaks of fish are sliced and laid in lines, and we hunch beneath the hordes of mosquitoes and blackflies.

In the wide evening of breezy summer, we walk along the coast of one-hundred-mile-long Lake Melville to find a graveyard, set on a rise in the forest, white flowers carpeting the floor of spongy lichens, Labrador tea by the old-growth trees. Under wooden crosses lie former tribal leaders. Shushep says later, put the lichen moss on the fire, and the smoke will send the mosquitoes away. It could be worse. Farley Mowat described the terror during summer over west. "They came in such numbers that their presence actually gave me a feeling of physical terror. An insanity would seize us. From behind our ears, from beneath our chins, a steady dribble of blood matted our clothes and trapped insatiable flies until we wore black collars." We make it back alive as the sun grips the far horizon. We stand looking out over the flat calm lake.

The next day, clouds seal the sky, and torrential rain patters on the canvas. The rusted stove glows, the crooked chimney pipe reaching through the canvas to the gray cold world outside. Tea brews in a blackened pot. Shushep and Sebastien, his granddaughter's father, and Tony Jenkinson's wife's nephew, lie on pillows and downs, smoking. Water drips through the roof, and they move the sleeping bags around. The tiny radio chatters, and we treat the ads for double chubby chicken as a permanent joke. Colin and I still laugh about these. Somehow the junk food's become stuck in our minds. All day, we lie on the sweet spruce. Shushep brings Sebastien out on the land to escape the trauma of the settlement. He left school at seventeen, was regularly drunk, taken by the Mounties, one policeman telling him, "Why don't you just commit suicide now?"

Shushep gets him out of jail on the promise of reform. His daughter is now seven months old, yet Sebastien tries to spend as much time in the country as he can. We talk of hunting: when Shushep was a young boy, he too used bows and arrows for hunting caribou. One monthlong trip resulted in four lynx, thirty beaver, and forty martens. But always there was self-regulation: beavers cleared from a lodge, but not another; rotation around hunting grounds, areas left alone for two or three years.

At mid-evening, the rain stops, and Shushep jumps up and says we must travel upriver in search of a birch-bark canoe he built with friends and family three years previously. We surge up the Kenemau, over scratchy shallows and still deeps, and moor by scrubby willow. In a line, we meander past sapphire patches of flag irises, the water of the marsh wet over our feet, accompanied by a mist of insects.

"Not far," waves Shushep.

The ground becomes drier as we climb a few meters, and the scrub thickens to dark and humid silver birch and spruce forest, rain still dripping from leaves. We find ourselves standing in a glade, the floor shimmering with the white stars of the frog flower. There is a hole in the world.

There is no canoe. We stand in silence, looking at the place where it should be. We can see the signs: three wooden posts in the ground for props, stumps of branches cut for tent poles, another space where a tent had been pitched, a birch stripped of bark for snowshoes.

Here, points Shushep, we pitched the tents, all round there could be twenty to thirty families, all of them working on the canoe over a whole summer. But now nothing. He looks around, an empty expression, touching this tree, pointing to another where bark had been taken for the canoe as they fashioned it. Over there they killed a moose that just strayed into the camp. Elsewhere, they hunted beaver, otter, and caribou, and gathered wild cloudberries. The place is thick with stories. I feel a dark shiver, a hesitation in the progress of time. On trees hang the skulls of otter and beaver.

We walk out of the trees, past a second campsite, and there, on the water's edge, is a sparkling settler's summer cabin, complete with deck, barbecue, propane gas stove, solar panels, and piles of freshly hewn logs. A bird skitters across the grass as the rain returns, a pied wagtail, symbol of the spirit of young boys who died too early. This land is designated for Innu use alone, yet others are claiming this new frontier for their own. Shushep says, "This is our land," yet with no animosity. Perhaps he knows it is too late. Or perhaps he is just more generous than we feel. We all walk back around the shore, and cast off into the wide brown river, clattering into the lake proper to check the salmon nets. The dusk draws in, and the wind whips white tops off the waves. Our hands are cold. The slate-gray water is unforgiving, smacking hard on the side of the boat. We look forward to lighting the woodstove in the tent.

This trip will end with us walking four abreast out of the forest into the village, smiling at the ordinariness of children on bicycles and wooden houses set back on their plots. We were at the end of a six-mile hike along the shore, weighed down by salt water, baggage, and fish. I swing right and bid goodbye, and head for Sheila Blake's shore-side house, where there will be warmth and food by the crashing waves. Colin heads for Basile's, but Shushep and Sebastien feel they are leaving home to come into the village. We have been wanting to arrive, they have not. Hugh Brody wrote specifically of Sheshatshiu, "It is like so many others, a place where most houses were built at lowest possible cost, and where people felt confined and demoralised."

We had just glimpsed our own disaster. We broke camp and packed the boat, checked the nets, patting one grand salmon a meter long. The wind was churning the lake, but there was no hint yet of worse to come. We crabbed along the shore, the lake water up and then down, then Shushep pointed to the far side, shouted, and we struck out. The swell rose, and now the open boat was crashing up solid wave walls twice as high as us. Suddenly water started topping over, and we were soaked. One second dry, the next wet and already cold. The three of us began bailing. The boat fell and crashed, one wave swamping the boat, and we wallowed horribly. The wind ripped across us, and still we were heading directly for the distant shore. I loosened boots and jacket as I baled; neither Shushep nor Sebastien could swim. Colin and I looked at each other, wondering whether we could do this. I kept my mind on one wave, then the next, still trying to get water out of the boat. Either time would pass, or it would stop.

And with no hint or warning, we burst through a wave, topped out, and were suddenly skating into a wide expanse of marshy grass. There was a wooden cabin all alone in the pelting horizontal rain. We pulled the boat up the shore, and now were shivering uncontrollably, not just from cold. Within seconds, Shushep miraculously started a fire in the lee of the cabin, and gradually our clothes began steaming. Cigarette smoke was whipped away in the wind. We all grinned. This was a good place to be. We pulled the boat across another bay, up to waists in water, and then left it tied high on the shore. Sheshatshiu was far around the bay, and we would have to walk. The black bears, says someone later.

———

People always had a good time in the country, laughing lots. "Everyone was happy and we felt free," said Kaniuekutat to Georg Henriksen. The land meant freedom. Thus the greatest threat to the Innu is loneliness, from each other and from the land. This loneliness and lack of hope corrode modern village life. Walking through Sheshatshiu one evening of cold blue light, a drunken man shouted at me from his doorstep.

"What are you doing here? Who are you?"

Inside, the single room had no furniture, save for single table and three chairs. Low sunlight streamed through the back windows, cutting through the blue pall of tobacco smoke. Another chair was cast in pieces in the corner. One window was broken too. The ashtray was full, and beer bottles were strewn across table and floor. A woman lay half conscious, then jerked up, frowned and demanded a cigarette. The man's anger diminished as we talked of hunting. He showed me photos on the wall of his granddaughter. No, she is not here, he said, shoulders dropping. There was a yawning space in this household. From a freezer in the kitchen, he pulled out a frozen goose, and slapped it on the table, its twisted neck splashed with red. This was his one remaining link to the land. There seemed no other food in the house.

He started shouting again, waving his arms, and I had to leave. Loneliness is a serious danger, more dreaded than death. Death is accepted, because of the harsh and arbitrary world in which random events cannot be controlled, nor monster beings and shamanic powers. But loneliness is much worse.

In *Make Prayers to the Raven*, Richard Nelson describes the lives of the Koyukon, a northern Athabascan group of central Alaska. To the Koyukon, "the surroundings are aware, sensate, personified. They feel. They can be offended. And they must, at every moment, be treated with utmost respect." Thus there is a moral code that defines and continually shapes interactions with all of the environment. At the time Nelson was writing, the Koyukon relied almost entirely on wild animals, fish, and birds for their food, supplemented by some flour. They made "strong emotional and psychological investments in the food they eat." The conservation ethic among all northern peoples is strong. One Koyukon hunter said, "I trapped all my life. But if you go there now, it's still good ground—still lots of beaver, plenty of mink, otter, marten; good beaver country. I took care of it, see. You have to do that; don't take too much out of it right now or you'll get nothing later on." The Koyukon, like other indigenous groups, are not accidental managers. They are aware of interdependencies and dynamics between predators and prey, and how change is a norm in an uncertain world. They say, "Each animal knows way more than you do." Like the Innu, they believe it is the animals that control the hunt, and such a belief brings a respect and a desire to behave properly. One hunter said to Nelson, "The country knows. If you do wrong things to it, the whole country knows. It feels what's happening to it. I guess everything is connected together somehow." This is why people stuck in the village feel lonely.

"The caribou are starting to come near," said Katnen, "because things are changing in the country." On our coming expedition into the heart of Nitassinan, though, we would have suffered hunger were it not for our supplies of flour and the ptarmigans and porcupine of the boreal forest. We wouldn't find the caribou, though we will search. Every Innu has noticed the changes in their movements. But it's all strange now, observes Katnen from her finely decorated wooden house. The salmon taste different, the porcupine are reddish in color because of replanted trees, the special flavors gone. Her parents died young, and she was sometimes in the country for a whole year with her grandmother, moving through the Mealy Mountains, over to Churchill River, Grand Lake too. Then they might stop awhile here by the coast in Sheshatshiu to meet other families, before there was a settled village.

In England, we had packed an old manual Singer sewing machine in a cardboard box, tying around much string, and carried it to Katnen's house. In the porch is a pile of caribou heads. With careful hands, she lays out on the floor a tunic, a child's red dress and hat, two pairs of delicate moccasins, and explains. It takes a week and a half to get one skin ready. First she scrapes the hide with a metal blade, making sure there are no veins or blood remaining. It's then treated with a mix of lard, brain, and water. A fire warms the mixture, and a moist atmosphere is important. Periodically, the hide is removed and stretched, dried, and rewetted. She used to do this in the house, but her grandson doesn't like the pungent smell, so this is a job for the tent in the garden.

"My grandson," she says sadly, "he doesn't eat any wild food. If I don't eat caribou meat for a week, I feel ill. Store food just makes me hungry."

Among the elder Innu, Dominic included, everyone believes store food makes people ill. This was evident almost as soon as the Innu were sedentarized when a Fr. Frank Peters quoted Innu at Davis Inlet as feeling hungry after eating processed food, and saying that chicken, pork, and beef were not as substantial as caribou meat. At the same time, he also noted the deterioration of teeth, which he attributed to the new availability of sweets and soft drinks. By contrast, a visiting physician reported that people in the country were remarkably healthy, with few cardiovascular or lung problems, and good dental health. Store foods contain on average 75 percent more energy per unit weight than country food, a third less protein, and more than four times as much fat. Country foods also contain more iron, three times the vitamin C, half more riboflavin, and two-thirds more niacin. These high concentrations of vitamins in country foods are important for people with little or no vegetables in their diets: ptarmigan, for example, has ten times the niacin as domestic meats, and caribou and duck are high in thiamin.

At the same time, there are stark differences in energy expenditure. In the country, most days are physically active. First, Innu have to get to camp. In the past, this would have been by walking, with loads carried, portaged, or pulled on sledges. Today, most use snowmobiles in winter. From the camp, men engage in hunting and trapping, and fuelwood cutting and hauling. Often they will be away for the whole day. Women gather plants and boughs of spruce for tent floors, snare rabbits, set fishing nets, prepare and cook foods, collect water, look after infants, repair clothes and tents, and take care of meat and hides. Hunter Jean-Pierre Ashini observed, "When I am in the country, I am 170 lbs; in the village I put on 20–30 lbs too easily. I eat a lot in the country, but it quickly burns off."

In the village, calorie intake greatly exceeds expenditure. This is a problem not only for the Innu. It is endemic in modern society.

A snowmobile engine lies in pieces, all the correct ones, but they do not fit together. The stove beats out heat, a file rasps on an axe. Snow drifts through the trees, and the boys chatter about the three *wapinau*, glistening white ptarmigans speckled with red, end of their lives too. The night was cold, the snoring loud. Nine of us in the tent, six feet above ground on layers of snow, up among the branches of these pencil-thin trees. As the stove guttered out, so the air congealed, and I pulled the sleeping bag over my head. Throughout the long hours, I feel cold leaching upward into dreams. Then I am cold too, and I slip in and out of sleep. The planned trip to the meteor lake at Kamestastin already looks unlikely, as this snowmobile is in parts, another won't start, and spring looks like coming early anyway. Perhaps we'll just get to the end of the Orma Lake Road and find the George River caribou herd waiting. Out on the land, all plans are shaped by the country itself, which is itself always changing.

We had arrived the previous day after several days of preparation in the village, accompanied by much discussion. Colin and I slept in Tony Jenkinson's basement, sleeping bags laid out among tools and machines, oiled or rusted, ready for action or abandoned forever. Five snowmobiles and four *komatic* sledges were loaded onto a flatbed truck, last-minute supplies bought, and then we were on the slippery road to the interior. Tony pointed to rivers yellow with meltwater, far too early for that. He noted that some migratory birds coming to the region do not have Innu names: shoveler, mallard, American coot. All around the world, there are animals and insects, fish and plants, creeping toward higher latitudes and altitudes.

All was lined up ready for departure, a squadron of red gas cans alongside sacks of flour, the square tent raised and wood chopped in a pile, when one of the snow-mobiles roared off by itself to crash into a bank of powdery snow. We all looked at each other. I had learned to walk with a light step to avoid the crump as gravity pulled me through the melted and refrozen ice surface, leaving me up to my leg tops in snow. The light finally gave way to a blaze of copper and gold across the boreal forest, then dripped away to leave a sky of spectacular purple. The tent filled with smoke as Tony baked bannock on the stove. Etienne Pone is not much taller than his two grandchildren, and wears what you would expect: modern clothes for the outdoors and cold.

One evening he jokes, "Do you think I should get a headdress of feathers, wear it out here?"

After breakfast, Jonathan and I set out to search for food, catching up with Alex on the way. Three of the four boys have slotted into country life without hesitation, as has Jonathan, who's along to help. A fourth never quite makes it. But Alex, who has the angular features of fetal alcohol syndrome, and was thought to be the hardest case, never has to be asked. He's working harder than anyone, swings an axe with skill, carries the gun with care. The country is a rapid healer. To the left is the vast Smallwood Reservoir, snow thick to the horizon. You can travel a couple of thousand miles west from here and only cross two roads. Over there, the tar sands of northern Alberta are today's Klondike, the bitumen containing low-grade sulfur-rich hydrocarbons, and requiring huge energy to crack out the oil. Two tonnes strip-mined for a single barrel of oil. An area the size of Bangladesh awaits.

We track for thirty kilometers through the forest, stopping to search for porcupine in the treetops, and then through the swirling snow I see two *wapinau* glide along a clearing, and Jonathan follows them into the forest. One crack and echo, and he returns with a ptarmigan dripping scarlet life into the shocking white. At speed, one snowmobile disappears with a crump into a water-filled gully. With hand winch and much effort, we crank it from the muddy water. Then the other becomes stuck. Alex then roars back home, over hills and down valleys, and I hang on the back for dear life. Back at the camp, all is quiet. It looks like we've been here for weeks. Tramped snow, more logs, and now feathers strewn across the clearing.

A teapot is permanently stewing, and Colin and I butcher the birds and lay them on a metal plate ready for the pot. We rub our bloody hands in the snow.

That evening, Jonathan and I volunteer to tow one snowmobile down to Churchill Falls to see if a repair can be effected. And here's one of the land's marked contrasts: from our seemingly remote camp we flash past the giant hydro plant ablaze with floodlights, then across silvered lands beneath the rising full moon. There are houses, a gas station, a shop even. We find the mechanic's house, and in his garage a diagnosis is conducted. He shakes his head. One down, until spring. On the way home, for it feels that way already, we tarry near a cabin that was Jonathan's grandfather's, and talk of wolves and caribou, of other homes and families. We arrive back at the camp to find everyone asleep, so we stand by the *komatics* and talk more. It is as if it were daylight, so bright is the moonlight. The snows seem to magnify and intensify the light. We huff plumes of bright air into the night. The distant hills are black and the land sparkles.

We hear the *hoo-up* of some bird or animal. It seems to come from one thicket, then a susurrus of branches and moving air, and the same call comes from behind us. We spin around. Then more movement and another call. It's as if it is playing games. We freeze to the spot.

In Henriksen's book, the famed hunter Kaniuekutat explains about the wild man of the forest, Katshimaitsheshiu. "I didn't see them, I only heard them. It was always at night, a very clear night. I never saw them in person, but people used to complain about them. . . . They just played tricks on us." The wild men of the northern forests were never the lumbering sasquatch of the lower latitudes. They ran swiftly, whispering through the trees, often trying to kidnap women and children. "Many Innu have seen Katshimaitsheshiu," said Kaniuekutat, "but never talked to him. They are in the country somewhere." Chuckchi author Yuri Rythkeu was the most famous writer to emerge from Siberia, observing that "people who live in cold climes keep warm by kindness." He described the infinite links between animals and people, and the *tery'ky*, changelings of the north, who go with the wind and carry off people to imprison them in ice. All we can do is stand taller and very still, waiting, breathing as quietly as we can. Silence comes again, under the moon.[2]

—◆—

Under a clear blue sky we pack and leave on three snowmobiles, taking icy turns hanging on to one of the *komatics* piled high with tent and food, with bags and gas cans. We travel 120 kilometers up the Orma Lake Road toward the boundary of the taiga where the trees thin and eventually leave only open tundra and barrens. We will travel an hour longer than I would have wished, and all warmth is leached away by the time we choose a campsite in a small hollow surrounded by trees. We travel through an intense landscape of radiant white and vivid green. Sparkling, shimmering mica, forests of slow-growth spruce where a finger-width could mean a tree of a hundred years of age.

Without warning, a *komatic* shatters, slews across the track, skids to a halt. Etienne and Tony head off into the land, and return with nails, and fashion wooden braces. The repair takes a couple of hours, but then what are hours out here. The two treatment boys are long gone, but six kilometers up the track we find them, Alex proud with porcupine strapped to his back. Tony and Etienne stand back, and smile. Jonathan makes the tiniest of slits in the abdomen and pulls out the intestines, then with a sliver of spruce stitches up the hole. There's a special way to remove the spines; the ceremony will come later.

We stop often, firing off shots at silhouetted *wapinau* that strangely seem to pose on ridgelines. We pass barchan dunes of snow, drifts sharpened by Arctic winds, and cross snowfields of glittering crystal, halting at caribou tracks stamped into the snow. Later, as the sun clutches low at the trees, the light takes on a polarized quality, as if it were moonlight, piercing the trees to cast long iodine shadows. The sun had faint warmth, but the light has come a long way through the atmosphere to acquire its blue-gray hue. Sometimes we are deep in trees, then rise up steep hills to see the land fall away to the north and west toward Hudson Bay. It all seems too large for humans, yet locally it is known and layered. Time has another quality too: there is no linear certainty. You expect things move in a general direction, but events intervene. Animals and birds appear of their own volition. Equipment breaks down and must be repaired or abandoned. In other habitats, you might be able to avoid such claims. Not here.

Overnight, another shift. We put down roots. The wind snaps at the tent with methodical violence. Snow sleets in horizontally, searching and piercing. We pile snow high around the tent, stamping it hard, and lie inside drinking tea, huddled by the glowing stove. We enter a half dreamscape, chatting, drinking, storytelling. During one venture out, we find two caribou hides and heads discarded in the snow by hunters. Leg bones lie scattered. The Innu would never do this—the tongues are valued, and soon are in the pot. Etienne cracks the leg bones to pull out the long strips of spongy marrow. Hunter-gatherers are constantly short of fat and sugar: wild animals are lean and so the marrow is much valued.

We hang the caribou heads on a tree. We just lie in the warmth of the tent, drinking more tea, cooking bannock, listening to the land being torn up outside. More wood on the fire; more snow in the teapot. We're living on tea with sugar. Then in the mid-evening cabin fever strikes, and I have to stray out. Etienne says stay close. The blizzard blows, then the western sky suffuses with orange, and to the east the moon has become clear. The cloud layer quickly departs, and the wind just falls away. Across the frozen lake, the sky above is bruised blue and purple, but the land below is calm and silvery white.

Jonathan arrives by snowmobile, and we take off in search of the caribou herd. The wind lifts the powdered snow into a laminar layer, racing like a river as wide as the whole land. The snow stings my face and eyes; my goggles back in the tent. The trees thin out, and suddenly ahead lies the vast open tundra. Like the steppe, not a tree to the horizons and beyond. We turn back, arriving in time to eat the smoky porcupine. This land lends itself to you. You borrow some space in which to survive, but can never assume control.

—⟶⟶⟶—

A vast stillness. A silent presence stretches the land from one horizon to another. The wind has gone, nothing moves. It seems that the land rings, an auditory hallucination in the cold. The moon floats in a blue-black sky, the distant mountains white as if lit by an internal glow. I crunch across snowfields, on the surface, then snap-snap and sink deep. The ice shimmers. Tonight is the coldest yet. In the dark, it is bitter, and I know there is nothing to do but lie and turn, then turn again, fending off dreams, to prevent the cold eating in for good. We had moved north in the bright morning sunshine, but another snowmobile breaks down. Kamestastin remains elusive, over the horizon. A temporary fix, and we make a few more kilometers, then it has to be abandoned for collection in the spring.

At the north end of the Orma Lake, we swing off to a small lake and set up camp by the ice. In a few hours, woodland is converted to camp, tent erected, spruce boughs woven together on the floor, trees made into stumps. When the snows have gone, these trees will look as if they've been pollarded at seven to eight feet height, and branches strangely stripped at height. On the lake, Etienne's grandchildren dig ice holes with Alex, three feet through snow, and another two through ice. The black ice finally yields to the axe, and a yellow gush of water rushes up. Alex talks of his freedom here to do what he wants. Tony is forever fashioning things with knives or files. Improvements to the stove, snowmobiles, his homemade snowshoes. His glasses are deep, hair always tousled, layers of jacket and shirts topped by a blue and white lumber shirt with only one button. By contrast, Colin and I wear bespoke gear, undergarments that wick away moisture, many layers, not for fashion reasons. I still look the more stunned in all the photographs.

I take a pot of warm water into the trees for a full body wash. Colin and I walk across the lake toward the granite mountains that somewhere contain the caribou herd. Are our minds settled enough for the caribou? Will they come? They do not. Beneath the limpid blue sky we stop at a pink rock with many types of bright lichen and spongy moss. We cross prints of fox, and some we think are bear. Another set looks large enough to be a wolf.

Now for another porcupine. It looks like a large beast, but it's mostly quills. With the body cavity sealed, I blow into the rectum to distend the body and cause the quills to point away in perpendicular fashion. The body is then laid on a fire of spruce to sear the quills, which are then scraped off with sharp knife. The quills are vicious, barbed, slide into the skin with silent ease. It takes a couple of hours to end up with a skinny carcass of now smoky meat. This is perhaps another reason why the country is healthy: you have to expend many calories to prepare the food. Then at the end of the day, the wind dropped, and I walked out through the trees to meet the moon high in a clear nocturnal sky.

Days pass, and now a dilemma. How to get back? Etienne would like his two grandkids to get home, and one of the boys from treatment is not coping. The others feel country is home, but the one keeps aggression close to the surface, dreaming of discovering a mother lode of precious metal. He's not the first or last to wish that winning the lottery will bring a new life. Perhaps a plane can divert from Shipiskan, perhaps we can get a subgroup back down the Orma Lake. In the end, the idea of leaving comes to dominate. One plane does comes to a lake nearby, but has insufficient fuel to divert. We are up and down, making plans then chopping holes in the ice to drop in lines and nets. Then the clouds close in and all the land and sky disappears. No planes will fly in this.

One day visibility extends to the far hills, and the radio crackles, a distant voice suggestive of hope. We stand by the tent in a row, facing southeast. The minutes pass, and then hours. We are ready. Inside the tent, I cut my hand slicing bread to toast on the stove. The red blood echoes the *wapinau*. Still nothing. Then a hum, and a single-engine Otter is coming directly at us low over the hills, tipping wings in acknowledgment. It feels like a desertion: Etienne, Tony, and Colin will stay, and arrange a later evacuation with equipment. I'll take the youngsters and boys. The skids touch down on the lake and the plane clatters toward us. We hump bags over, climb up steps, and strap into the bare cold fuselage. I sit up front with the young pilot. He chatters as we lumber across the lake, clawing at the thin winter air. It is frigid, and through the thumping engine noise now we can see all of Labrador laid out before us, gray, cold, white.

At Goose Bay, where my uncle flew in the 1950s with the RAF, the sun is shining, and life seems to go on as if nothing has happened out there in the country. I pop Dean and Montuakiss in a taxi, and the owner of the charter company runs me round to the commercial airport. I jump on a flight to St. Johns via Deer Lake with minutes to spare. At St. Johns international airport, it all feels far too hot; I reek of wood smoke. My face is scorched, gray-bearded. My name is called over the PA: they have found a seat. In London, I hoist the black bag over my shoulder, and engage with morning tube and train. People blankly rush for work. It seems to be a desperately full world.

⸺◦◦◦◦◦⸺

Inspiration for a cultural revival has come from within. The Tshikapisk Foundation was set up by Innu hunters who had a plan. Find a way to open the door to the country, especially for the young, and perhaps a few individuals or families would go. The elders could teach the young traditions, tell stories, share values. The young could develop pride in their identity, then see a future that was worth pursuing. Jean-Pierre Ashini, George Rich, Tony Jenkinson, Michel Pastitchi, and others began building a permanent camp at Kamestastin in the center of Nitassinan. Journeys began to be made. Some elders had never stopped going, but now others went too. On one trip, Tony and Colin took a young and very tall Michel Andrew, and they watched the caribou herd of tens of thousands swim across the lake. There have also been efforts by Natuashish's Gerry Pasteen to revitalize country connections, organizing annual canoe trips and walks in the tundra territory, sometimes involving thirty or more young Innu.

One winter, Michel, known better as Giant, decided he would walk from Sheshatshiu to Natuashish to draw attention to diabetes. He walked the three hundred kilometers, pulling his own *komatic*, and everyone was amazed. Two Mushuauinnu women, *Manin* Mary Lucy Dicker and Kestin Rich, walked many miles over the sea ice to the Inuit village of Hopedale to meet him. They then walked together to Natuashish. Since then Manin has organized walks for Mushuauinnu young people. The Innu were always known as great travelers, but settled lifestyles had eroded this belief. Giant changed this, and people felt pride. The next winter, fifteen more joined him, and the Young Innu Walkers tramped from Sheshatshiu to Pukuashipit, though warm weather brought an early halt.

The following properly cold winter they walked from Pukuashipit to Sept-Îles, picking up more walkers from Innu communities along the coast. The summer after they walked from Sept-Îles to Schefferville, and the next February from Schefferville to Kauauatshikamatsh and then across the tundra to the Atlantic coast at Natuashish, so completing a huge circle of healing. One iconic image depicts Giant leading the group across a frozen lake on snowshoes, staves in hand, a toboggan behind each, snow glasses and traditional pale canvas trousers, tops, mittens and hats, each edged with fine decorations that Katnen would be proud of. This was not a return to the old days, as some might have put it, but a step forward to create a new future. Everywhere they went, they received heroes' welcomes.

Social media has done something new too. Now all have mobile cell phones, and updates can be made on the land, and others can be at home watching. One page is filled with thanks and congratulations from those who could not go physically, but traveled in mind. "Memories have been made," said one, "friendships formed and your traditions and culture are living strong." Another wrote, "They have inspired me to take my own health into my hands, and start leading a healthier life, for myself and my family." Stories travel far now. This could be a good thing.

Jack Penashue then led Sheshatshiu to gather the community's voices into a vision for a healthy community. One villager observed, "I cannot think of one person who has not been harmed or challenged by this progress of Western society."

"Faith in progress," wrote Hugh Brody, "is itself a kind of religion."

One Innu man concluded, "Giant is taking us by the hands and is guiding us. The Youth Walkers cannot solve all problems, but they have become an inspiration."

10

FARM-CITY

Amish Country, Ohio, United States

262° West of Date Line

Mose Herschberger holds the camera in his huge callused hands. His eyes twinkle beneath the wide brim of a straw hat.

"What do I do with this?" he laughs.

We've just eaten in a bustling restaurant in Charm perched high on rolling glaciated hills of the northern Appalachians. This is Holmes County, the center of a successful way of living at the heart of America. Amish farming culture seems to mainstream moderns to be stuck in the past, and yet it has a small environmental footprint, a high level of contentment, a deliberate rejection of many contemporary values and technologies. The resilient Amish have, as Donald Kraybill of Elizabethtown College has put it, "dared to snub the tide of progress." How, then, can they be doing so well?

The Amish arrived in North America in the 1730s, having fled persecution in Europe. The Anabaptists were reformers of the 1500s, and thousands were pursued and killed by civil and religious authorities. Every Amish house today has a copy of the 1,100-page *Martyrs' Mirror* book that chronicles the carnage, name by bloody name. They took their group name from the Swiss Jakob Ammann in the 1690s, who taught against trimming beards and wearing fashionable dress. Many things have not changed since their arrival. Mose wears denim trousers and braces, fixed with hooks and eyes, denim top and white shirt, and has a graying chinstrap beard with no mustache. He has never driven a car, nor had electricity run from the network to his house; never used a mobile phone, and farms with horses. His religious beliefs are strict and he knows everyone in his community on first-name terms. Yet though his farm is both innovative and highly sustainable, many view him as an anachronism.[1]

When we talk about the contradictions in cultures, Mose leans forward and smiles, his eyebrows bobbing. He's interested in the rest of the world, too, what we know, how we might help. We walk around his farm, past the chicken barn and the housing for his thirty dairy cows that are intensively grazed using new pasture management ideas that came from New Zealand. In some ways, it's a very traditional method: shepherds used to move fences and manage their flocks and pastures actively. Such grazing requires large inputs of skill and knowledge, and improves grass yields and cattle health, increases organic matter in the soil, up half a percent over a decade, so sequestering carbon too. There's a new milking parlor, too, to increase labor efficiency: it is solar powered. Six Belgian horses stamp in the yard, chestnut in color with a white blaze on their foreheads, and tan manes and tails. There are other new practices: solar telephone booths for the business, a dog-breeding operation for the pet industry, and composting of chicken waste for the cornfields.

This question of innovation is often perplexing for outsiders. A seemingly unchanging culture that on the inside changes. Kraybill suggests there is no riddle at all. The Amish are clear: they innovate, but on their terms. And only if new technologies and practices help to build social capital. Modern society is good at pulling things and people apart, separating family, work and play, destroying social relationships. But the Amish engage in both resistance and negotiation, and in turn will ask tough questions: Why do the civilized people deposit their elderly in bleak retirement homes? Why do they move house so often and lose touch with family and friends? Why do home-owners sit on ride-on lawn mowers and then drive to the gym? Perhaps we should ask such questions of ourselves.

To the Amish, a key term is *worldliness*: they do not like it. To be worldly is to be *a little on the fast side*, to move away from the established norms. They say you should think before you speak, take a long and slow stride, and brake deliberately to slow things down. *Gelassenheit* is a further important principle, and implies submitting, yielding up to a higher authority, a further sharp contrast to the individualization of modern society. There are two ditches along every road, goes a saying, and it's easy to fall off. Emphasizing separation can be a key strategy for cultural survival, particularly if you can choose which new technologies or practices are appropriate to adopt.

We travel to a farm at Rolling Ridge to see how other new ideas have been taken on, passing on the way many different vehicles: open buggies, spring wagons, market wagons, two-wheeled carts, and open carriages. Matt and James Schlabach are the sons, and meet us in the yard. Both wear woolen hats on this chilled late-winter day. We begin at the new polytunnels for tomatoes and cabbage. They are on a slight slope so that the heated air travels up the length of the tunnels. Their dairy cattle are also rotationally grazed. The horses are stabled, quietly chewing on sweet hay. James runs the wood shop, making mainly garden furniture. It's a sub-business that has done well in recent years across the county, using new technology but also giving young Amish men the opportunity to expand their skills and interests. James, too, is interested in our agricultural practices and policies, but knows he'll never come across the Atlantic unless by ship. We talk more about innovations and why some are accepted and some not. A vibrant example of social capital in action is barn raising: in eight hours, one hundred men can raise a single barn.

The telephone is a link to the industrialized world, and as the Amish prefer spontaneous visiting and face-to-face communication, they were initially banned. But community phones did then appear, and next were formally permitted for businesses by some churches. Electricity leads to worldliness, and was long banned in houses. Diesel and hydraulic pumps are used for farm equipment, but then a deal with struck with church authorities over generators in the 1970s, and inverters were permitted to make homemade 110-volt current. Electric fences are vital for grazing, and batteries are needed for flashing lights on the back of buggies—too many are hit by speeding cars on darkened lanes. Home freezers are owned to preserve produce, but are kept on neighboring non-Amish farms. In the fields, the horse is preeminent. It is central to identity and practice. In Holmes and Wayne Counties, the Amish have been using horses for two hundred years and the land is healthy. But in the farmyards, small tractors are now allowed by some churches for moving feed, harvests, composts, and wastes.

Education is an awkward riddle: high school is rarely attended. If you face cultural extinction, says Kraybill, you must indoctrinate your children, or at least prevent them all being wooed away by the sirens of modernism. The Amish fought hard in the 1950s for their own education system; some were jailed. Now, though, most children attend Amish schools and are taught by Amish women. The teachers' pay is low, and they themselves have not been trained. And here lies another riddle. The Amish value their separation from the world, but nonetheless share many cultural objects with the rest of America: they read newspapers, barbecue hamburgers, jump on trampolines, and hunt. They use antibiotics, but do not train as doctors or lawyers. Society is virtually free of crime and violence, and mental illnesses are substantially less prevalent than in mainstream society. Divorce is unheard of. They are not free to buy a car, but avoid the frustrations of commuting. Dress is not individually defined, and is seen as something that unites rather than constrains. Women do not cut or curl their hair. However, few people from the outside ever join the Amish.

Oddly, the Amish towns and counties have now become a tourist destination, and many thousands come, clogging up the streets with cars. Like some indigenous tribes, the locals in their distinctive clothing have become objects. Visitors buy mementos and furniture, eat and drink, and on driving away are probably held up behind another horse and trap. I suspect the last thing they consider is the possibility that the Amish have found some solutions to the astonishing contradictions of industrialized society. When the credit crunch struck, the Amish, like many indigenous groups and remote farmers, hardly noticed. The Amish are often curious about the idea of *progress* and the seemingly desperate efforts we make to have all the benefits it offers. I had first traveled to Holmes County with the distinguished environmental educator David Orr of Oberlin College.[2] We walked around David Kline's 120-acre organic farm under wet occluded skies. David's elegant book, *Great Possessions*, documents the gentle rhythms of Amish farms and their abundant wildlife. He was once asked by a magazine editor to write about the advantages and disadvantages of their way of life.

"This bothered me all summer," he says. "Quite honestly, I couldn't think of any disadvantages."

———

At the top of the state of Ohio, it seems no one saw the economic tsunami coming. It roiled across the financial landscape, ripped the heart out of communities, and eventually brought down a few of those who had played loose with the rules. As rough waters retreated, governments plundered from the future to save some of their banks, and now we're all going to pay for years. In this way do empires eventually fall. Too many of us in industrialized countries, and increasingly in developing ones too, aspire to consume goods and services that are stretching this planet's capacity to supply them. It would have been fine if those dominant aspirations were for ways of living that trod lightly on the planet. But they are largely not. The financial storm was only a warning. The environment, which is the economy after all, was sending a signal.

Wake up. Do something different.

Up here in the rust belt, Cleveland was one of the worst affected by the credit crunch, and is now trying to think differently and map a route to some kind of new future. The town was established in 1796 where the Cuyahoga River flows into Lake Erie. It grew rapidly through the nineteenth century on trade from the Great Lakes through the Ohio and Erie Canal. It rose further on steel manufacture from iron ore shipped from Minnesota by boat and coal by rail from the south, and became the country's fifth-largest city by 1920. Its population peaked at 915,000 in 1950, but then it stuttered. Heavy industries closed, the urban raced to suburbia, unrest grew, industrial waste caught fire on the river. The city defaulted on loans, and the population plummeted to 480,000 by the turn of the millennium.

It was, though, to get worse.[3]

Steve Billington of the Cuyahoga County treasury's team meets me at bustling Tower City at the end of the clattering Rapid line. Standing tall among the crowds, he's the only person waiting. He's wearing a dark raincoat, plain suit, and yellow tie, shoes scuffed by long hours prowling streets and court corridors. His was a Mayflower family, the only one to make it through the first winter complete. His mother is a much later migrant from central Europe; Cleveland is now Hungary's second city after Budapest. We drive first to Slavic Village, a neighborhood of detached houses on their own plots. The shingles are pastel blue and green, the windows and doors bright in the hard winter sunshine. But as we walk, it is through deserted streets. In the city, we do not wear paths into concrete and pavement, though nature is coming back anyway.

Almost all the homes are abandoned. Long shadows from bare trees stretch across the road. The children's play area is strewn with shards of glass. Fixed chess tables glint in the sunlight. A sheriff's car drifts by, driver staring at us. Within seconds, I can't remember his face; just the sunglasses mirroring this cold outside world. One house has cars parked on the drive, and is well-maintained. Another has a yard sign: *House for sale $20,000; or put down $500 cash and move in now.* No one will. We walk around the back of one home with powdery blue sky showing through broken upper windows. A pale raccoon pokes its nose out of a basement hole and snarls.

People moved to neighborhoods like Slavic Village because of sub-prime and predatory loans. Scandalous is a good description. Many were offered to people with irregular incomes or even no job. All were sold the idea of an American dream: you can own your own home. But no one said you could lose it too, and fast. Only a month after the mortgage company or bank decides you have a problem with repayments, it forecloses on the loan, assuming there is someone else in line to buy the house. The predatory loans are worse: knock on doors and sell the idea of a loan to someone who doesn't need one. Steve met an elderly woman who had cleared her mortgage, but on her doorstep took out a loan for $57,000 for home repairs, paid the money to a builder working for the mortgage company, who then disappeared. She lost her home.

Cleveland is in intense trouble. There are thirty-five thousand vacant properties in the city, fifteen thousand of which have already been condemned. They will have to be demolished. All those destroyed families and livelihoods. Once a few houses go, the community unravels, the school comes under threat through falling rolls, bus routes move, local shops struggle. There are too few eyes to keep foreclosed properties safe. Boarded windows have curtains painted on them, a strange effort to make the place look alive. But as soon as the signs go on a house, thieves circle: they break in to rip out the sinks, metal pipes, copper wires, aluminum shingles. The speed of the descent is breathtaking, as is the shift from private responsibility to public sphere. Twenty-eight days after the issue of a warning for a late payment, the bank or mortgage company hands papers to a court. The following Monday morning at ten o'clock auctions are held, where the price begins at 75 percent of the value of the property. There is usually only one bidder: it's the bank buying it back. The residents have to move, often thinking the process is over. But unless the ownership has passed to another loan-holder or householder, they are still liable to pay at least $10,000 for the home's eventual demolition. Those bankers probably deserve another bonus for their good work.

As we drive away from Slavic, we see a determined man pushing a shopping cart overflowing with the metal intestines of a house. He is close to the gates of a scrap yard, and twitches as we pass. We drive past closed factories, and then swing up to Cleveland Heights. Only a few minutes away are mansions on wide tree-lined streets, land donated by Rockefeller to the city. Here are cars, people, and no sign whatsoever of the abandoned neighborhood just down the road. We pull over at a coffee shop; inside are piles of books on tables by padded sofas. A good place, full of people.

We continue to the Hyacinth neighborhood, and stop at a corner shop. Marianne James has been here since the late 1970s. She grew up in Berlin, was bombed in the war, survived but always hungry, had no shoes for years, then migrated to America, and has seen her community fall apart again. She's about five feet nothing tall, with gray hair and half-moon glasses, a silver cross outside her dark blouse, working jeans and a cell phone clipped to one side of her belt, a bunch of keys to the other. Ten years ago, after fire damage to the shop and home, the whole neighborhood helped her rebuild. But then came robbers, five times, the last man putting a gun to her chest. Now she's the one jailed in, behind bulletproof glass with a rotating unit to deliver goods and take money. Mostly she sells lottery tickets and cigarettes, but there are soft drinks and bread loaves too. But it's still her community. She's seen children grow up and have their own children. A little girl was born up the road two days ago, she says proudly. The kids in the neighborhood call her Mrs. Mary, unofficial grandmother to all. But next door, more thieves broke in and stole the sink and pipes. They bashed a hole in the wall to snatch the boiler too.

"I'll never leave," she says defiantly; "it can't get worse." The dark shop window blinks with red lights: *lottery*, it invites.

We trek through more raw streets of cold skeletal houses. In yards are collapsed sofas, rolls of old curtain, other discards. Two men stand by a plain white van outside a boarded house, and stare unspoken challenges as we walk by. There's an air of menace. No gardens are cultivated, there will be no flowers this spring, nor vegetables. There are broken windows, scattered glass fragments, paint peeling, piles of tires on the corner. Technically, these properties are OVV: *open, vacant, and vandalized*. Past the distinguished Brost Foundry building, established 1920, closed too. What is clear, though, is that most of the houses are structurally sound. These fleeting achievements shouldn't have been abandoned. These ruins in the making challenge assumptions about the inevitability of human progress.

Christopher Woodward observed in his *In Ruins*, "When we contemplate ruins, we contemplate our own future." He was talking of the likes of Rome, a city of eight hundred thousand people in AD 400, and only thirty thousand by the mid-sixth century. At its height, there is no evidence that any writer, painter, or politician imagined such an outcome. Oddly, in these modern ruins, there can be a sense of absolute peace. The people have gone. *Home improvements*, says a sign. *For sale*, again *$500 down*. At a shopping center there are no banks, only centers for cashing welfare checks, and fast food outlets. A dream has destroyed these places and their people, breaking hopes and aspirations, causing the collapse of city and security. In the past ten years, Cleveland has lost another fifty thousand people from within its borders.

Jim Rokakis was county treasurer, and spent much effort trying to navigate out of this storm. We talked at length.

"It's a profound crisis," he said, as cascades of out-migration have scoured out the inner suburbs. "We've been dealt a horrible hand," and his public office had to pick up the pieces. But he did believe there were some new opportunities: "A crisis is a terrible thing to waste." Perhaps the rust belt will become the green belt. Jim persuaded the state legislature to pass a new Land Bill. The condemned properties would have to go, perhaps most of the abandoned thirty-five thousand. They would have to rebuild and repair, offer completely different deals to home owners, and green the city by putting in urban gardens, wetlands and community gardens. Growing food in the city could provide both an environmental benefit and get food to those who most need it. Alarmingly, some thirty million mainly urban Americans are food insecure, which is official speak for hungry, and Cuyahoga County already spends more than $2 million annually on providing food to its own hungry population.

"Why not grow some here?" Jim asked. Where poverty and hunger stalk today's streets, maybe a garden city will emerge. Just up the road, David Orr and colleagues are redesigning the town of Oberlin around green space, local food and energy generation. What does it take? Vision, and diversion of some of that money.

It has begun to happen in forlorn Detroit, once capital of cars, also now half the population it was in the 1950s. It too has more than thirty thousand deserted plots and vacant houses. But the city government is out of money, and with industry in freefall, has few prospects. Abandoned houses and empty plots take up forty square miles of Detroit, nearly the size of San Francisco. There is not a single national grocery chain in the city: no Kroger or A&P, no Walmart or Costco. It is as close to a food desert as can be imagined. Yet urban farming has taken root, and small farms are appearing out of the rubble. Some are run by families with no work, some by community groups. Some like Hantz Farms are large operations intending to create commercial city farms that would bring jobs, something that has eluded economic planners year after year.

In the 1990s, seven hundred GreenThumb gardens emerged to great success in New York City, but then were swallowed up by developers. This does not look likely to happen in these former rust belt cities, at least not for some time. There are many institutional models: community gardens of orchard trees and vegetables that make all the produce available free to locals. Such gardens are never vandalized. Rich Wieske runs Green Toe Gardens, an apiary with sixty beehives across Detroit. "There is so much forage now," he says, "so much land for bees." They sell thirty-three hundred pounds of honey annually. Some nine hundred food gardens have now appeared in Detroit. One retired truck driver shoots raccoons and sells them for twelve dollars apiece. Pheasants have become abundant, and also favored for the pot. A wild and agrarian city is emerging. It will have low food miles, a small environmental footprint. But not everyone is in favor. Some have declared "this is a city, not a farm!" and are waiting for the revival of the old model. Others are disturbed by the small-scale agrarian vision. There is green where there should not be.

In Cleveland, the current mayor has stated a willingness to reform the city land-use plans, to set aside land for urban agriculture. But it is an oddly top-down model, half grudging, not really believing this could be a viable future. But residents are taking up the gardening options. Food author Michael Pollan said at one lecture to local people: "So, you want to be a farmer? Well, good, because we need thirty million more of them. And soon." Urban Growth is a half-acre intensive vegetable garden on the west side of Cleveland. With Erie's Edge, they run a new Community Supported Agriculture operation. Each CSA is just a start. These frontier people are reshaping a food system that has been characterized by an enormous environmental footprint and damage to local communities. Except down in Amish country.

Cuyahoga County's new County Land Bank was established in 2009, and the county's Save the Dream program helped more than seven thousand people stay in their homes. The land bank is buying up mortgages and helping people to stay in their homes. But the costs for this new future are staggering. It would cost $125 million to demolish every property that is now condemned or abandoned. As time passes, so the urban farms and gardens will spread. But one estimate suggests that Ohio as a state has $24 billion of sub-prime loans, 40 percent of which could still go bad.

"This was the Wild West of lending," says Rokakis, "and there was no sheriff in town."

They did try: Cleveland passed an ordinance to discourage predatory lending, requiring prospective borrowers to seek pre-mortgage counseling first. The banking industry responded by threatening to stop making loans in the city, and it successfully lobbied the state to prevent its cities issuing such ordinances. This crisis is not over. Each year, there are thousands more foreclosures. Cleveland's rate of foreclosure was the highest in the country in 2007; then it was overtaken by parts of California, Nevada, and Florida. Steve's experience here on the wild streets will soon bring him promotion as an appointed official on the county Board of Revision, adjudicating complaints about property.

How much are these dying cities a sign of something more problematic with the global economy? Two things are kept secret from children: birth and death. "I am afraid of death," said Gilgamesh, "so I wander the world." Death is hidden behind many strategies. Oddly, though, dead bodies are treated with a respect that the alive often do not receive. This is a little like ruins: once fully dead, the ended civilization is treated with restored respect, visited by tourists. But unlike human deaths, which have many and diverse rituals and ceremonies, there are none associated with the dying of cities and their civilizations. These cities of the former rust belt may evolve into new ones with green economies. But maybe they will not. Nature invades empty plots, descends on semi-demolished buildings as they crumble into grass and scrub. We may have to practice these responses to city death in the face of climate change, sea level rise, much wind, too little rain in some places, much in others.

At Cleveland airport is a large billboard with six smiling men and women advertising Shaker Heights: *an outstanding community*, it declares, *for those outstanding in their fields. Find your dream in Cleveland's premier suburb.* Does someone need to launch a rescue mission for modernity? Or should we just post a sign above the bed—do not resuscitate?

—◦◦◦◦◦—

At first light, I slip out of the large bed and its crisp sheets to gaze from the window up in the farm's eaves. Outside, mist is clinging to the fields, and light glows from a farm pond. I hear the soothing twittering of the cliff swallows, and in the distance geese call with noisy *kronks*. Two doves coo right above my head. A horse with buggy trots up the road, traces rattling, both hidden in the gloaming. No dogs bark. I sit on the white bedspread, and listen to the slow steady silence of a two-hundred-year-old house. I hear a cough, the clink of kitchen pans. The clock ticks, and morning light shines on the polished floorboards. Above the bed are two red candles, on the table a battery-run camp light. It's been ten years since I'd been on David Kline's farm near Mount Hope, though it shocked us both when we had counted back over dinner. I had thought it half that.

We had arrived the previous mid-afternoon, the sun shining and everyone smiling. It's been the wettest spring since 1950, with the winter weather system stuck for weeks mid-continent. A spring marked by slugs, and by bees staying in their hives. David finishes mowing the grass around the farmyard as Leah Miller and I sit under an old apple tree. This was their first day of sunshine for months, in complete contrast to our hot, dry spring at home. These glaciated rolling hills of central Ohio are at the top of the Mississippi watershed, and those spring rains have now reached Louisiana. The Morganza spillway had been opened to save the Mississippi and New Orleans, and water was pouring into the Atchafalaya Basin. My friend Ricky e-mailed to say all the egrets and their young were now lost. His neighbors' plots on Bloody Bayou were deep underwater. His camp had just escaped the flood.

David, Leah, and I walked the farm in the glare of rare sunshine. David has a gray chin-strap beard and wire glasses, and wears a panama straw hat, short-sleeve shirt, and dark trousers held up by braces. He walks with the roll of a plowman.

"My knees," he winces. "I'll have to get them replaced."

Rotational grazing is practiced here too. All the feed for his forty-five Jerseys comes from the farm. We walk down a track scarred by two inches of rain falling in one half hour last weekend. The fine auburn cattle follow us down the hill, munching, chewing, dry and watching us with wide eyes. There are more than fifty pairs of bobolink, the New World blackbird, nesting in this legume-rich pasture. They rise with the bubbling song of the prairies, and will fly back to Argentina later in the summer. David pulls up invasive bulbous buttercups, a species donated by the chicken industry. They add the flowers to feed to make yolks look like they are from chickens fed outdoors on pasture. But seeds set, are eaten, and are spread through the use of chicken manures. We stop at a nest box on a post, and find two slender tree swallows huddled together. Dead, from starvation this cold spring. The iridescent blue-green bodies seemed tipped toward each other. They had waited and waited for warmth and insects, but neither came. The eggs are pulsing with maggots, and a pair of bluebirds have begun to build their nest on top of the birds.

"The first time I've seen that," sighs David, who takes out the swallows and their original nest, and replaces the bluebirds'. The sky is cloudless.

David used to be Old Church, but is now back in the New Church. This is how it is in communities: to the casual outsider, it looks homogeneous. Inside, though, there are subtle differences in position. David is a fine author and editor of the respected *Farming Magazine*, which represents the perspectives of small farmers of all stripes. Many Amish, though, do not like to see their names in print. One day, I talked at length to an Old Church member who has led innovation in developing and spreading cooperative markets. He was very direct: "I don't want to see my name in your book!"

We stop at the creek where the children regularly find arrowheads.

"Every child should have a creek running through their childhood," has written David. The creek line is also a place for many wild foods, morels, berries, deer. We climb over an electric fence to avoid David's son-in-law's large mules, and walk up to his farm on the ridge. David and Emily Herschberger have thirty-seven cattle, and they are walking with us up toward the farmyard. The Organic Valley cooperative was originally set up by seven farmers, and has grown rapidly in the past decade: now sixteen hundred members have a turnover of $650 million.

David junior explains, "In conventional markets, you're not used to the company batting for the small farmers, but here they do."

They arrange third-party certification, manage quotas and prices, keep the suppliers content. David grew up on commercial orchards, and knew nothing about pasture management. Like other farmers hereabouts, he has learned quickly. We sit in the shade by the house, and talk as swallows swoop across the yard. With her brother, Emily is choosing flagstones for the front yard and path. Then it is time for milking, and they head off for the barn. Over dinner, Emily and I will agree on a new column I'll write for their magazine.

We continue the journey the long way round, stopping at neighbors' farms to talk about vegetable operations in polytunnels, and flower cultivation, also in tunnels. These small plots of land are highly productive. Children in bare feet run through the yards, and the lawns are clipped to perfection. The white farmhouses gleam in the sunshine. The sun has dropped low by the time we walk back up the road, and now the view of David's cliff swallows is perfect. On his red-roofed barn, ancient and tall in this land, some three hundred pairs of swallows are nesting under the eaves. Mud nests are plastered to the white wood. As individuals approach the barn face bright in the evening light, each bird and its shadow converge as it effects a perfect stall and slips into the narrow opening. On leaving the nest, they simply peer out, and stone-drop, spreading wings to swoop away.

David stops, looks around. "There are not many insects on my farm."

Ohio farmer and writer Gene Logsdon has written extensively about being a contrary farmer.[4] Small, biodiverse, community oriented, unstressed, and above all successful. "We are pioneers," he writes, "seeking a new kind of religious and economic freedom." Such contrary farming depends crucially on reducing labor to a minimum by skill instead of expensive machines. Gene's twenty-acre farm has 130 species of birds, 40 of wild animals, 90 of wildflowers and trees, and several million weeds. The more diversity on a farm, the better is self-regulation and balance. He does not spray: "It's not a problem." He writes that the Amish are geniuses: they produce at low, horse-powered costs, and sell at high, tractor-powered prices. Moreover, there is something else about this farming style: "The era of horsepower was just as much fun and far less stressful than the high-tech days of later years."

He asked of one of his neighbors, why keep sheep? "Well, there's little money in it," she conceded, "but the real reason is my sheep make me happy."

He too is an adopter of rotational grazing, the practice that has transformed livestock production in recent years. "To understand a meadow," he writes, "you really need to sit down in one awhile. Maybe like for twenty years." Farmers who pay attention, in short, are likely to be successful. And this suggests a size of territory that can be known, a land that can be managed and loved whether rural or urban. "My animals notice more about me than I do," he notes, observing something important about the body language of farmers and their animals. "Thousands of us contrary farmers are the village idiots of agriculture. We farm because we like to make little paradises out of our land while growing good food on it." This means these farmers are able to ride out financial messes in the way that large indebted farms cannot.

David Kline has also written, "I think we farmers must be the most fortunate people on earth in loving the independence and modesty of our life close to the soil."

⟶⫘⟵

Leah Miller and I started one bright day over in Coshocton County at Clarence Miller and David Erb's grazing farms at Brinkwater. Clarence moved from the heart of the Amish community in Holmes County to start a new settlement. It is not surprising that schisms have occurred, that different churches and orders have evolved with slightly different norms. You would expect the same of any community of some two hundred thousand people. The soils here were not so good, and when they came there were no livestock. We turn down a track where a groundhog lumbers across the shadows, red-tailed squirrels flitting up trees, and come to the two farms. As we set off, David warns of ticks. His daughter has recently caught Lyme disease. Both Clarence and David are slim, tall, wearing dark serge trousers with wide braces, lighter blue short-sleeve shirts, and straw hats, this time with a dark brim band. Their large rubber boots are turned over like those of musketeers. I change sandals for boots.

In the cattle barn, swallows cleave the shadows and streams of sunlight gathering motes of insects. "We have to shoot the sparrows and starlings," explains Clarence, "to allow the swallows to survive." The dairy is sparkling, the milking parlor with eight places marked by red head-locks. It takes about forty-five minutes to complete each milking. Clarence started with Holsteins, but they just produced too much milk. It didn't add up: overproductive means hard work. Holsteins have also not been bred to walk on pastures. You cannot turn them out of an intensive barn: they do not know what to do. He's switched to Jerseys. All over these counties, farmers are now selecting cattle with strong, wide front ends, large rumens, large mouths for grazing all types of pasture plants, and shorter legs. They are no longer the cattle of billboards.

The system of intensive grazing deliberately constrains the cattle to small patches of pasture for short periods. They eat quickly, fill up, and make milk while resting. The fencing is then moved each morning and noon. The cattle are thus encouraged to eat everything, and not just their favorite plants. In the distance is an old oil well, a reminder that these lands have produced oil and gas since the 1920s: a few Amish landowners still have income streams from leasing land for wells. Across the pasture a turkey vulture circles. On a harrowed field we find the stony nest of a killdeer, one chick lying in the open. The adult plover pipes in agitation, trying to pull us away with a broken-wing routine. David says his children love to find nests, and they come back each day to observe progress. We find a tree sparrow's bower nest fashioned in the long grass by a lane. Here is a farm good for culture, makes money, is good for nature. The children are racing around on bicycles as we say goodbye, leaving books as presents.

Leah drives us back to Holmes County, where she served as an elected county commissioner for years. The devolution is considerable: handling finance, job, and family services, running the jail, water and sewerage infrastructure. She now runs the Small Farm Institute, and knows what farmers need to make their new operations work. We arrive again at Rob Schlabach's farm near Berlin, where I had come that winter's day. Rob is a minister in the New Order church, and is leathery from decades of outdoor work. Matt joins us for an instructive walk up to where a neighbor on the ridge is going out of business. Both Rob and Matt have straw hats with a dark strip, Rob in blue-gray shirt, Matt in burgundy, Rob with bushy gray beard, Matt's brown. Matt has a permanent smile on his eyes, content with the world. Rob's great farm hands wave expressively. Like his feet, they have come to know every part of his farm. Before the year is out, Emily confirms Rob has suddenly died, and now his sons will run the whole farm.

"Back in the nineties," explained Rob, "it wasn't going well for us. We were trying to push production to the maximum in a mix of conventional and Amish ways." It wasn't working. "We didn't have the mechanization of the English farms, and yet were trying to follow the same path."

"We made a 180-degree turn," said Matt, and they took up a smaller-scale system of production that lets the animals do the work.

Their 120-acre farm is a half mile long and a quarter wide, and almost all under grass. The polytunnels are now full of many more types of organic vegetables, watered by a new drip irrigation system. Onions and squash are on the top of one hill. We walk up a green lane cooled by the shadows of trees. "This is all new," observes Rob, walking slowly. "I used to cut all the trees down to make use of every inch of the farm. Now we let nature do the work for us." He can remember the soil washing fast down this lane when any rain fell.

Over the fence, the neighbor has just applied herbicide to a field, and it is yellowed and dying. Over here is a way to survive, yet he made a bold emotional statement in the early days: "I'd have to have brain surgery to farm like you do," he had said to Rob. And now, he can't seem to find a way to swallow those words.

"Why are we so foolish?" asks Eugene Anderson in his *Ecologies of the Heart*. "It doesn't matter about the beliefs; what matters is the end." On this side, the soil is deep, full of organic matter and carbon. They too are redesigning the genetics of their animals, more toward animals of the 1950s. The health of animals has improved too. Organic cattle produce about 12,000 pounds of milk per year, perhaps only half that of conventional animals. There are savings, too, on trimmings of hooves, as the cattle are out on the land. Barn owls have returned, taking to flying behind the cattle who walk up mice and voles as they graze. The produce-more, get-more paradigm has changed.

We eat lunch at the kitchen table with Mary, Matt's wife SuAnn, and their four young children. They stare, blue-eyed, faces not yet farm-burned, and speak only what they call *Dutch*, evolved from the original term Deutsch. We talk of the far future. No radical changes now, concludes Rob, just building and improving fertility on the farm. Matt observes that it is the constant observation and management of pasture that makes him a better grass farmer. Indeed, young people have come back into farming because of the high knowledge input required for clever rotational grazing. The next generation of innovation may be around anaerobic digesters and solar photovoltaics, but the knowledge base will have to expand on integrated pest management, cover crops, and soil amendments too.

"How to observe is an art to be acquired by observing," said Darwin's mentor, John Henslow in Cambridge of the 1820s. What is quite clear is that traditional here does not mean simple and unchanging. Practice, beliefs, and behavior are not frozen. It is also interesting to observe the fiercest opposition to environmental causes comes from fundamentalist and entrenched hierarchical establishments. The Amish have rules, but they are far from entrenched. They have shown how to create new traditions from engagements with the land.

At the supply shop, we hear how produce auctions have been established to help farmers sell directly with low overheads. It's another institutional innovation that helps to ensure that small farmers can thrive. David Raber describes his vegetable business that sells to Green Field Farms. Amish frown at corporations, but not at cooperatives. The credit crunch? They felt the effects, he says, but less than conventional farmers. David is a member of the Dan church, who permit no bicycles, tractors, or milking machines. Hand milking takes ten minutes per cow, and with lack of cooling machines it restricts the chances of any kind of economic success for dairy operations. But he says they now make more money on twelve acres than they ever did on a hundred.

Back at David's, we lever the pump to fill a jug with cool drinking water, and sit again under the apple tree. Later, Emily, David, and young Noah arrive on bicycles, and we all sit around the table to eat dinner.

"All the food is from the farm," says Elsie.

We talk as dusk arrives and the warmth of the day disappears. "Real proof of a truly sustainable agriculture will be when we can romance our children into becoming farmers," says David.

Then Elsie asks, "Shall we have ice cream?" and fetches a large plastic tub.

Later, David, Elsie, and I sit inside reading, talking about what's in the books about faraway places. This is a life built in the presence of the wild shaped by intentionality, built too on the slow sedimentation of centuries.

11

SWAMP
Atchafalaya Basin, Louisiana, United States

271° West of Date Line

Mud-brown water sluices at the eroding bank, eddying around drowned willows still thick with trailing leaves, and races up a swollen bayou of old-growth cypress. Beneath a watchful osprey, an egret harshly cries, alabaster flashing into the dense forest. A heron stately sails on a raft of plant debris, yellow eyes intent. Deep in these swamps, the water levels are higher than anyone can recall for the time of year. The flat-bottomed skiff scuffed by a quarter century of duty skids across the surface. There are smiles: for a while we're free from the relentless persecution of mosquitoes. A swimming raccoon, head held high, unblinking at first, is swamped by the rushing wake. A sleek black moccasin glides from matted water hyacinth, and glares as it has to twist away.

Ricky Carline turns the aluminum bateau into the baylet on Bloody Bayou, and we jump ashore to walk a narrow dappled track invaded by brambles and clutching palmettos. In the high canopy hidden birds sing, and then the brooding forest unfolds. Before us is Sawyer's Cove, an inner lake stretching far. Here are old-growth cypresses, with buttresses wet in water and branches wreathed with Spanish moss, and beneath our feet are young bullfrogs leaping in the yellow marigolds. An early flock of ducks clatters down on the sunlit water. Ricky and Calvin Voisin, friends since childhood this half century, clear debris from their pirogues, and pull them up from the shore. The water has some more rising to do. Last year, Hurricane Gustav ripped through here, putting down trees, tearing roofs from camp houses, flattening houseboats. Today the sky is pure blue. In all swamps, nothing remains quite the same.

The wild Atchafalaya Basin: twenty-five hundred square miles of the largest contiguous bottomland forest in North America, a land of many thousand bayous, lakes, ponds, rivers, islands, levees, and mounds. It's a refuge for endangered peregrines, Florida panther, the ivory-billed woodpecker, and another three hundred bird species. The 135-mile basin begins near the Red River's confluence with the Mississippi and ends at threatened coastal marshes, and is constrained mostly on each flank by the ninety-mile Eastern and Western Levees built by today's mound builders, the water engineers. It's a liminal land at the end of a funnel that channels water and silt from thirty-one states and a couple of Canadian provinces. What happens up there acutely affects what goes on down here, as it does out on the Gulf too. Louisiana was once the richest state of the South; after oil it became one of the poorest. Its hardwood forests are now mostly gone, the ancient bottomland cypress logged out for ships and housing.

It's the sister Mississippi, though, that is best known. River pilot Mark Twain called it "eluding and ungraspable," and T. S. Eliot in *Four Quartets* "a strong brown god—sullen, untamed and intractable." A river of assumed darkness and clashes, a river that at all costs must be kept open, whose industrial shore between Baton Rouge and New Orleans is hemmed by one hundred miles of refineries, shipyards, grain silos, aluminum factories, chemical manufacturing. Tocqueville thought the lower Mississippi "the most magnificent dwelling place prepared by God for man's abode," but he didn't predict industrial intrusion.

"Go look at the weather," sang Muddy Waters up on the delta, "I believe it's going to be a flood." When Katrina thundered in, vehicle gas prices leapt across the country. So much oil and natural gas industry is here that national city lights depend on Louisiana and its half-forgotten swamps and coast. At first colonial contact, there were fifteen thousand Native Americans in twenty-two language groups across the region. They were farmers of corn, beans, and squash, hunter-gatherers of nuts, berries, roots, wild fruit, deer, bear, wildfowl, and turkeys, and fishers of clams, mussels, crawfish, and shellfish. The earliest records are from the Poverty Point culture of 2000 BC to 1000 BC, one of many mound builders of the South. In the northwest of the state is an earthwork six hundred feet long and seventy high. The mound builders built a hundred cities, all long gone, and from the Choctaw came *hacha* and *falaia* to name the Atchafalaya River.

Contact was fatal for many. On Bayou Teche, the Attakapa collapsed from 1,750 in number at contact in 1700 to just 175 a century later; none survive today.[1] The Chitimacha in the central swamps numbered three thousand, and almost all were killed or enslaved, survivors hanging on at Bayou Teche. Waves of colonists came—first French, then the Spanish held the region from the 1760s, giving it back to the French again until Louisiana became first a territory and then a full state in 1812. But it was events far north in Nova Scotia in the 1700s that shaped the creation of a distinct culture for the Atchafalaya swamps. The original Acadians emigrated from France in the early seventeenth century. But Britain acquired Nova Scotia in 1713, and the governor in 1755 ordered the wholesale deportation of ten thousand Acadians. Many died in awful conditions aboard cramped ships, as Longfellow later related in his epic poem *Evangeline*. Some headed for Haiti, others landed on the Gulf Coast, intending to overland to Quebec. Others later stopped in what would become Louisiana and declared it New Acadia. Acadian shortened to Cajun, and the name stuck.

The Cajuns have a proud heritage, and have retained identity and customs more than most in North America. But like all distinct groups, this comes with casual stereotyping: they are swampers, devoted to a good time, eat well, sing and dance. By the mid-twentieth century, Cajun had come to refer to a culture of poor, inbred, and ignorant swamp dwellers. It became an insult. Many Cajuns were punished if they spoke French in the classroom. But the late 1960s brought a cultural revival, with the import of French teachers and a growing sense of pride. French speakers settled not just from France, but also Belgium, Switzerland, and lately Vietnam, Cambodia, and Laos, all now seeing themselves as honorary Cajuns. Stereotypes can help cultures retain their own identity, yet also bring unfair characterization. It is often difficult to have one without the other.[2]

Almost all early visitors thought the cypress swamps were dark and dismal places, beyond civilizing tendencies. In 1816, William Darby's geographical description of Louisiana drew attention to the "deep, dark and silent gloom of the inundated lands of the Atchafalaya," and the "dead silence, the awful loneliness and the dreary aspect of the region." Searching for woodpeckers, Audubon wrote of "gloomy swamps . . . oozing, spongy . . . where the sultry, pestiferous atmosphere nearly suffocates the intruder." The cypress itself is rot-resistant with a deep taproot, and withstands strong winds well. The seeds root in mudflats bordering rivers, but die if covered by water. Once old enough to reach the canopy, the trees can stand in water, and develop the distinctive buttressed base with unique cypress knees that are part of the root system. The wood is called eternal: hollow logs used as water pipes in New Orleans in the 1790s were still serviceable more than a century later.

These cypress swamps are, as Anthony Wilson observes, "a challenge to the imposed order," an obstacle to prosperity and thus often inhabited by unofficial peoples. Missing from the official histories of the South are the swampers, poor farmers, Acadian trappers and fishermen, Native Americans, free mulattoes, swamp Maroons, and escaped slaves. Their annual cycles mixed trapping, moss gathering, fishing for catfish and crawfish, seine netting, frogging, alligator hunting, and gathering of wild honey. They thus seem to occupy a strange place in the imagination: the last vestige of a threatened southern culture, but also shadowy, entangled lives alongside *traiteur* healers and loup-garou spirits. Swamp gas was always associated with fairies, and sometimes balls of fire roll through the wet woods, leaping from land to ride on the bow of boats. Thoreau, as ever, called it right. The swamp, he wrote, is "a sacred place, a sanctum sanctorum."[3]

Today the swamp is still more likely to be portrayed as menacing rather than a fragile wilderness. This land remains forbidding for most people. Luckily.

I had come to the Atchafalaya swamps from the low deserts of the far West. Flying into Baton Rouge, I looked down and saw much FEMA blue: tarpaulins still cover thousands of destroyed roofs. In the distance, a haze of chemical smoke wreathed the Mississippi. It was five years after Katrina, and the population of New Orleans was still one hundred thousand down. Roofs across this southern state will probably stay blue forever. I drove across the iron bridge high over the Mississippi, and was immediately assailed by vertigo. I wanted to look at the river, but dared not. I stared at the road, white lines flick-flicking by. And concentrated on driving on the wrong side, for me, of the road. I passed along the long elevated section of the I-10 without fully realizing we were over water, swinging south to McGee's Landing, a place of music and food, to stay in a houseboat moored on Henderson Lake.

Gwen Roland, author of *Atchafalaya Houseboat*, had said, "You have to go." She lived out on Bloody Bayou with Calvin in their own gimcrack houseboat for near a decade in the 1970s and 1980s. That first evening, I sat in the porch wrapped in the sound of croaking frogs and sawing crickets, the occasional splashdown of fish or alligator. Across the dark swamp of cypresses was the distant line of flickering lights on the I-10. Another fish jumped, and a wind whispered through the trees. Sometimes all we need is a place to sit and absorb into the world.

I realize the moon should be up, and step outside the screen. It is climbing through the black cypresses and washing ghostly silver onto this inky waterscape. Earlier, the sun had slid blazing orange into the water, and everyone had gone home, leaving me with a couple of beers. Since Katrina, there are few visitors, the restaurant no longer opening nightly. The contrast with the desert could not be greater—so much blue water, verdant green and gold of autumn trees, bottle-green water hyacinth. Clouds of insects, and also a stab of loneliness. In the distance, geese gabble, then a harsh caw, and a laugh. Inside the houseboat, moonlight now streams through the windows and across the floor, and there is no need for artificial light. I could live in a houseboat like this. The creaks and sighs, the rhythm of water, the response of the boat to walking. Then silence, which becomes a kind of presence rather than absence.

The next morning, Vonda of McGee's makes arrangements, and I fly into the swamp by airboat with Weylin Blanchard, his ancestors one of the families from Nova Scotia. Henderson is fine under a pure cornflower sky. We stop in cathedral cypress groves silent above a layer of waterweed, looking from a distance like meadows on solid land. Hard shadows stretch long across the weed in the streaming sunlight. An egret stands still and bright. On an islet of thick vegetation, a small gunmetal alligator is warming in the sunshine. In open groves the water is reflective as polished glass, the trees trailing tumbling moss. All are 130 or so years old, dating from regrowth after the Civil War. Since then the water in the basin has been constrained, managed, released, and now there is no time dry enough for cypress seeds to sprout. Yet with normal freshwater at the right times and depths, they will grow thirty feet in a decade.

In some lagoons the surface is choked with hyacinth, introduced in 1884. It's difficult enough keeping invasives out of wetlands; even so, its arrival was unique. At the International Cotton Exposition in New Orleans, a Japanese exhibit featured a purple-flowering aquatic plant from South America. Every visitor was given a specimen as a souvenir, and encouraged to plant it out. It loved the swamps. It's been forked onto bayou banks, chewed to pulp by sternwheelers, treated with dynamite, fire, arsenic and 2,4-D herbicides. It flourishes still. But it's now been joined by hydrilla, the Esthwaite waterweed, first appearing in Florida in 1960 and becoming established here in the 1970s. Now it too clogs waterways, reduces water flow, and is sloshed with many herbicides.

The boat binds us to water and sky, skimming between blue and blue. We swing out of the deep shadows, past more egrets and flocks of cormorants, and glide under the concrete bridge. Finished in 1973, its eighteen miles link Baton Rouge with the Lafayette side of the basin, the second-longest such span in the country, the sixth in the world. Parallel piles stretch to the horizon, carrying cars and trucks that rattle and roar. Originally a railroad ran across the swamp too, and up sprung the two towns of Atchafalaya and Pemba. But then water was diverted from the Mississippi one year to save New Orleans, and all the houses had to be raised on stilts. Then came the 1927 flood, the century's worst, and the rail bridge was washed away. The railroad fell into disuse, the two towns quickly populated only by ghosts. In a cove opposite an abandoned oil rig, an eleven-foot alligator slides off the shore and watches us from the surface hydrilla and marigolds. It could weigh more than two tons. Weylin has never known anyone to be attacked, unlike in Florida. They are protected, except in September, when each landowner is given a hunting quota. Metal hooks baited with chicken are hung from tree branches, the alligator then dispatched when caught aloft.

"When Katrina came, it was a day like this," says Weylin, sweeping his arm across water and sky.

Fine, sunny, wispy stratus. No hint of the terror a hundred miles away in New Orleans where levees collapsed and drowned the poorest parts of the city. But when Gustav fled through last year, it tore off roofs and ripped up the land, and no one down in New Orleans would have noticed. Except they were not there. Gustav had formed up southwest of Haiti, and marched north to crash into Louisiana west of New Orleans at Cocodrie. Almost entirely because of the mismanagement over Katrina three years before, authorities overreacted and triggered the largest evacuation in U.S. history: two million people in the southern parishes were evacuated and a dawn-to-dusk curfew imposed. The Mississippi was closed to ship traffic. The hurricane smashed up the Atchafalaya Basin, but quite left alone the east of the state under clear skies.

During a hurricane, there is a rapid drop in air pressure accompanied by eerie silence. Birds begin to wail in advance of the coming violence. Fish die by their thousands. No one is sure why: the exceptionally low air pressure, high winds churning the water, leaves blown onto the surface and mixed in, the water becoming deoxygenated. Alligators benefit, but the Fish and Wildlife officers don't miss a trick: they get out on those levees looking to book anyone who dares gather them. Down on Bayou Sorrell, Ricky and Teri-Ann remained at home but were to be without electricity for two weeks. Ricky has stayed for every hurricane over the past forty years. Gustav brought consistent hundred-mile-per-hour winds when it reached them. Trees came down all around.

"You think they are never going to be that bad until they get on top of you," he tells me. "The force of the wind is chilling, bro. All you can do is sit and wait it out."

Weylin brings us back past Prayer Cove, where a beseeching Jesus with arms outstretched is pinned to one cypress tree. Air vines climb the thicket of willows, and the water is lime green. The sky is now streaking up with more cloud. At another grove is an abandoned houseboat of weathered cypress, with red corrugated iron roof. It's tipped half over into the lake, the porch's swing seat at an extreme angle. The owner of McGee's, David Allemond, admits to me later they towed it out there for the tours. Everything is not what it seems. Fellow visitors from New Mexico advise me to drive back into Henderson, away from the levee, to pick up food from the dollar store. There I see customers with full baskets racking up bills of just a few bucks. I pull across the road to try the sprawling modern store where the car park is smooth instead of cracked with potholes, a policeman eyeing me from the gas station forecourt. My heart sinks, but perhaps he sees the rental car. I stock up for the houseboat.

"Are you English?" asks the girl at the checkout. "Can you help with my homework?"

Her papers are spread by the till. I offer advice, and one of her fellow workers brings over her homework too.

⸻⚬⸻

I talk with David and his wife Peggy one evening in the empty bar. The darkening lake is awash with pink, the groves of flooded trees now deep in shadow. Since Katrina, it's been bad. Just not enough customers. Gustav, though, clean tore the roof off, dropping it behind the western levee. It took months of hard work to repair, longer to obtain any compensation and insurance. That afternoon, I had walked several miles south along the crown of the western levee, a berm one hundred yards wide and twenty high. Lime-yellow butterflies and coppers with brown spots had accompanied me, and beetles, bees, hoverflies, wasps swarmed through the grassy sward. Cackling egrets called from the pellucid fleets on the inside. A flock of piping redshank were a welcome reminder of home. Another laughing call from the forest, perhaps a woodpecker. A vehicle rumbled toward me on the top of the levee. Two men stared ahead, and I jumped aside. A plume of dust followed, swirling around me. A sign says *Trespassers will be prosecuted*.

"Drivers," explains David later, "not walkers." When the levee was first raised up, the only road was along the top. Now there is a crumbling, slipping one on the toe of the lower outside slope. Why is the freeboard so high, I also wonder? The water will never overtop it, he agrees. But the Atchafalaya Levee Board does what it wants. As do the U.S. Army Corps of Engineers. They listen to no one, especially not the locals.

In each of the years 2007 to 2010, the Army Corps spent $120–140 million in Louisiana on dredging, canalization, levee works, and algal cleaning. Some $8–10 million was spent annually on the Atchafalaya and Bayou Chene. On exactly what, you wonder? Then in March 2010, the American Recovery and Reinvestment Act was signed to put public money into jump-starting the economy. A total of $4.6 billion went to the Corps' civil works. You can see how such spending power trumps the values of local people. Or maybe there'll be a change of approach. Some are now talking of the need to restore wetlands along the Mississippi, as they hold water and prevent downstream floods. But Army Corps official documents say, *through deeds, not words, we are building strong.*[4]

South Louisiana is partly defined by the long-running history of conflict over water. Engineering is precise, and engineers measure, calculate, and predict. But water engineering is political. The 1927 flood, caused by deliberate diversion to prevent the Mississippi flooding New Orleans, put sixteen million acres under water, destroyed forty-one thousand buildings, and drowned 250 to 300 people. It provoked another reevaluation, leading to the 1928 Flood Control Act, which was subject to the usual political wrangling. The plan called for extensive leveeing, new spillways, reservoirs, and floodways, and was picked apart little by little. One result of this constant tinkering: Grand Lake has turned from a twenty-five-by-five-mile lake into a series of streams, willow bars, and silted pans over a fifty-year period. From the mid-1970s, the oil industry then cut six hundred miles of new canals across the basin. In May 2011, the five-thousand-foot span of the Morganza spillway was opened for the first time since 1973, and the Atchafalaya was again sacrificed under an unnatural flood. Perhaps ecological restoration would indeed be better than hard engineering, more through-flow to the coastal marshes to ensure sediment deposition at the coast and not in the basin.

My feet and ankles had come under attack on the levee walk, and would bear the scars of mosquitoes and biting ants for weeks to come. I should have worn boots while walking, and covered up at night. Maybe it was fire ants, as they head for levees at times of high water. Famed swamp and coastal photographer C. C. Lockwood has seen the extraordinary behavior of these ants when they need to escape rising water: colonies form a ball that rolls over repeatedly so that individuals take turns underwater. On the dock, I drink a beer under the external light, the restaurant dark. Many mosquitoes come, but then so does a swift who perches on the railings by my arm. On the wooden houseboat, creaking in the dark, I drift off peacefully.

—◀▥▥◗▥▥▶—

In the cool veranda shadows, I sit with David's ninety-year-old father, Curtis. He's thin as a rake, wearing overalls for pottering around. It's a morning for quiet conversation, ducks circling the lagoon, alligators mostly holed up in their winter dens. He was born in the swamp, his daddy a nomadic fisherman like many others who towed their houseboat to fishing and trapping grounds during the year. He points to my houseboat. About there, he says, that's where this levee broke in 1927 and the water scoured a great hole. In front of us is a line of trees in the water marking the original levee. The water ran to Lafayette. It was 1973 that saw the greatest rise of water, though, when it made it to the base of the new levees. The problem now is that the basin is filling with silt. Curtis can remember when channels were fifty feet deep, the water so clear you could see the bottom. This silt partly comes from soil erosion on farms in the upper states, but also from the diversion into the Atchafalaya of more than half the Mississippi's sediment load at Simmesport.

"People who make the laws," he states, "have never been in these areas. They don't know what we do, no."

We talk about this month: he's never seen the water this high at this time. It shouldn't happen until spring with meltwater from the north.

"When I was a boy," he remembers, "it would freeze a week or two in winter. But now Arctic fronts are mostly replaced with wet Pacific ones, yes."

It was rare until the 1950s to hear anyone speaking English here in St. Martin Parish. Today, many older people remain much more familiar with Cajun French than English. "We didn't know how to speak English, no. That first oil well was drilled north of the I-10 in 1935, then a bunch more." The wells might give a certain impression, but oil allowed many families to remain in southern Louisiana.

I ask about the ivory-bill. He blinks, hesitates.

"I saw them when I was younger, about the size of a crow, larger than a pileated."

Still there, do you think? "Yeah, I reckon they are there now. You better believe, we know stuff!"

Alcide Verret of both Bayou Chene and Bloody Bayou, friend of Gwen and Calvin, used to come to McGee's when he was young. Alcide had wild hair, front tooth missing from some event on water, and wore braces embroidered by Gwen. He said he often saw the silver-beaked woodpecker with the red head. Curtis has never seen a panther, but knows deer hunters who have flushed them out. He's heard them growling at night too. And Louisiana black bear? Oh yes. There was one over near Weylin's in Henderson yesterday, even though they tend only to be common in the coastal marshes and the *chenier* forest edges.

He looks over the swamp, and smiles: "I can still make a living here, really survive without money. We wouldn't be hungry, I guarantee you!"

Later, over on the east side near Plaquemine, murky rain clouds have sealed the sky, and the air is dense. The wind smells of wet trees and grass. The skies grow angry, and stormy winds blow the curtains, and then pellets of rain dash against the windows.

Gwen e-mails from Georgia: "Have you seen the news? Ida is coming."

That Sunday night, the hurricane is four hundred miles south-southeast. Suddenly the region is making preparations. At the front desk, everyone is maintaining calm.

"No, sir. Nothing to worry about."

On the TV, the news reader furrows his brows, and says "You should get out of the coast."

The clouds are bringing much wind, more rain. Red taillights snake into the distance, reflected in pools on the wet road. The coastward side of the road is empty. I imagine the view from above, all those FEMA roofs.

Then, after some hours, Ida chooses to swing east for Florida.

We leave Ricky's swidden camp in the clearing edged by Bloody Bayou, just along from Calvin's moored houseboat, built on pontoon pipes dragged from an oil field by Gwen and him thirty years ago. We flit upstream, which used to be downstream, points out Calvin. We are aware of the many moods of water. Some bayous seem to flout hydrological norms, with sleeping water, dead streams, reverse flows, every willful behavior. The boat skims out of the enclosed bayou onto the shimmering Atchafalaya itself. On the far side a line of trees hugs the horizon. Ahead the lunging, turbulent river swirls with debris from the north, great logs lurking just beneath the surface, ready to send such a boat straight to the bottom. With no warning, a cohort of water gives up it geographic origin as we slice through an invisible patch of icy air hugging freezing water that's come thousands of miles from the Rockies.

A towering double barge pushed by a thudding tug blots out the sun and proceeds downriver. We angle across the current in search of the ghost town of Bayou Chene, once a thriving settlement of some seven hundred people. We moor to a willow, and push through dense undergrowth. This forest is tall with cottonwoods, also invasives that came by water. The *chêne* oaks have gone, long since destroyed by high water and the silt. A few mature cypress and tupelo remain. Dense clouds of insects join us as we strike inland in search of the hidden graveyard. In the thick forest, it is twilight in the middle of the day. We push on, and there, in a clearing, tender sunlight streams onto a white marble cross and two headstones inlaid with brass plaques.

Mrs. Joe Diamond, b. 1880 died 1927, age 47; Veries Diamond, b. 1914, d. 1933; Addie Seneca, b. 1910, d. 1935. A blue-and-white china Virgin Mary stands cracked in the brambles that seem raised to swathe this place of young ghosts. Deep under our feet lie fields and pens, houses and paths, churches and shops entombed in silt.

All once made up Bayou Chene, established in 1795, thriving in the 1800s, dead under sand by the mid-twentieth century. In 1803, C. C. Robin called Bayou Chene the bayou of the live oaks, a place "overhung with enormous trees, impenetrable by the rays of sun, interlaced with dense vines and loaded with grayish streamers of Spanish moss . . . an enchanting sight." Ancestors of both Ricky and Calvin lived here in 1860, and the history of Bayou Chene illustrates how easily our imprint can come and go.[5]

Gwen's grandmother, Mawmaw Josephine, was also born in Bayou Chene, and they moved to the levee when their first children reached school age so that they could avoid the dangerous school boat. Her father was a Union soldier from New York who settled at Bayou Chene when he married the daughter of a large land-owner. There were not many black people in Bayou Chene after the plantations were destroyed in the Civil War. Gwen's friend Peter Bunch remembers someone snagging a body weighted down by two iron cooking pots. He'd never seen a black man before, and the body was buried between two trees near Calvin's houseboat. Even today, there appear to be few black hunters and fishers in the swamp.

At the time of the Civil War, Louisiana was one of the most prosperous states in the South. But it also had three hundred thousand slaves. In 1860, Bayou Chene was also at its height with 670 people, of whom 60 or so were officially free people of color, 30 Chitimacha Indians, and 90 slaves. People grew sugarcane, corn, potatoes, beans, raised fruit trees in orchards, kept cattle, hogs, turkeys, ducks, and geese. We search through the forest, but find no signs that agriculture was ever practiced. The main industry was extracting old-growth cypresses. Ricky explains the technique, as taught by his father. Two men in a pirogue would cut slots into either side of a tree, and drive in two boards. They moored the boat, climbed on the boards, and bent their backs with cross-saw until the giant fell. The log was then floated out. By 1915, one billion board feet of cypress had gone from Bayou Chene alone. Apparently great damage was caused at Bayou Chene by Union gun-boats. I look across the bayou and realize how much silt has been deposited since then. Large-scale logging, though, was virtually over by 1925, another economic pulse expected to go on forever, yet guttering out within a couple of generations.

Luckily, for those who continued to live near the swamps, a new extractive industry had arrived. It was the miracle and curse of oil.

———

At the bottom end of the basin at Patterson, Ricky, Teri-Ann, and I drove to the Cypress Sawmill Museum in its modern hangar—one side for trees and logging machinery, the other for shining acrobat planes and waxed antique cars, glitzy and silver and every primary color. The museum official likes this side more than the swampy part. Someone slips on the polished floor and grabs at a wing of a red plane. "Watch out!" he barks.

On the other side is a piece of cypress trunk a couple of thousand years old—half the age of the oldest individual recorded. No one is concerned about what we touch: wood, rusted machinery, toothed saws. Monochrome photographs show steamboats pressed into the swamps to provide power to haul logs on vast chains into the bayous. Groups of grim-faced men stand in thickets with axes and saws, hands on hips awaiting the photographer's slow cameras. Cypress and tupelo are still being cut today, now for conversion to garden mulch. Logging is good for jobs and mill owners, and after Katrina and Rita home construction jumped. More mulch was the call. The Louisiana Forestry Association claims it replanted four hundred thousand cypress trees last year. The Army Corps says it knows of no swamps that have been replanted.

Bayou Chene was known for its frontier character. Farming, trapping, fishing, and moss picking all brought vital income. At that time, alligators were killed to prevent them from eating the hogs: the gators would club them with their tails, and then pull them underwater. Spanish moss, an epiphyte of the pineapple family and not a moss at all, gave a uniquely brooding presence to the forests. The French called it *barbe espangnole*, the Spanish *peluca francesca*; the French won. The Indians clothed infants with it, used it for mattresses and insulation, and it was medicine when boiled. Then distant markets were found. Ford used it for stuffing upholstery in its cars. Men in low pirogues stood with perfect balance with long poles to pull down moss. At the museum were photographs of moss pickers by their houses in the 1930s, loading trucks, laying it out to cure and darken by the bayou banks. It was dirty and dangerous work, says Ricky, who recalls it from his youth. Snakes commonly came down with the streamers of gray moss. But huge amounts had to be collected to make a living. In the Atchafalaya, twenty-five moss ginning plants were active in the 1940s, the last closed in 1967.

It doesn't take much to guess who made the money: the owners of the wood yards, timber operations, and moss gins. Today, Louisiana remains one of the poorest parts of the country, yet is the center for oil, gas, and chemical industry. Someone's still making money.

In Greg Guirard's fine record of Cajun families of the swamp, Alcide Verret remembered living in Bayou Chene when it "was pretty near as wide as the channel of the Atchafalaya is now. Steamboats would run through it." It was the massive 1927 flood that just about did for Bayou Chene. "They got so much sand deposited on the soil people quit farming," said Alcide. "Man, the timber was big, virgin timber, up to 62 inches wide and 60 feet long. We had some of the most beautiful oaks that ever existed, but that sand will kill a live oak."

Alcide died in 1998, a man who lived across a whole century. He lost his first wife and two children when they were killed in a gas explosion on their houseboat. "If only I'd stayed at home that day . . ." he never stopped wondering.

Another of Guirard's profiles is about Myrtle Bigler, who lived at her camp on the Atchafalaya River until she died in 1995, age eighty-nine. She married Harold in 1946, and they left Bayou Chene in 1954 for their new camp. "I been satisfied; that's the most important thing in life. As long as you keep wantin' no matter what you got, that's no good. I like my life." I wished I could have met her or her husband, who died four years before her. "Oh man," he had said, "I wouldn't give this life up for all your town life. This is too much better."

Wild food at Bayou Chene was abundant, the seasonal calendar diverse: deer, doves, duck, snipe, woodcock, squirrel, raccoon, opossum, rabbit, turtle, crawfish, alligator, oyster, shrimp, crab, and freshwater bass, bream, crappies, *sac-a-lait* perch, and catfish. The golden age was probably 1907 to the 1927 flood, when the tide ended up seven feet above the bank of the Atchafalaya River. Most residents had to be evacuated; only those on houseboats remained. One goat was stranded in the Methodist Church and survived weeks by eating wallpaper and hymnals. The floods and then the Depression of the 1930s pushed Bayou Chene further to the edge, though still the school roll averaged one hundred students. But then came another flood in 1937, and by the late 1940s many homes, churches, shops, and businesses had gone. The people had modified their lives to accommodate the amended water management: they raised floors of houses, built rafts for the cattle, raised their levees. Myrtle and Harold were among the last to leave. Bayou Chene ended up under twelve feet of sand.

We head downriver to a clearing in the forest, where an automated oil platform and gas plant quietly do their business. Cattle graze the meadows. A rusting quay is tipped on one side, half submerged. A gray building on twelve-foot stilts is streaked red with rust from the tin roof. *Bayou Crook Chene Field*, says the sign. *Warning. Gas pipeline crossing.* Trees crowd the edge of the clearing. White nimbus are streaked across the sky. It looks like the weather is about to change. We head along Crook Chene, past the site where stood the grand white wooden Catholic church of St. Joseph. We stop and look on forest where once it was. Now there are only camps in the forest and deer-hunting concessions, many with their own warning signs. Baseball was popular at Bayou Chene. It's difficult to imagine. There is no open space at all.

Gwen and Calvin lived on Bloody Bayou near Alcide's home. Then, Calvin was just as thin, with long beard and unruly hair, caught up in a ponytail when working fish or boats. Like all of us, Calvin's become grayer over the years, but unlike most he is just as skinny. No beard now, but a broad overhanging mustache under quiet eyes that crinkle when he holds up a large catfish caught from the silty waters. Gwen wrote her swamp-gas journal to record a life among the shimmering lakes, old cypresses, and lavender hyacinths.

"It's always about the water. High or low," she wrote. "Each year of swamp life reaffirms that flexibility is the key to surviving the wilderness."

Their life was finely photographed by C. C. Lockwood, who came every month. With old swampers like Alcide and Myrtle, they were the last remnants of the Bayou Chene community. Theirs were lives spent cutting wood, fishing for catfish, hunting frogs, canning vegetables, raising chickens, making blackberry wine. Gwen wrote that she often wondered why people "ever left this paradise for the stark, unlovely settlements perched along the levees." The biggest inconvenience, she observed, to living so far out was going in. The swamp offers slim connections to the modern world, tied as it is to the older rhythms of the wet world.

We go in search of further industrial monuments, leaving Chene behind, surging back over the racing Atchafalaya. We turn into an enclosed bayou to look for beavers. Their musky odor is strong, and we nose through the dense cattails, more invasives. We don't find them, but there are two old platforms, and a rusty derrick, toppled in the forest. *Texaco producing*, says a fading sign, *well number 25*. Bound cypress timbers make up the platform, and show no sign of deterioration. That rig was one of the first oil producers here, explains Ricky. The impact of these automated platforms producing oil or natural gas has probably been less than the lumber industry, and certainly less than the continuous tinkering that stands for water management. They bring income to small landowners who house the platforms, and to locals who work in the industry. This may indeed have helped protect this distinct culture of the swamps, allowing people to stay and keep their lands. It's an odd realization. The other source of income to the region should be tourists, but since Katrina and Gustav they have stopped coming. They seem to think the region is closed, damaged perhaps forever.

Then came Deepwater in 2010.

Back at the camp, the three of us sit on the porch in hammock and deep chairs. Back of the clearing the forest trees rise sheer and dense, entangled with vines. Wild turkeys venture onto the pasture in search of feed. We talk fish. Especially crawfish. Of the twenty-nine species in Louisiana, the red swamp and white river are the most common. Crawfish further define identity of the basin. Some are now raised, but both Ricky and Calvin say wild is best, a slightly muddy flavor, something extra. They are smaller than lobsters, caught with traps similar to lobster traps but fashioned of black chicken wire. Fish or corn bait is dropped inside, and like a lobster trap, once in there is no way out. Every fisherman has his special places. Those with camps also know who has rights. But sometimes outsiders steal. Ricky came upon men emptying one of his traps: they pulled a gun on him. Decent prices are possible early in the season, but they tail off as the farmed fish come to market.

As I sprawl in the hammock, beers in the ice bucket, shirt crucially rucked up my back a few inches, one thing lazily strikes me about life in the swamp. Where do you get your exercise? I ask. There's not much land to walk upon.

"Set a hundred crawfish traps," smiles Calvin, "and empty them too, and you'll soon know you've done a day's work."

Night closes in and now we watch the ball game, LSU at bitter rivals Alabama, the jungle television bright from batteries. We are missing C. C. Lockwood on this trip. He wanted to come, but was called to Afghanistan. Meanwhile mosquitoes work their way silently across my back, leaving, I see the next day, weals of red bites like bullet holes. But it could be worse. Charles Simpson in the 1920s wrote of mosquitoes in these swamps: "The insects covered the exposed parts of my body until the skin could not be seen, and when I wiped them off blood dripped on the ground. With puffed cheeks and eyelids I could scarcely see." We retreat inside, and eat fried catfish and bullfrog legs, one of the few places outside France where frogs' legs are on the menu.

A treat: Calvin serves his best blackberry wine, and we talk of the animals of the forest. Louisiana black bear, red wolf, river otter, and panther. Poor old coyote is formally called an *outlawed quadruped* by the state wildlife authorities, as are feral hogs—escapees from the days of farming—nutria, and nine-banded armadillos. Nutria were introduced in the 1930s for fur, and the armadillos marched north through Central America and then Texas. But there's one bird that is internationally iconic to these southern swamps—the ivory-billed woodpecker, also called the Lord God bird. Calvin says he thinks he saw one once, Ricky too. Its silvery beak and large size are distinctive. I tell them about Curtis Allemond.

But all of them must be wrong, as officials have deemed it extinct. The ivory-billed woodpecker's habitat was the cypress and tupelo groves, and it has been recorded extinct since the 1940s. It was then sensationally rediscovered by a group of Cornell scientists who filmed a snatch of video in 2005. The fleeting image was disputed, not good enough evidence for skeptics. Then Mike Steinberg of the University of Alabama revealed another angle. He spoke to local people, and documented their stories in *Stalking the Ghost Bird*.[6]

He observes that there are "simply too many knowledgeable people who have reported seeing the ivory-bill to dismiss them all." He also asked why the stories of the bird weren't going away. Rural Louisianans eat more wild food than anyone else in the United States, so they are out on the land a great deal. There are 678,000 registered hunters and anglers in Louisiana, who spend $1.6 billion annually. They also watch, listen, and use their knowledge and skills to obtain fish, birds, and game. They take pride in this knowledge. Many were surprised to find their bird had been rediscovered: they didn't know it had gone. Steinberg also revealingly documents the testimony of experts, who consistently indicated there was too much to lose professionally if they claimed to have seen an extinct bird. Colleagues would say you had caught swamp fever, said one. A skeptic emphasized, "People want to see the ivory-bill so badly they convince themselves!"

One Louisiana Department of Wildlife and Fisheries instructor said she was endlessly teased by colleagues when she mentioned she'd seen the bird twice. She was so tired of being hassled she never mentions it now. The contrast is striking. If you want to see an ivory-bill, said one duck hunter, then birders will have to "rub elbows with some of the other creatures that occupy the habitat, such as snakes, bugs and hunters." One woman, given a pseudonym, described how she phoned a college academic, who then belittled her report, and refused to come to her land. She felt he was calling her a liar.

Hunter and writer John Dennis describes seeing or hearing ivory-bills through the 1950s to 1970s, but then doubters seemed to increase and start saying it was extinct. There's been a backlash. *Kill the woodpecker* mugs and T-shirts have become common. Ironically, the early impetus for environmental awareness in the basin came from sport hunters, who had noticed the falling numbers of migratory waterfowl because of the loss of habitat. One local pointedly asked Steinberg, "Since you're an environmentalist, are you here to find the bird and confiscate our land?" Fielding Lewis describes seeing an ivory-bill in the late 1960s in a cypress swamp, then a pair in the 1970s. He too writes of being exposed to the deep suspicion by a member of the Museum of Natural Science. Yet when he described his observation to other hunters and fishers, he found they too had many sightings. One man said to Lewis, "I see those big woodpecker with the white bills pretty often. They're all over that area. They are definitely not extinct like they say in books."

The core of local silence centers on worries that big government will take their land away if they report a rarity. Their fear is really about their own extinction. Lifeways of rural people have disappeared so easily in the past, oddly now as much in the face of conservation as development.

Ricky splashes out brandy in the moonlight, the bayou shrouded dark and lapping at the shore. I sleep on a rusting sprung bunk rescued from a World War I troop carrier. All around is the deep penetrating silence of the night forest. I wake in the darkness, and watch it gradually retreat as a gray light fills the clearing and leaks through the windows. Under the covers it is warm and dry. Inside the cabin, the air is cold and still. Before long, Calvin is up and cooking breakfast. The eggs bubble in the heavy iron skillet, and deer sausages crackle and fill the cabin with sweet aroma. On the stove bubbles a tin pot of coffee. There are cold fish and frog pieces from the night before, and pickles in a glass jar on the table. The air is cold, yet Calvin's warm scones are piled high.

Mist clings to the water. The land is still quiet, the waters swirling. It has come up a couple of feet overnight, further reminder that these are unusual times. If it were not for locks and diversion channels, it is conceivable that by now the Atchafalaya would have captured the Mississippi and they would be one. Baton Rouge and New Orleans would be stranded, as would all that heavy industry. The barrier islands and coastal marshes of Louisiana perform a vital function by absorbing the energy of hurricanes and storms, preventing saltwater intrusions, protecting communities and industry. But starved of silt, they are disappearing. In the past century, nineteen hundred square miles of coastal marshes and islands have been lost. The rate is now up to thirty square miles a year. C. C. Lockwood spent 2004 traveling six thousand miles of the wetlands, documenting the interwoven maze of oil, industry, and nature.[7] He saw more brown pelicans, egrets, bald eagles, raccoons, deer, and alligators than in the 1970s. But the losses at the coast were devastating. Places once inhabited are underwater. And now climate change, too, will raise sea levels, change the frequency and violence of storms too. Yet at an earlier evening up at Lafayette, I was having dinner with a lively and hospitable family when climate change came up. A conspiracy. I hesitated, and shrugged to myself. There's a time and a place for discussion, and it was not in someone's home. Maybe that's the problem.

We prepare to leave the camp. Today, Ricky's got on his Muddy Water Tours purple T-shirt with gold compass, colors of LSU's football team. Summer will bring sticky heat and the whine of many mosquitoes, and then everyone will remember these cool mornings with fondness. Calvin is checking a dozen catfish lines he set yesterday, tied to overhanging branches and marked with blue ribbon. Five flatheads and blues are caught, one large, perhaps three pounds. They lie in his boat, gasping. Good food, but people don't eat much catfish these days. The clouds are low and gray now, the wind is up. We look to the south, out over the Gulf. Ricky and I head off, a little wave to Calvin at his houseboat. We head tens of miles south, along pipeline cuttings, into dark and silent cypress groves, past a place where a frog hunter holed his boat on a cypress stump, was stranded there three freezing nights before he was found, kept only warm by pouring gasoline on the water and setting it alight. Over the years, Ricky's laid pipes through these swamps, checked oil platforms, come to know much of the land for oil as well as for hunting and gathering. In one bayou, we throttle back and watch a poisonous cottonmouth, swimming with its head above water and body close to the surface.

We bring the boat ashore at Bayou Sorrell, and drive over the eastern levee into the land of cane fields and dry woodlands. At the back of Ricky's house is a pond covered with duckweed, but the resident alligator is hidden today. In the forests beyond have come reports of panthers, another animal whose presence is dismissed by officials but acknowledged by locals with simple nods. Two weeks later, Ricky and Calvin will go back for bullfrogs, lamping in the dark, pulling nearly four hundred from the lake by hand, each animal itself larger than a hand.

—◁◁◁∩◁▷∩▷▷—

We come back in cool spring to find watery sunlight on the flooded forest. Earlier in the darkness awaiting the arrival of dawn, heard but not seen, a red-tailed hawk keened from a nearby tree. We would be fishing, too, this Saturday morning, quieted in the swamps. We drive over the levee topped with a long concrete wall with blocky white over-painted graffiti, and launch the skiff into the bayou. Early leafing trees are a haze of green in the sunshine. We tramp along the now-flooded path to reach Sawyer's Cove, and launch the green pirogue through the cypress. Ribbons tied to nylon string mark the traps, and as we proceed, a black-and-white woodpecker with red head flits across the clearing and perches on a low branch. Could it be, but no, it is not large enough. A black-headed, or downy, or hairy. The traps in the deeper swamps have crawfish, and the bucket begins to fill with clicking crawfish, reddish-purple and glistening in the hard sun.

The simple task of clearing traps ties us to the place. Some have been torn open by otters. Cold water drips from the mesh traps. It's yet early for spring, and the canopy above the young cypresses is open to a sapphire sky again stretched with cirrus. The heron is generally worth watching closely. When their nests are low, you can put short strings on your crawfish traps. High nests mean floods. The quietly thumping engine takes the metal pirogue deeper into wet forest, the land for several miles around five to ten feet below the surface. Later in the year, we would be able to walk along paths and levees beneath this boat. The rising water allows the crawfish to harvest grasses and vegetation that were once air-side. To thrive, crawfish need dry summers and autumns, standing water in winter, and then a gentle spring rise and warmer water of summer. These will be an excellent gift for neighbors or family. Later, in the main channel, we chat to Ricky's brother working with men swathed in yellow and green oilskins, pulling in great looped nets set in the slower waters by the shore. Their metal skiffs are soon full of fat buffalo fish, silver and red, twitching and leaping.

Beyond the swamps, the southern Louisiana landscape grades into fields of rustling sugarcane, only the electricity poles by the road bringing anything vertical to this land. This is the true delta of the Mississippi, thousands of square miles of open marshland, sugarcane fields, and strings of islands that survive into the Gulf of Mexico. The economy is in bad shape, rows of boarded-up shops in small towns, for-sale signs abound, stoplights bright in the gloom. Yet a couple of months later, the Deepwater rig explodes and for ninety days washes this edge-land with viscous sludgy oil. In the whole United States, twenty million barrels are used a day. Now five million barrels daily drown fishing and tourism in the country's worst-ever oil spill. By e-mail, Ricky says the shrimpers and oystermen are worst affected, and the $2.5 billion Louisiana commercial fishery is closed down. But it's not good in the basin either. To try to force the oil away from the coastal marshes, diversion channels were opened, and the water levels dropped six feet in a week. "Crawfishing has been dealt a season-long blow. I cannot even get to my traps," writes Ricky.

In the long-running efforts to cap the cursed leak, and the messy cleanup of beach and marsh, the chief executive of BP, Tony Haywood, wailed "I'd like my life back," and was photographed sailing his racing yacht in the clean waters off southern England.

Louisiana has lived with such turmoil since the beginnings. First French rule, then Spanish, then entrance to the United States, joining the Ordinance of Seccession in 1861, four years of civil war in which it sent fifty-six thousand troops to the Southern army, and saw twenty-four thousand of its own black people serve in the Union army. After the war, black Louisianans helped form the Republican Party, yet were oppressed by the Ku Klux Klan. In the late 1880s, 128,000 black people were registered to vote, along with 124,000 white. But the 1898 constitutional convention adopted new terms for voters—literacy was dictated as a precursor alongside property ownership. By 1900, only 1,342 black people still could vote; twenty years later only 600. Between 1882 and 1951, 391 people were lynched in the state. The phrase *sold down the river* came from the practice of selling black slaves to Louisiana cotton or cane plantations, which had the worst of reputations in the South.

It is bad, still, for the Houma Nation. In Raceland, we slip down a track behind the Relief Center, white paint flaking from the wooden walls, the lettering bright with the nation's colors of red, yellow, and black, a crawfish painted on the wall too. In wide fields, smoke curls from cleared sugarcane. The Houma have a long tradition of women leaders dating back to the 1700s, and the elected president is Brenda Dardar Robichaux. After Katrina and Gustav, their task remains as great as ever. Many Houma Indian families lost their homes, and in disasters, predators swarm in beside those that bring charity and aid. The Houma have a nation, traditions and culture, bound up now in bayous and fields. They know where it is, where it was. But the politics of land intervenes.

The United Houma Nation of seventeen thousand to twenty thousand people is located in the coastal parishes of St. Mary, Terrebonne, Lafourche, Plaquemines, Jefferson, and St. Bernard, and Brenda has black-and-white photographs of dignified families standing before their wooden houses roofed with cane, girls with long braided plaits, all wearing clean white shirts. In a bayou is a punt piled high with Spanish moss. A man in rubber boots pulls a net into a trawler at sea. These are the tanned faces of outdoor people. And then color photos of modern girls practicing basketry, groups learning about the uses of indigenous plants, the nation in full ceremonial dress. We can see the busy hands of the girls, trying the old techniques. They are reviving other traditions of songs and stomp-dances, the music from drums, alligators skins, gourd rattles, and flutes.[8]

The Houma have never received recognition from the Bureau of Indian Affairs. A letter was filed in 1979, but it took the BIA fifteen years to reply. They rejected the case. Since 1994, there has been no response to every single further request. Their history has been recorded since contact with the French explorer LaSalle in 1682. The problem is the one year of 1809: the BIA says there is a gap, which means no continuity for the tribe. They are thus, ludicrously, seen only as individuals, not a tribe, and thus not permitted a reservation. The Houma were both cultivators and hunters, growing corn, melon, pumpkins, beans, and hunting with blowpipes made from cane reeds. At the boundary line of the Houma and Bayougoulas was a tall red pole topped with a bear skull and fish heads. When the French saw it, they called that place the *bâton rouge*. From contact, the Houma became closely tied to the French, and indeed helped the French to negotiate a treaty with the Chitimacha in 1716. Their main language is now Cajun French, and about a fifth speak English only poorly.

Brenda is off to D.C. again soon, wishing they would listen more. In all, 565 tribes have been federally recognized with membership of two million people. It makes you wonder what exactly is going on. We talk about the black dolls with sequin eyes, dresses of cane grass, and find they are fashioned from the Spanish moss. Basketry, doll making, weaving, drumming—all these are traditions known well by elders, but less by today's youngsters.

"We are making efforts to revive this knowledge," says Brenda, but they are short of moss down here.

The next day, Ricky and I spend time pulling moss from tree limbs in the swamp near Bayou Chene, packing a sack full with the gray fibrous epiphytes. A hard dusty job, and we see no snakes. Brenda's doctor husband, Michael, will come to treat many fishermen, shrimpers, crabbers, and oystermen of these coastal areas for illness arising from the clean-up operation after Deepwater. There are still a lot of blue roofs down here too.

Only one Native American nation in Louisiana has control over its own homeland, the Chitimacha at their 260-acre reservation at Charenton. We drive around the bottom of the Atchafalaya Basin, across box-iron bridges over bayous crowded with cranes and docks and floating casinos. Every gas station has its own casino, a room filled with slot machines. The big casinos are either paddle steamers on the rivers or situated on reservation land. For the next four miles, says one sign, bears might be crossing.

We turn off the cracked and potholed main road toward the Chitimacha reservation, where wide avenues of smooth blacktop are lined with large bungalows on wide plots. Four fire trucks are drawn up on the lot by a large station, and a smart school is corralled by a picket fence. Every home seems to have several SUVs, parked under the live oaks and cypresses. Just off the res, the houses are trailers on bricks, old cars subsiding into the long grass of yards out front. A red tower marks the money machine. Tall yellow lettering says *Casino*. There are also restaurants, gift shops, coffee bar, grill, and nightclub. We sit at the bar. There are no windows, creating a timeless zone where the worries and concerns of the world cannot enter. All the bar and restaurant staff are local non-Indians. It's the middle of the day, and the glittering, clunking, tinkling slot machines are being fed by legions of hopeful visitors, many elderly. Savings, pensions, and incomes are being swallowed up. The house always wins. And so, in this case, does the tribe, for the profits from the casino go to all members.

In 1900, only six Chitimacha families of some one hundred people survived from twenty thousand at contact. They were granted federal recognition in 1917 with the Charenton reservation. Four sacred cypress trees marked the corners of their territory. In 1985, a bingo facility was built, and then 850 slot machines added in the early 1990s. The Chitimacha nation now is able to say it is "facing the twenty-first century in perhaps the best position it has ever been." Dance and music are practiced at the school, though the language has long been lost. They also speak mainly Cajun French. At the new museum, a history of the Chitimacha is depicted behind glass panels and painted on murals. A pirogue of elegant design and smooth lines hangs from the ceiling. The baskets of red and yellow geometric design are woven so tightly they can hold water.[9]

The young woman in charge says she recently came back to the res with her two young children, her marriage dissolved. To qualify for financial support from the nation, you must be at least a sixteenth Chitimacha. This would seem to be straightforward, but a new problem has emerged. The tribe now receives hundreds of letters every year from new claimants, mostly spurious. The total tribal membership is 950, of which 350 live here. What an historical twist: now that there's money involved, people want to be Indian, having spent centuries trying to ignore or get rid of them. Above the photographs of eleven past leaders is written, *weavers of the past, weavers of the future*. Perhaps this is a danger too: the loss of some identity in the face of casino income. Nonetheless, the Chitimacha are expanding: they have bought more land, and now have a thousand acres.

Dramas have emerged elsewhere around the expansion of Indian gambling, and the subsequent claims for citizenship. Some tribes, such as the Ho-chunk of Wisconsin, Chukchansi of California, and Eastern Cherokee of North Carolina, have begun to use DNA testing. But this apparently rational system to reject false claims has now led to many existing citizens being traumatized by their loss of identity. Existing tribe members have been stripped of their identity and homes. In California, twenty-five hundred Indian people have lost citizenship. The problem is that DNA tests ignore the realities of cultural history, as in the past many tribes adopted children and adults with no blood connections. To be Indian was simply to be accepted. This opens up "complex, intractable and perhaps ultimately unanswerable questions," James Wilson has observed in his *The Earth Shall Weep*. But such questions about identity and meaning are relevant for all of us. We're all trying to make sense, to find the right stories to tell about ourselves.

The clouds have dispersed by the time we leave the darkened Cypress Bayou Casino. To the north, we pass through St. Martin Parish, one of the poorest in the state. White plantation homes with wooden verandas, lawns and specimen trees, then a main street of painted houses and shops. This is a place deserving of serious dedication: it is the home of one of America's best living writers, James Lee Burke. We stop for bowls of fish soup. Ricky's family owned sugar plantations hereabouts before the Civil War, and were original landowners at Bayou Chene. They have since stayed close to the swamp, even though the land was lost. He says they always will.

The evening sun now washes the cane fields and wooden houses, and we turn inside the swamp and drive north along the cracked road outside the western levee to McGee's. The restaurant is almost empty, and Ricky and I chat with David over a beer. Everyone here's the worse for drink, even though the evening is yet young. Peggy looks through me, but then it is her birthday. Teri-Ann checks the slots. No live music, few customers, for a Friday night again not so good. The economy has declined yet further. At a table with checkered tablecloth overlooking the darkened lake, we work on a heaped dish of red-hot crawfish. Before these journeys, I had not been a great fan of fish, certainly not seafood. Oysters grabbed up from an Irish bay by an enthusiastic owner, shellfish in a Philippines cafe: both bringing on days of dreadful illness, seared deep in memory and taste. Yet here I am with cold beer and fiery crawfish.

Ricky sighs. "I have to spend the next few months over the border in Houston." But then, he and Teri-Ann will get five weeks straight at the camp later in the year.

As we prepare to depart, I notice the houseboats have been removed from the water and are now on pilings at the shore. Insurance, explains David. All I can think about is the moonlight on the still lake, on the floor of the houseboat sharp shadows, croaking frogs beyond the mosquito netting. It was sad to see the houseboats grounded. No more feeling the creaking of the boat in your bones, watching a moon rise through the trees and filling the windows with light. Somewhere south, deep in the swamps we cross a clanking bridge, and stretching backs and legs, walk into a bar in a shambling wooden building. There are no other lights in the swamp. Inside, local friends leaning against a bar are shouting over the music.

You could have it all, sings Johnny Cash, *my empire of dirt*. Neon blinking, eyes smarting, beer at the bar.

Outside, I stand and listen to the frogs out on the bayou.

12

DESERT

Timbisha (Death Valley), California, United States

296° West of Date Line

Deep in cold shadow our truck is stranded on ice just over the top of a steep pass. It slews toward the edge. All is quiet, apart from our slamming hearts. We try chopping away the ice, and develop an ungrateful nickname for the vehicle. Then over the rise floats a small four-by-four, and the man steps out, sniffs, and sighs.

"People die out here, man," he states, but fixes a tow strap.

Their little dog skitters on the ice; inside his wife waves. They surge us back to the pass, and depart. My old school friend Kev and I retreat down to the stands of Joshuas on Lee Flats, brew tea on the flatbed, and reconsider. We're not bothered, we nod, and stroll slowly out into the dry land. Walking, said desert-man Edward Abbey, stretches time and prolongs life. The craggy yuccas spread across the sandy saddle, each tree lonesome in its own water catchment. The oldest known is nine hundred years of age. From far, they appear delicate as lilies, up close their tough leaves are curved sickles. The winter sky is hard blue, the desert crushingly silent. A wake of dust appears, the motorcyclist slows, stares, and guns away. We head back to the Panamints before long. It seems we are done with the first plan.

The night before we had pulled over on the long road to Lone Pine to watch the moon rise over the Inyo Mountains. It first lit up a strip of cloud, then grew as a sparkle on the dark horizon, turning the starry sky silvery gray. It leapt away from the hills and climbed, a couple of days past full. At the lilac dawn, we shivered in a paddock crusty with frost and the bleached white bones of plant stems. Mount Whitney and the rest of the Sierra Nevada were bloody icebergs ragged beneath the moon. Then the sun-shadow front raced down the slopes, past pines and snow meadows, over crests and hanging valleys. Distance was hard to judge, but the line lunged over the brown foothills and swept right at us, the sun itself now exploding from the hills behind. Immediately colors began to bleach. After breakfast of coffee and boiled eggs, we left the cold empty streets of this wild town favored by film directors of westerns, to the north Manzanar where Japanese Americans were interned during the war, and head past the Paiute-Shoshone reservation. In the grip of the Sierra's rain shadow, this desert whispers of layered and contested history.

We turned east, and the first sign of water was stolen Owens Lake, sixty-five miles from Death Valley and flash point for California's first water wars, inspiration too for Roman Polanski's *Chinatown*. In 1903, Mary Austin described Owens as "jade green, placid, unwinking and unfathomable," and others wrote of flocks of avocets and ducks, and many orchards. Steamships carried silver and lead ore across the twenty-five-foot-deep lake. But this was not to last. All that remains today of the two-hundred-square-mile lake are bitter salt flats and a patch of super-saline water far out in the shimmering middle. The villains were from Los Angeles, a small town on the coast constrained by its lack of fresh water. It began in 1898, when the former head of the city water company, Frederick Eaton, was elected mayor. He appointed another self-made water engineer, Belfast-born William Mulholland, to run the Department of Water and Power, and together with *Los Angeles Times* publisher Harrison Gray Otis they came to be known as the San Fernando Syndicate. Privately they bought farms in Owens Valley to acquire water rights, and tracts of the unirrigated San Fernando Valley. They persuaded thirsty voters of Los Angeles to issue public bonds, and the construction of a 223-mile aqueduct began in 1908. Violent tactics forced the last Owens farmers off their land.

"There it is. Take it," said Mulholland, as water flowed from the aqueduct in 1913 to transform city and farmlands. Mulholland has a drive named after him in LA, and a memorial fountain on Riverside Drive. Owens has alkali dust storms. No signs of orchards and fields remain.

We drove into lakeside Keeler at the base of the switchback road that climbs nine thousand feet to Cerro Gordo mine. Keeler rose and fell, fleeting like so many booms and busts of desert mining country. There were five thousand people here a century ago; now just sixty-four remain. Two wide roads amble down to the old lakeshore. We passed the old saltworks, trailer homes, yards jammed with cars slumped on axles, windows gaping, rust spreading. The abandoned swimming pool was blue with cracked tiles, surrounded by a wooden stockade topped with barbed wire. The concrete paths were broken by weeds that had pushed and bent the very earth. We walked out onto the bright flats. To the west the snows were glimmering, down here the sun blinding off the white mineral trona and halite salts. Capillary movement had lifted salt over plants and posts. A nearby field contained two crumpled house trailers and the accumulated detritus of years. A surfboard had been raised up. *Keeler Beach, provided by LA Water*, it said. *Swim, surf, fish. Have fun. Safe beach!* We saw no one. This place was doomed to extinction by LA's swimming pools and green lawns. The water wars of the future will set cities against farmers, just as they did here.

—⟫⟪—

Somewhere in every desert is an oasis. Tiny patches of rich, wet life, they speak of mystery and surprise. We turn into Darwin Canyon and walk the track around

Zinc Hill, then climb a couple of miles up a narrowing arroyo. It is utterly silent. Nothing moves in the intense light. No smells, no sounds, except our own breathing. I stop: a long nothing. No rocks cracking, no soil moving, no mountain ranges crumpling, just many creosote bushes. Later a wandering row of tamarisk salt cedar appears along the center of the canyon. To the side are dry gulches. Then come bulrushes and phragmites reeds, and we can hear a tiny trickle. We climb on past willows and cottonwoods, and many birds are chattering now. At the base of sheer rock is a pool of dark glass. Branches and tree trunks lie shattered, plant trash caught among the rocks and high branches. It has the appearance of a dynamic place suddenly arrested at the close of a traumatic flood. It is dank, but somehow somber. As we walk back out we cross the distinct thermocline: the air sharply shifts from cool and damp to hot and dry. Within paces we're back into the dazzling and everlasting silence of the desert.

Though Death Valley was designated a national monument in 1937 by President Hoover, parts of this territory were not included. The Panamint mountains are in the park, the valley not. There is no warning: three F-111s flash up the valley, breathtaking jet roars bouncing off the slopes, and flip back over the road so close we see each pilot's mirrored mask. By such partial preservation, we permit the non-preserved to be harmed. We pass hillside Panamint Springs and its cluster of cottonwoods and drop down to the dry lake either side of the shimmering blacktop.

We get out of the car. Kev sits on a dune to play his' mouth organ, and I walk with fading music a mile or so south across the empty flats. Unheralded, I stumble on a mystery. For here are lines of stones stretching down the valley, each a couple of paces equidistant, pieces of black and bruised-purple lava. Wind or water has scoured the sand to create small craters in which each stone sits. Some run at right angles, across the valley toward the hills. They must have been placed— perhaps piles of mud put by prospectors making claims a century ago, which through capillary action have become salty stone. But no, they are heavy as rock. These intaglios mean something, but what? Who put them here, how long ago? You can't see them from the road, nor from Telescope Peak either. Later, we ask a tall ranger with pink glasses and gray ponytail.

"People," he says. "Must have put them there. Not animals." We look at each other. We needed to ask someone else.

Later, I read Charles Hunt's fine geological account: on the edge of the Panamints are "carefully placed lines of rock stretching for hundreds of feet . . . probably ceremonial mesas of an unknown people dating back thousands of year when the valley was a freshwater lake." There are many geoglyphs in these desert mesas and arroyos. Some of the most famous are at Blythe on the California-Arizona border, giant humans with arms outstretched, tiny heads and great hands, and spindly legged horses. Horses died off eleven thousand years ago, and did not come again until brought by the Spanish. Some of the glyphs in the Panamints and Death Valley are larger: at the mouth of Wildrose Canyon is an alignment of colored rocks almost fifty yards long. A rectangular design in Death Valley is seventy-five yards of circles and spirals, which could be mazes, in which haunted people might have run to lose a ghost. Some circles are designed with an opening that points toward water. There are many other petroglyphs: bighorn sheep and snakes, chevron symbols, circles, circles with pendants, more stick figures with large hands, segmented wheels. Some were painted with organic pigments, most pecked, chiseled or scratched into rock surfaces, by method and design many like those of distant Murujuga.

<hr>

We camp five feet above sea level at Stovepipe Wells in a park full of vast RVs, hitched to their own four-by-fours for local mobility. Part of a growing cohort of middle-class American itinerants, selling up and following the weather south in winter and north in summer. In *Ghost Riders*, Richard Grant says there may be millions of these snowbirds, new nomads of the American West. We are content with our life sprawled around the tent. The simplicity, the deepness of sleep, the vivid dreams. We light the wood in the fire pit as the sun drops fast. Soon the heat of the land has leached away and cold is pouring across the flats. We eat noodles and soup, gazing into the blazing fire, hunched up. Just cooking, just sitting. Nothing more. We never see the coyotes, though in the morning there will be paw marks and droppings close by. Darkness advances and the sky convenes with three-dimensional stars. In this crystal air, they are not flat against the dome of the sky, but separated, near and very far, going on forever. But there is more local source of light too, for toward the southeast is a pale line on the horizon. Sound travels far in the desert, vehicles are heard long before you see them. But the Las Vegas Strip, just a mile long and a hundred away, intrudes much further into the wilds.

Then all change. Another moonrise brings us back, spreading a line around the bowl of the horizon. Distant stars blink out one by one. The effect is breathtaking. Just look at the sky, we want to shout. Just look. By the time the moon has risen with a slow seepage and then leapt from the Funeral Mountains, there are few stars remaining. Our shadows grow distinct and dark. The landscape is silvered below the pale sky, the night bone cold. Later I pull the sleeping bag over my head. When I get up, the desert is acute and monochromed. There is not a sound, no breath of air.

At dawn, we watch with cawing ravens the salmon light spread across the mountains again, and set off toward the distant dunes on Mesquite Flats. We are walking across salt flats of polygonal cracks and gray gravel washes when the sun appears, first on the Panamints to the west, and again charging across the valley floor. Among the coarse sands, scales of mica and quartz, fragments of agate and carnelian, coppery shales and patinated rocks we find signs of nighttime warfare. Chains of twisting, turning scorpion tracks, the meanders of rattlesnakes, the double-prints of sidewinders, the two prints of kangaroo rat. Then by sagebrush, tracks of a bird join those of a scorpion, a scuffle, and disappearance of scorpion as it is briefly lifted, then more scrapes, battle continuing, more scorpion tracks and chasing feet, and then nothing. One lifting, the other lifted. Under creosote bushes are many burrows, where dwell the poisoners of the desert, rattlesnake, trapdoor spider, tarantula, and scorpion. Add us to that list too.

We climb the barchan dunes, hundreds of feet high and said to be ten thousand years stable at this place. In the overwhelming silence, not a thing moves save for running grains of sand beneath our feet. No shift of air, no whisper, no birds, no voices either. Pure air, pure sunlight, "far beyond the wire fence of civilization," as desert writer John van Dyke put it a century ago. Coyote tracks, two paws and two more, walking, and then stretched out and running down the slope. A leap, and then four prints together. Tickety-tick of another eight-legged scorpion, up slope, down the other side. In the valley are a thousand species of flowering plants, deer, mountain lion, bobcat, coyote and fox, much maligned burros set free in the 1880s, and bighorn sheep. In the salty springs are tiny endemic pupfish. This is why deserts and knowledge go together. You need to be able to read the land to survive the apparent austerity.[1]

This is what the Newe people, later known as the Western Shoshone, did so well. There were four phases of Native American culture here before the 1848 discovery of gold. To 10,000 years BP, the Nevares Spring people lived in a wet and game-abundant landscape. By 6000 BP, the Mesquite Flint culture is recognized as distinct, and their land was becoming drier. By 2000 BP, the Saratoga Spring people watched the last lakes disappear as the land became arid. Bows and arrows began to be used at that time; before that the spear and atlatl. The nearly forty-thousand-square-mile Western Shoshone homeland of Pia Sokopia is centered on Nevada, and the Timbisha Shoshone, who inhabited Death Valley for these last thousand years, are at the western edge of the tribal range. Historian Hubert Bancroft wrote in 1883, "They are lovers of their country," then slipped: they were "lovers not of fair hills and fertile valleys, but of inhospitable mountains and barren plains." But by then, it was already too late.

After ten thousand years, it took only two decades from first contact to destruction. Horse traders first came to Pia Sokopia in the 1830s when this was in the Mexican state of Alta California, then were followed by bands of raiders and English-speaking fur trappers. One of the earliest, Jedediah Smith, crossed Nevada into California in search of beaver, and described the natives as the "most miserable of the human race having nothing to subsist on except grass seed and grasshoppers." Visitors found it hard to survive, the Spanish trail was soon labeled the *jornada del muerto*, and thus the myth making began. The moniker Death Valley would come later. To the Shoshone, it is a source of irritation. Their home is *timbisha*, red ocher paint.[2]

The patchy natural resources of the Great Basin meant that the Newe lived in small family groups and moved regularly. Dome-shaped winter homes were fashioned from mesquite and willow. In summer, they moved up into the mountains to conical homes of pinyon branches and bark. Sweat lodges were packed with mud to hold in the steam. The main staples were *ovi* mesquite pods and *tuba* pine nuts, supplemented with sand bunchgrass, wild rye, sunflower, wild grapes, lily bulb, Joshua tree buds, and cabbage greens. Like all foragers and hunters, they actively managed the local environment, building artificial ponds to lure ducks, and brush blinds of sage leading to deer corrals. They seeded wild grasses, also cultivated corn, beans, and squashes, like farmers. The regional chief was the shaman *pakwinavi*, but there were no formal political structures. The largest social gatherings were for the pinyon nut collecting, when each individual would hope to gather over two hundred pounds in two to three weeks of autumn.

Water bodies were unsurprisingly important. All springs, hot and cold, housed water babies, dangerous spirits that could lure especially women and children to their deaths by drowning. *Puha* was the guiding life force that connected diverse spirits, and was associated with water. Animal and human trails that linked watering points guided the flow of *puha*, perhaps, too, the intaglios and stone lines. And then new people came, claimed this land, and unraveled a culture. The Timbisha received federal recognition as a tribe only in 1983, then had to wait until the year 2000 for the Timbisha Shoshone Homeland Act. It granted them 314 acres of Death Valley near Furnace Creek: the National Park alone is ten thousand times larger.

When gold was found, California still felt remote to the Europeans. The year of 1848 saw an end to the Mexican-American War, the treaty granting America control over vast areas of the West, including the lands of the Western Shoshone. The year before had seen the arrival of the first Mormons in the Salt Lake City area, and then the rush began. In the spring of 1849 alone, one hundred thousand people were lured into California in search of gold and hope. Later in the year, a thousand impatient people gathered with two hundred wagons and two thousand horses and oxen. The passes across the Sierra Nevada were closed, and the wagon trains had to travel south an extra five hundred miles into an area the maps depicted as empty. Trappers had good relations with both Paiute and Shoshone, trading food for clothes and respecting local gardens. But this did not occur to the argonauts, or forty-niners as later they were known. The Jayhawkers, Bug-Smashers, and Georgians headed into the heat of Death Valley, and simply blundered around. They did not know the land, did not think to ask.

William Manly and John Rogers were members of the Bennett-Arcan group. Manly wrote an account of crossing Death Valley, though he waited thirty-five years for his memories to mature before completing his account. "We were," he wrote, "badly deceived as to the distance," and they were soon in trouble. He noted signs of Indian settlements and their conical baskets, and also the dry cornstalks of last year's crop. He wrote of peaks of many colors, and the "wonderful picture of grand desolation." They found minnows in springs, and clay bowls attached to canyon walls to collect drinking water. Near the little stream at Furnace Creek, they fell hungrily upon a stash of buried squash, which he "did not approve of for we had no title to this produce." But they ate them nonetheless. The local women and children retreated to mesquite thickets, the watchful men trailed by day, careful to remain invisible.

Some groups went north around Tucki Mountain and up Darwin Canyon; some went back south through Death Valley. By Christmas, most were running out of food, worrying that they might never escape. Yet the argonauts were suspicious both of each other and the locals. Records show the Paiute helped some groups find their way out. The Bennett-Arcan group, crippled by scurvy, tried to cross the salt flats at Badwater; it took them two days. At water holes, they found mostly slimy mud, and water the color of wine, alkaline and slippery to the touch. "On the edge of the desert stretching out before was a long dreary trail with bones of animals alongside," Manly wrote, which rather contradicts his other testimony that "ours were the first visible footsteps." Manly and Rogers volunteered to go on alone to find food. They were away twenty-six days, walking a hundred miles to San Francisquito ranch near present-day Los Angeles. They returned, heroically, and it was one of them who then declared "Goodbye Death Valley" as all finally escaped.

Yet after all this effort, all those dreams, none found riches. Most returned east, disillusioned. The impacts on the Shoshone and other tribes of California would be far from temporary.

Death Valley is not really much drier than other deserts. But it can be hot. Rather than rising, the heat sinks back into the valley, is compressed, and so generates more heat and raises the temperature yet further. An 1894 newspaper claimed it was "the most deadly and dangerous spot . . . a pit of horrors. . . . It breeds only noxious and venomous things. Its dead do not decompose. It is surely the nearest to a little hell upon earth that the whole wicked world can produce." Maps now have the new names: Coffin Peak, Funeral Mountains, Deadman's Pass, Dry Bone Canyon, Dante's View, Hell's Gate, and Devil's Golf Course.

In a fault of Tucki Mountain, once hoped to be a fabled mountain of silver, lies a marbleized copper-and-amber watercourse called Mosaic Canyon. The breccia and smooth dolomite were formed on a seabed 750 million years ago, pressurized and baked, and recently eroded by water. The canyon drains four square miles of mountain, and is a place to avoid in rain and the wrath of flood. We walk up past swirling marble walls, across sandy shales, and then up into a silent amphitheater topped with towering peaks and clear sky. Somewhere are bighorn sheep, perhaps five hundred in all, lions and burros too. Most of the fans are stained by iron and manganese oxides. The most stable and oldest surfaces are dark satiny varnishes. But the sun steadily leaches the color from the land, and from the shadows on the way out we see Stovepipe Wells down on the far valley floor. Translucent mirages shimmer, so we can't be sure.

Coming out of the desert we smell the rich citrus airs of orange groves east of Bakersfield, and are astonished at the emerald land. A prison bright in its neon wash is an island in a dark field, then we swing north, vigilant for weaving night drivers and the jackrabbits of tiredness.[3] In the early hours, burned and bristled, we stop on Treasure Island halfway across the old Bay Bridge to gaze upon the lights of San Francisco. And wonder, why do such city nightscapes look so attractive?

—⬥⬥⬥—

Las Vegas works best at night. Close up, the Strip glitters with the warm embrace of Christmas and every birthday you've ever known. The old adobe hotels by shiny walls of glass, lasers arrowing into the dark sky, reds, greens, and golds, a roller-coaster wrapped around one hotel, the dancing fountains lit before another. You can see all from the windows of the plane, the airport enticingly placed alongside the southern end of the Strip. In summer, the heat of the desert beats and wraps itself around you. In winter, the winds whistle through the streets, but still the doors to every shop and casino are wide open, and screens the size of houses glitter. Palm trees line the street. The citadel, the crowning glory of consumption. You come to be happy forever, again forgetting that the house wins.

We begin in this town named after meadows. Mid-century, tourists came here to watch the Nevada nuclear tests. Now we're in the latter part of the credit crunch recession. In the previous decade or so, the numbers of permanent migrants to Vegas had grown to about eighty to ninety thousand a year. We walk the Strip, this time quieter than usual. An illuminated sign asks *Got a traffic ticket?* and offers a lawyer's number. There are more hustlers on the exposed streets than gamblers, handing out cards, *girls to you*, trying to divert us. Waste collectors are swathed in many layers; a figure dressed as a branded candy sweet stamps his feet on a drafty corner. We had intended to stay at a particular motel, but it was shut. The neighbor, just by that famous diamond sign, is dark save for its female hustlers. We see that several tall hotels are lit only a third of the way up, the upper floors locked down. Inside, though, there is bustle around blackjack and roulette tables. Many more stand by rows of slot machines, faces bleached older by the artificial light. There's an end-of-era feel to it all.

At dawn inky clouds race across the sky, the wind scooping up cartons and paper in mini-tornados. Vegas is one mile of Strip and three hundred square miles of housing sprawled toward the hills in every direction. "If the sun, smoke, bugs and arthropods don't get you . . . it's Las Vegas, more sickening by far than the salt in the Death Valley sinkholes." Edward Abbey was desperate to protect the desert, and I suppose the people there too.

"Anyway—why go into the desert? Really, why do it?"

We are going to the real desert, but dwell first in the suburbs. They do roads here very well. Each development is built around wide blacktop roads, which at their ends simply halt at a brick wall or piece of scrubby desert. Squares of land are oven-ready with lights and telegraph wires, road and drains. But no houses. It's Sim City for real. A bank of clouds flames sunrise pink, but down here all feels unloved. To the west, mountains rear out of the shadows, and the wind surges through empty streets. A ghost town that hasn't even been built yet. On other streets, adobe and gray houses are packed side by side, some with Halloween decorations. A few front gardens have desert shrubs and stones, but this is a rare concession to local ecology. Most have green lawns bright and manicured.

We drive to the southern edge at Somerset Hills, more imported names. There are no signs of foreclosures here, but arrested developments are marked by rows of red cones and blocked gates. Cactus Twilight is one, by a field of stones. There's been no effort to clean up trash—perhaps the more there is, the better people feel when such land is converted to housing. Highlands Ranch, proclaims a billboard, *for a new brand of lifestyle.*

For this is what is really for sale. A dream of a way of living, and of fabulous riches. At the edge of another development with a golf course snaking through an arroyo, a double line of metal fences prevents anyone getting out onto the hill, where there are signs of natural vegetation, how this place once was.

We turn into a wealthy development, and two security guards jump up. We're English, we say, as if this will do. Roberto, in sparkling black uniform and pearly white gloves, asks if we're really secret shoppers.

"We don't allow anyone in who's not been invited," he states firmly. He's guarded and guarding. We don't give away any information, he says, about the housing or people or anything. But it doesn't stop us standing around for a chat. Amran turns out to be from Lahore. Cricket, we ask, and he smiles. Here we are in an invented place talking of a game mostly played on the other sides of the world. As we leave, we observe that every community is gated, inward-facing. Even the malls are fenced. One way in, one way out. "It's us against them," Roberto said obliquely. You can't go for a walk here even if you wanted to. Then we see that's not entirely true. Gangs of gardeners and street cleaners are pruning the green hedges along the main drive. As we leave we pass one development behind a long brick wall in which none of the houses have outward-facing windows. A space station. No need to look outward if there is nothing there.

"Goodbye to Las Vegas, but we'll be back. Unavoidable. Las Vegas is creeping out everywhere." Abbey saw Vegas for what it is; and how its allure damages us all. Twenty years ago he was right. Today, he'd still be, just more so. Time, then, to call upon the barbarians of the twenty-first century, to tear down some walls and create something new.

The contrast with the intensity of place over in Death Valley is acute. On the way, we pass through Pahrump and eat late breakfast at the casino with neither windows nor clocks. The slots are crowded, the café too. At Death Valley Junction, once called Amargosa, the desert opera house of white adobe and pale blue doors and windows is flaking in the desert air. Elegant wrought-iron seats face a grove of wind-torn tamarisks set among rusting agricultural and road machines: a grader, cart, fire hoses, and red wheels. This was the launch, before any of this was built, of the descending journeys into Death Valley. Once with its own railhead and population of three hundred at peak, now it's a historic monument. Tumbleweed spins, head over tail, down the hot street.

<hr>

We turn off the main road and bounce down toward the tribal offices and a dozen houses on the Timbisha Shoshone reservation. Mesquite trees provide shade near the homes, but the adobe offices stand alone among the low creosote and salt cedar. From the Timbisha tribal office, the air to the west is clogged with sand, the sun watery and Telescope Peak invisible. The wind roars down the valley. To the north is the oasis that is Furnace Creek motel, museum, shop, restaurant, and bar. Over there, preparations are under way for Forty-Niners week, when descendants of Manly and others will come again to celebrate. Barbara Durham is tribal heritage preservation officer, and welcomes us to her office piled with papers, computer blinking, tribal ornaments on the shelf. She has narrow eyes above a broad smiling face, flat nose, and jet black hair.

"People often ask me," says Barbara, "why do you live in Death Valley? I tell them, this is my home."

Barbara graduated from the high school in Shoshone, and has a daughter and grandson over in Reno. She often brings him to learn about life in the valley. It was her great-great-great grandfather who saw the first white men come into the valley, the beginning of an end. This was their valley, mountains and pine forests, their water and game. The Newe did retaliate, taking horses, cattle, and weapons. Periods of conflict followed, and a Colonel Connor instructed his troops at Ruby Valley Fort to hunt down all Newe and kill them: "Leave their bodies thus exposed as an example of what evil doers may expect. . . . This of course may seem harsh and severe, but . . . I am satisfied that in the end it will prove most merciful."

Suspicion grew. There was mass settler hysteria in the early 1860s when the Shoshone were thought to be organizing to attack. But it was autumn: they were simply gathering for the communal pinyon harvest. Yet key decisions were being made by Bureau of Indian Affairs officials. Jacob Forney, Utah Territory superintendent, concluded that the Shoshone must live on reservations and learn to become farmers. With the 1863 Treaty of Ruby Valley, the Western Shoshone agreed to end the war and allow the United States access to their land, though they did not formally cede it. The Newe were a flat heterarchy, highly effective for living lightly on the land. But this put them at a disadvantage when dealing with the centralized organization of the pioneer cultures. Still the government sought to acculturate. Shoshone were settled as farmers, and their children sent to distant schools. The explicit aim was that native identity would be crushed. The campaign was long. One of the first actions after the 1933 declaration of the Death Valley National Monument was to force relocation of remaining Timbisha camps. In 1945, the U.S. government conceived of a national policy called *termination*: Indians would be emancipated by assimilating into mainstream America, all in the name of progress. Anyone feel guilty at all?

"It was hard work," says Barbara of the battle for tribal recognition. "We had to shame them to the table." The first round of talks in the mid-nineties failed, and at the launch of another in 1998 the park superintendent baldly stated, "you will never get lands in this area [the park]." It's a common theme across the world: that land is an emergent property of thousands of years of interaction between the people and the place is irrelevant. But then in 2000, President Clinton signed a national act granting them this small reservation.

"We had always gone out to gather," remembers Barbara, and points out of the window toward the high forests, hidden by the raging sandstorm. "Autumn was our favorite time." Up in the cool groves, there was collective celebration and stories. Spring, though, was special for honey mesquite, the wiry ocher pods collected and the beans ground to flour. But now salt cedars are taking over, and young mesquite trees will not grow.

"Now we need more people," says Barbara, gazing again out of the tribal offices. There are only fifty here, just a few families, and numbers do count in the constant negotiation for resources. There are just four kids, and they have to travel sixty miles each way by bus to school. "In the summer, that bus was so hot. No air con. You just hoped you went to sleep." To the south of here is the lowest place in the North Americas, Badwater, at 282 feet below sea level, and uniquely hot. I remembered one evening at Furnace Creek a few years back, when we as a family had stood blinking before the outdoor thermometer that read 115°F in the late evening. It was not just hot, it was an oven. Any activity seemed a struggle, yet we needed to move to create some kind of air movement.

"Yes, like that," says Barbara.

This is why water is the most revered resource, and always was. Yesterday, Barbara found two sandstone pendants and a couple of grinding stones near a spring. They are laid out on cotton wool in a box. Traditional lifeways have not been abandoned, and this gives everyone hope. Pine nuts are gathered, wild foods for medicine, game and fish hunted, willow gathered for baskets and tools, and spiritual healing ceremonies held. There are plans for the reservation—a museum, an inn perhaps. Not a casino, says Barbara. There are hopes for solar and wind power, for attractions to bring in the visitors. Most drive past unknowingly.

"You must go up and look at our grinding stone," urges Barbara, and when we leave we drive back to Furnace Inn perched green on the course of the old stream. In the car park is a sunken pink stone where dancing ceremonies led by *pakwinavi* were held, all night long so much stamping that they created their own dust devils. In this stone are three perfectly circular pits a hand's breadth deep: where the querns were turned and the mesquite ground, and thanks given. Today, there are many parked cars. I am no fan of the interpretation board, but this would be a good place for one. We point to the stone as a pair of visitors with serious cameras walk by, but they shake their heads and walk on, intent only on the rock formations above.

In the small museum down at Furnace Creek, an end wall is devoted to the Indians. A dozen beautiful baskets of willow and grasses illustrate skilled handiwork—cream with black, red, and yellow designs, the dyes from yucca root, willow, sumac, and devil's claw. Tight weaving produces flat plates, parching trays for roasting pine nuts, cradle boards, bowls, necked vessels, and most remarkably the tightest twining for a water vessel, additionally proofed with pinyon resin. In another glass case are nocked stone arrowheads so thin they are translucent. On the floor are two rocks pecked with petroglyphs, geometric patterns that could be a map. This part of the museum is empty; visitors focus on souvenirs of the postindustrial era. In the yard full of carriages and pumps, flatbed trucks, and the sixty-six-ton rusting locomotive that was the last to make the run to Death Valley Junction, we find a gray-green mesquite bush, and I pick up a crescent pod from the ground.

We had thought to camp at Stovepipe, but there was not a single RV at the site, the wind driving so much sand that our teeth and eyes filled with grit. The granules blasted exposed skin. We too retreated back across the valley. At the Devil's Cornfield, the sand tore across the road in laminar flow, submerging bushes, accreting sand dunes. The mountains appeared wrapped in turrets of mist, but it was the air filled with sand, and the sun not a disk but a massive diffracted source of yellow light. Yet we are fortunate, for on the road south on the clear east side of the valley we catch sight of a rock line in the low evening sunlight. Easy to miss at any other time of day or angle of light. We walk far out across rock fields, jump a tiny stream white with encrusted salt, and there, looping over rises and dips, is the single rock line, pointing toward the rising moon. Perhaps toward water too. It's a foot wide, constructed of multiple rocks, and a hundred yards long, and with one perpendicular spur. To the north a single con trail white in the sky echoes this line below. It may be ancient or very new. Nearby Kev finds a slab of orange sandstone lined with the fossils of filamentous plants, and we hold it up to the light.

For an hour at dusk, we kick a ball back and forth. Kev's long been involved with the football scene here. We spent many a Saturday following our clubs when younger, sometimes happy, often miserable. The sky flares fully salmon and orange, and a coyote trots across the salty playa by our tent.

———

Before first light strikes the Panamints, we are brewing tea and making ready. Ravens own these salt flats and mesquite clumps too, their cries widening the land. Furnace Creek airport is 210 feet below sea level; the golf course the lowest too in the world. No green grass anywhere in the valley except here. Water creates this place, diverted away from the Timbisha's mesquite groves. There's a sharp border between golf course and the salty sand. In the low sunlight we come upon another coyote, sitting on haunches, ears pricked, white mouth and chin beneath russet head and piercing eyes. With a kinetic blur of legs, she eases away, bushy tail swinging from side to side. Most people today think of them as cunning and insolent.

The sky by now is flawless blue. The wind has flat died away, the tearing storm blown out. On both sides of the valley the sandblasted mountains rise up clear and majestic. We drive over to meet one of the five tribal elders, Pauline Esteves, Barbara's aunt. We stop on the way at Furnace Creek restaurant for a full breakfast: fry-up, easy-over, grits and all. The tables are populated with Forty-Niners. They're mostly big people in khaki, and we suspect they should be having salads. We, though, clean our plates, and could eat another. Pauline's trailer is painted green, the veranda with latticework along the front. A large mesquite shades one corner, and a knoll of palms is by the track. The ground is all sand. Nothing else grows. We knock and enter. Pauline wears a simple blue dress, and tells stories from her armchair. Her wrinkled face often cracks with a deep laugh, eyes tightly closed, gray-white hair combed from a parting above her left eye. The sun shines on the floor, and she has a flyswatter close at hand. On the wall by the kitchen are pictures of bald eagles.

"I am the oldest here now," she smiles, head tipped to one side, her eighty-five-year-old hands clasped on her lap. She's part reflective and wistful, but also angry. Piles of official reports cover chairs and the desk. A plaque with her name handwritten is propped against the wall. "It is up to the tribe to stand up for ourselves," she says.

We talk of water. There is a lot in the desert, if you treat it well. There are two hundred natural springs in Death Valley: not that you'd know it without local knowledge. Miners on arrival identified the best springs, and promptly used them up. She remembers the days before the spring was diverted for the inn, motel, and golf course; it flowed across the surface from up on the hillside. They wanted the water first for the gas station, and then the first aid post, the doctor and nurse flying in periodically.

"That was neat, we all used that facility." But now there's not enough to keep their deep-rooting mesquite alive. "It was lush and cool in those groves when we harvested in the early mornings." Water to the Timbisha was not simply a resource or commodity. It contains the most powerful of spirits.

"You never misuse water," Pauline says, "and never go to the source. It is bad to walk right in and use water without asking." They first acknowledge the creator, and before drinking, they would sprinkle some on the land. Its healing properties are deep. Water in the desert also perfumes the air, changes temperature, gives places extra significance. "Once my aunt forgot to ask for acknowledgment. Her and another woman walked up to a spring, and the spirit rose up and gushed into the air, and they rushed back. They knew they had failed in some way."

We settle in deep, the sun shining brightly, and talk about hunting deer and sheep. This also requires a proper approach to the land. "We'd go and camp out, build a fire so the spirits of the birds and animals would know we were there. It's surprising, you build a fire, and the birds will come." We know, thinking of the ravens we have met. And some people had the gift to call the animals. "Animals would offer themselves to us, if everything was right." Pauline's mother and aunt had this gift. They would gather watercress in spring, and would call in the deer too. Hunters sometimes whistle to bring in the spirits of the land. But Pauline doesn't know how, women being only allowed to whistle when calling for a winnowing wind.

The most important desert character is coyote, whose stories are key to defining moral behavior. Stories, indeed, are not just happenings. They locate the present in past events, and those events dictate behaviors. Above all, they indicate right and wrong. Coyote is the trickster, like the wolverine of the northern forests.

"When we see coyote crossing the road" points Pauline, "we'll say, there he goes; he's supposed to be our father, but what a father! He's always teaching us." Generally, wolf's younger brother, coyote, was the contradictory being representing both good and bad. As he was cunning, the Newe told their children, "don't be like coyote."[4]

Many stories expose pride: coyote is tempted to look down into water, but terrible things happen when you adore your own image. "Pride is like a sin to us," observes Pauline. Coyote once mocked a bird about flying, and sun helped him build his own wings, but then melted them when he flew too high, to show that pride was bad. Over the hills on the Amargosa flats is a place they call the Brains, says Pauline, nodding east. This is where coyote ate his own brains. The story relates to pregnant women, who never say anything about the baby: "You don't even talk of it: it is so sacred." When the baby is born, the chord is put in a particular place on the land: near plants if a girl, near an animal trail if a boy, so that they may become good gatherers and hunters.

Stories are also tied to intaglios, rock lines in alluvial fans, stones piled to indicate paths to pine nuts or water, rock piles to attract chuckwallas, which were caught and eaten. The greatest density of petroglyphs are in the eastern Panamints, confirms Pauline. There are sun symbols, water, rain, meandering lines and linked parallel lines. Petroglyphs near springs are no surprise. "There's quite a few of those [petroglyphs]. There were certain rocks for identification, for signs, pointing to water. They would place the rocks in a certain way for migratory paths. There would be others up in the mountains for the best pine nuts. There's monuments all over the place—but some are modern practices from visitors. We take those apart."

"I was taught as a child to go out and gather willows," remembers Pauline. "They had to be soft, not brittle."

The sun has moved, as have the shadows on the floor. We are talking of basketry, made from willow twines, others from coiled grasses wrapped over sumac or willow. She made her first basket with a zigzag pattern, but her mother said she had to give the basket to the land. She said, go and wedge it there between two boulders. Animals will use it. Her second basket she gave to a friend. "There was this little white girl, and we were friends. I had no dolls, and admired hers. When the basket was complete, my friend liked it. We traded basket for doll."

Now, though, she needs the time to prepare for the Forty-Niners. Each year they have a taco stall, and sell to visitors.

"They've got to be made with Indian hands. No secret ingredients. Just our own hands." The Forty-Niners do say they're the best they've ever tasted, states Pauline.

We stand on the shaded veranda. Pauline recalls how nuclear weapons were air-tested over on Yucca Mountain and Area 51 on the Nevada side. The growling rumble, the tumbled rush outdoors, and the sight of the great mushroom cloud billowing over the crumpled Amargosa Mountains. "We could feel the ground shake. The houses were creaking. There was this big cloud. . . . It was yellowish-sun-clay, a dirty-clay, cloud color."

Because the Shoshone were not a registered tribe, they were not counted by the Department of Energy as *down-winders* of the 100 atmospheric and 928 underground nuclear tests. Thus no compensation. Today, the sky is clear, and we gaze up at the jagged edge of Murgu, also known as Telescope Peak. Beyond the house, a car is settled on axles in the sand, all the windows gone. We stand together and gaze at the land.

Next spring Barbara e-mailed an update. A fire burned along the highway by the inn, clearing underbrush and killing hundreds of imported palm trees. A little bit of land had been made healthy again. She said, "The wild flowers aren't as spectacular as years past, but they're still lovely. The mesquite trees are blooming and have turned a real pretty green."

—⟨⟨⟨⟩⟩⟩—

Today, what we see in this landscape is not as it was. It was degraded by mining that used vast amounts of water and wood. These are hard lessons. Minerals without cheap water, energy, and transport do not give a good return. Dreams of immeasurable wealth drew in the hopeful, and investors parted with their capital with remarkable abandon. Pocket miners carried samples of ore to the stock exchanges of San Francisco, Chicago, and New York, and by spinning stories got rich quickly. The romance of remoteness was an asset, for few investors could be bothered to check claims in person. Capitalism drove mining, and the clever realized you got rich by selling dreams, not ore.

Then the Panamints became famous. In the 1870s, they became known as *a wonder of the world*, and attracted vast investments. In eighteen months, a settlement sprang up, and by 1875 Panamint with its two thousand people had become the largest town for a hundred miles. Senators John Jones and William Stewart of Nevada used their influence to inflate the bubble. They constructed a twenty-stamp mill one thousand feet above the valley floor, and a one-mile supply pipe for water. Panamint was served by three stage lines daily, to and from Bakersfield, Lone Pine, and Los Angeles. The town had two banks, three doctors, four lawyers, several general stores, butcher, barbershop, bankers, assayers, boutique, and the *Panamint News*. But up in Wildrose, one silver mine's furnace consumed three thousand bushels of charcoal daily. The Modock Company built ten beehive kilns in the spring of 1877, twenty-five feet high and thirty in diameter. Each held forty-two cords of pine, some 90–130 tons of wood. They burned slowly for a week, each producing two thousand bushels of charcoal. Forty men were employed to cut trees from one to two miles around the kilns. But just a year later, the Modock ore was finished, and the kilns abandoned. By now Panamint itself was imploding. A House committee in Washington had begun investigations into false sales of silver in England, and suddenly Jones and Stewart could sell no more stock. Their Ponzi scheme collapsed, and so did the town.

Oddly borax created more wealth than silver or gold. Sodium tetraborate was used for the manufacture of detergent, disinfectant, water softener, weed killer, fertilizer, and insulators. The Eagle and Harmony Borax works opened in the early 1880s, and led to the famed twenty-mule-team wagons, giant operations each pulling thirty-three tons of borax, and making a 330-mile round trip in twenty days. Yet by 1888, these teamster operations had ceased too. There were other frenzies. Copper in the hills near Furnace Creek led to the towns of Greenwater and Copperfield, for whom water had to be hauled eighteen miles overland from Furnace Creek. A hundred mining companies were formed, and $250 million of stock was sold before any ore was removed from the ground. But Greenwater declined and dissolved, as did others.

All this time, the mythology about Death Valley grew. It was a "death pit . . . from which there is no escape," wrote one commentator. "This is the dominion of death," said another. The editor of *Scientific American* commented on the valley's awful "climatic violence" and lamented that "no man could survive there long enough to secure continuous observations." The wood having been used up, gasoline came to the rescue in the 1890s. To this point, no one had even thought of tourists. The Stovepipe Wells Hotel was opened in 1926, then the Furnace Creek Inn. John Thorndike dreamed of building a hotel up on the top of Telescope, but settled on tourist cabins at Mahogany Flats. Annual visitors to Death Valley grew from ten thousand in the early 1930s to half a million by the 1980s, and then to near one million now. The hell-hole became a tourist paradise, and probably saved the region from becoming more military bases, weapons centers, test sites.

⊸⫘⟡⫘⟞

In the desert, animal life is often hard to come by. Mostly the land is quiet, secretive, apparently resting, but then a coyote trots across the playa, head swinging from side to side. Ravens in the morning and evening narrate our every move. One attacks a jackrabbit as I stand to watch the sun creep up, swooping and scattering the rabbit, giving silent and deliberate chase across the flats. We begin the climb down at Badwater, where the heavy air fills the wide valley and the light is blinding where the alluvial fans meet wide salt pans. There are two hundred square miles of salt playa, desiccation cracks, drying and shrinking muds, polygons and salt wedges. It is constantly mobile. Capillary rise of salt can burst wooden posts set in the ground, and raise up and shatter muds. From a distance it looks flat. But this is another illusion. Beyond the patch of standing water that houses endemic Badwater snails and pickleweed, water spirits too, is the harsh saltscape of sharp crusts that could rip feet to ribbons.

Painted on the rocks far above is a white line indicating sea level. The clear blue pool reflects hills as well as sky. When it does rain, every few years, the pans are covered briefly with standing water, soon driven off to leave salts behind. In places are perfect hexagonal patterns formed by alternate freezing and thawing, and in others miles of crumpled fractal hills that are no more than a foot high but could easily be a continental mountain range. The ground has been shattered, forced up by tectonic movements, salt creating filamentous networks and accreted around slabs. I lie down, and it is a brown and white sea frozen in stormy conditions. Silent waves in a dry land. In some places the gray and white salt is several feet thick, elsewhere it is dangerously thin above sucking muds. The silence booms across the valley, and we walk out further, deeper, a mile or more, soon becoming thirsty. We'd like to continue, for Telescope and the foothills of the Panamints are ahead of us. But distance is hard to judge in the heavy air: "Who in the desert has not spent his day riding at a mountain and never even reaching its base," asked John van Dyke. Instead, we walk up Golden Canyon to the red cathedral of iron oxide. Beyond is a single white cloud of feathery cirrus in the shape of a mushroom. In the baked canyon, we find not a single plant. We were letting time be curved rather than linear.

Kev and I intend to climb Telescope Peak, the highest point in the Death Valley park and Panamints. We are apprehensive. It's not so high on a global scale, but it is top of this land. On its slopes are forests of pinyons and juniper, above them ancient bristlecone pines, the oldest living beings on the planet. The approach, though, is roundabout, a sixty-mile drive from Badwater basin to the camp on the far side of the range. First we go in search of ephemerality. In such an ancient landscape, everything modern was short-lived: Wildrose, Harmony Borax, Panamint town. Individual bristlecones have looked down on thousands of years of cultural adaptation to this desert environment, watching too the mining towns briefly flare and gutter out. We cross the Funeral Mountains, and pass over a high plateau of perfectly equidistant creosote bushes and slip back into Nevada. At the base of the first hills are slopes where emerged the famed towns of Bullfrog and Rhyolite.

On August 4, 1904, prospectors Frank "Shorty" Harris and Ed Cross found gold bedded in green quartz on a hill they then called Bullfrog, and staked their claims. Shorty went on a six-day bender, selling half his claim for drink. His loose talk caused a dramatic rush. Twenty-five years later, he recalled, "I've seen some gold rushes in my time, but nothing like that stampede. Men were leaving town in a steady stream with buckboards, buggies, wagons and burros. . . . Timekeepers, clerks, waiters and cooks—they all got the fever and milled around, wildeyed, trying to get to the new strike." Within two weeks, the population of the new town of Rhyolite ballooned to twelve hundred, and to twenty-five hundred by mid-1905, by which time there were fifty saloons, sixteen restaurants, and public baths offering *all kinds of baths, massage and manicuring.* The main street of Golden was choked with traffic; four daily stages connected the region, including to Las Vegas 120 miles away.

Two hundred Bullfrog companies were floated. *Buy Bullfrog shares and watch them jump,* said the publicity. *The Greatest Gold Discovery of Modern Times,* claimed another. Pittsburgh steel magnate Charley Schwab put in an eleven-mile water pipeline, contracted electricity supply from the Sierra Nevada one hundred miles away, and brought in the first railhead from Las Vegas. By 1907, four thousand people lived in Rhyolite, which now had telephone, an ice plant, a water main, three railroads, a daily newspaper, an opera house, school, bank, and its own stock exchange. With electric lights on every corner, Rhyolite must have lit up the desert like Vegas does today. There was an active civil society. The nine-hundred-strong Bonanza Miners Union opened the district's first hospital, offering health care to its members for one dollar a month. There were unions of carpenters, joiners, electrical workers, newspaper boys; then too the Arcade Opera House, pool and tennis tournaments, basketball games, and a bookstore. But Panamint Joe, one of the last *pakwinavi,* predicted at the time, "Someday white man gone, Indian sleep here."

It was distant stock markets that spelled the end, again. Schwab's mine produced gold, but no payments were made to shareholders. Over three years, the value of shares fell to a tenth; then an independent analyst announced the mine was *distinctly unfavorable*, and stock crashed. The mine closed with shares at four cents apiece. Rhyolite itself was now in trouble. Other mines failed, and residents departed. By 1910, only six hundred remained, and then the bank failed and the newspaper shut down. The last train ran in 1914, and the Nevada-California Power Company turned off the lights and took away the power lines.

This day, we walk past the facades of bank and school, past the narrow hand-dug mines of this brief settlement. Rhyolite's pride was the John S. Cook Bank, a three-story, four-floor concrete building, with locks on its vaults, Italian marble stairs, stained-glass windows, and Honduran mahogany trim. It had electric lights and steam heating, the post office in the basement. I pick up the rusted top of a tin embossed with lettering: *satisfaction guaranteed, not bite tongue.* Alcohol in a tin. A cold wind whistles across the plateau, and in the distance straight lines mark trails into the valley and toward passes over the Amargosa. There are dozens of rattlesnake holes in the stony ground. Today, the ghost town's remains are before us, the grand rail station at the top of the windblown hill. In the main street, I turn around slowly; in the ruins of the bank the floor joists are long gone, and the whole building is open to the sky. At the front, tall empty windows give upon what was once the busy street. On the corner of Golden and Esmeralda, a bristly tarantula picks slowly across the stones, its limbs black and brown. I put down a quarter for sizing, and it looks tiny by the spider. The old schoolhouse is complete with four walls, two stories of windows but no floors. The fascia is cracked, the door with two fine timbers framing a view across to the Amargosa and Panamints beyond.

Behind the general stores, H. D. and L. D. Porter written over the door, are hundreds of mine shafts to the underworld. Where now live more spiders, scorpions, and rattlesnakes; where once men dug and burned their hopes in the search for gold. We walk over sprawling middens of rusted tin cans, thousands flattened, broken, some of later welded design, some originals. Ghosts of writing hint at meats, soups, more alcoholic drinks, oysters. Belt buckles, kitchen ware, ribbed tins, cans with handles. Too precious to pick, too precious not to pick.[5] Geologist Charles Hunt observed: "Abandoned mines possess a certain romantic fascination . . . yet an active, productive mine is regarded as lower than a burro." One hundred years of slow absorption into the land lies before us.

We complete our delaying tactics, and head back toward the Panamints. We are hedging: being there is what matters rather than getting to the top. On the mountain, though, this will change. At Stovepipe Wells we buy supplies, take a refreshing shower, and fill up with water. I find deet has leaked and eaten right through a bag, melting it like a fire. I throw it all away, an action I later regretted in the swamps of the South. We drive through sweeping Emigrant Canyon and twist thirty miles over more plateaus, past the ghost town of Skidoo, and up Windrose to arrive at Thorndike camp while the sun is still bright. We camp by sagey chaparral in a narrow, steep valley of pinyon and juniper. All the juniper are infected with mistletoe, giving them a pale yellow cast. I sit on a fallen log to read, and Kev walks with guitar and spreads music over the meadows. The shadows advance across the steep hillsides. Sunlight flares in the grasses and wildflowers. The air is quite still. There seems nothing left to do but wait. In the forest will be mule deer and mountain lion, bobcat, fox, and coyote. On the scratchy tops, rare bighorns. We're marking time. We ready the fire for the evening. No more of those wild days of felling for charcoal kilns. Now we carry everything in, and take out what is not burned or eaten. The pale pine in the fire pit has been cut and plastic-wrapped in British Columbia. The lettering is in Spanish; *100% natural*, it states. Something is not quite right.

The sun drops across the slope, and suddenly we are inside cool shadow. The temperature plummets. Sunset floods the sky with mauve and rose. In deserts, each day is made by dawn and dusk. We are at seventy-four hundred feet, and tonight it will be cold. While there is a gray light in the sky, we decide to walk the mile up to Mahogany Flats, the start of the summit trail. The moon is up, chasing Jupiter. Through the dark woods we can see across Death Valley. Beyond the hills is a grid of neon light on a plain, the sodium wash of Vegas, twinkling across the desert. Modern civilization has chased us here, consuming all. We trudge back in the silvery moonlight that casts dark shadows, lights our way too, and then sit around the spluttering fire to eat and wait yet more, flickering shadows dancing in the thin resinous air. We're not high enough for ancient bristlecones, but still the night freezes our drinking water. Up here trees are squeezed into a narrow band: below six to eight thousand feet, summer heat and drought are too severe; at higher altitudes it is too cold and windy.

We rise as light begins to wash the east. The empty skies promise warmth, but you never know at this time of year. There may be blizzards. The boiled coffee is only warm in the thin air, and we're off up the same road as the previous evening. Above Mahogany, the pinyons and mountain mahogany grade into open hillsides, and now we can see down to Badwater, across the whole of Nevada too. The ridges of hills are blue against the sun this very morning. We gaze into canyons and their shadowy depths where the mountain air is so dense that it seems to have something of the sea in it, as van Dyke put it. Once, of course, these woods would have been full of Timbisha harvesting pinyon, living the summer and autumn above the blistering heat of the valley floor. The trail continues steeply, and we come upon the first of the resinous bristlecones in the high chaparral buzzing with grasshoppers.

As we climb, the sun does not seem to rise above our horizontal. My lips will be chapped and face burned by the end of the day. We had been the first on the trail, but gradually pairs of climbers stride by, mostly younger but then one old and lean and as grizzled as a bristlecone. It's nice to know we're not alone on the mountains, but faintly dispiriting as they all surge on. The sun warms the trail, and we unzip jackets. Beyond the Panamints is the line of jagged white that is the Sierra Nevada eighty to a hundred miles distant. Ahead the rocky trail sweeps over flats and then across slippery slopes, around minor peaks.

Telescope looms, simply looking far too steep. Vertigo could be a problem. Our minds play games. Emotions soar and fall. We walk an hour across flats and saddles, and seem to get no closer. Then a slope of switchbacks brings the peak suddenly and alarmingly closer. We stop to investigate these special pines that seem to have the edge on us. White healthy bark, red striated wood where the bark has parted, a natural dieback strategy to save water, focus nutrients, and limit exposure to lightning and fire. They are weather-beaten, wind-and-ice-scoured like driftwood, drifting up here, nine thousand feet and more above sea level. Other trunks corkscrew, as if the very land has turned sharply and twisted these ancient giants under the cornflower sky. I wanted to climb down to one; its trunk must be twenty-five or more feet in circumference. Perhaps it's close to the individual record of forty-eight hundred years of age, but a slip and it's a few thousand feet down into Hanaupah Canyon.

The final climb rears up, and the altitude is playing games. Oxygen seems hard to obtain. We are on the eastern slopes and the trail jags sharply through the thinning trees, then we reach the last saddle and the view to the Sierra Nevada opens up and we feel we can see half the continent. We clamber across scree and stand on the peak. Clusters of walkers are here already, eating, chatting. To the west, Panamint valley and its lines of stones, where we will walk tonight in the dark and lose our car, and beyond the Inyo and snow-covered Whitney. To the east, Vegas marked even today by a haze of dust, and beyond purple lines of mountains striding across the land. We can see a hundred miles in every direction. Thirty thousand square miles of territory before us. Below is Badwater still, trembling with phantoms. Up here, the light is crystalline.

Summits make temporary friends of people. We talk to fellow climbers, and gaze down upon dry Southern California and its 8,800 square miles of no-go lands: Nellis Air Force Range, Ridgemarsh, China Lake Naval Station containing ten thousand petroglyphs, Fort Irwin to the southwest; to the east, the Nevada Test Site. At the peak both of us are battered and burned. You go through many emotions on a mountain: each is engraved on your soul. We rest for an hour, and head back on the eight-mile trail. We skip past the bristlecones, then the downside, a long walk that feels desperate at times. But as the light is bleeding from the sky again, we slide into the pinyon forests and are striding again down to the camp. We sweated and drank so much that we would have to change plan again. Even if tightly rationed, we would not have enough water. We are thirsty, and have to leave. The row of beehive kilns is in deep shadow as we pass. Inside, people have camped, made fires, left detritus. Great skill went into their construction, the two-foot-thick rock walls tapered to an apex. The low sun fires up the hills of Emigrant, then the moon rises.

We stop to watch the sunset. The mountain will have been a savior of Kev. He decides to give up smoking, and succeeds.

Down on the Panamint flats, we search again for the stone lines. Far from the road they remain in place, but near the blacktop they have been shuffled. If they are ancient, they should be left alone. Some have been formed into circles, spirals, and names. By now the stars above the flats are glittering. The playa shimmers mercury under the gibbous moon, hanging over the Telescope and smiling on the land. We continue further into the playa, and smile now ourselves. We are tired after nine hours of walking on the mountain, but down here is a kind of magic. It warps time and space, makes us want to stay forever in the wrecked perspective of the desert.

We come back to the road, and promptly realize we have lost the car. It's not possible. Just this one straight road across the playa. We walk west, and can't find it. Retrace our steps. Worry mounts. This is mad. And then, there it is, parked at the base of the hills. The desert changes so much in the mind. In Lone Pine, the shower is hot, and the late-night food satisfying. The next day we swing over the Sierras at Yosemite, and reacquaint with humanity and the parkland that John Muir championed.

"A world without wilderness is a cage," predicted Abbey, and there is some wildness in the relationship between people and the land. It is not separation. Pauline Esteves reminded us, "The Timbisha people have lived on our homeland forever, and we'll live here forever. We are people of the land." Edward Abbey's other plea works too: "Stay out of here. Don't go. Stay home and read a good book. . . . Even if you survive, which is not certain, you will have a miserable time." But our greatest danger is that society may reach a point where too few people see the planet as worth preserving. We humans make sacrifices for what we love, not for rational or material ends.

We come back in the dark again, across the bridge to the seven-by-seven-mile city bright with lights and tall buildings. The next morning at dawn, the Pacific swell drives rollers crashing onto the empty Ocean Beach, and hazy salt spray fills the air.

So much water. We sit and drink our coffee.

That's the way it was that morning.

CODA
Dreaming of the Day After

Sun rises again.

It was cooler.

There were many people, but they seemed happier. Afraid it could all fall apart, but hoping it might not. There was much history to make, many paths to walk.

The barbarians had come, welcomed inside the city walls. Inventors had decarbonized economies, allowing consumers to buy goods and services that only improved the planet.

Black gold was long finished. It had been a century and a half of miraculously cheap energy that was easy to transport. It had blackened the sky, expanded the oceans, melted ice. But science did have solutions, turning to light, waves, wind, and plants for energy, packing it up, transferring it, which now all drove the environment-economy.

The short experiment in fat carriage was over. But it had taken transformation of living and working space to ensure such regular physical activity so that now gyms were only populated by those planning sporting glory, rather than the guilty. Calories in food mattered less now that more were being burned off. Tofu and hamburgers were both fine. New personalized medical treatments had helped too. There was enough for food for those formerly hungry. Humans were all walking, far and often.

No one talked of the economy anymore. People called it the environment. Growth in gross domestic product meant people had on average more, but so did the planet. There had been a grand rapprochement between science and religions, whether formal institutions or animist spirituality. Instead of distrust, there had grown an appreciation of similar aims regarding human and planetary well-being. Diversity of cultures and beliefs had come to be valued; everyone was right, everyone was wrong.

None of this had meant the end to pain. Or of disagreement. Each place was the center of the world, the best there could be. Communication had become immanent. It built linkages and relationships, encouraged more gatherings and rituals in the physical world as well as in the virtual. Someone realized that giving made people more happy than taking. Time spent helping others, people, animals, the planet, became a valued currency, and no longer a distraction from consuming. Thoreau long ago argued that wealth should be calculated not by how much we own but by how much free time we have.

As a result, people had come to value things that used to have no monetary value. Sitting in nature was known to benefit mental health, so was encouraged. Growing food and flowers was satisfying for children and adults. Walks in the country or visits to the beach were no longer seen as escapes from another busy stressful life. They were life itself.

People paused. And stopped. Took ten breaths. And ten more. Looked around, noting changes from day to day, hour to hour.

Mind met land.

Each day: sun rose, and then sun set. Dreams arrived, then receded.

And so it ends.

NOTES

PREFACE

1. On happiness and well-being see Frank 1999, Kasser 2002, Nettle 2005, Layard 2006, Wilkinson and Pickett 2009. See also Action for Happiness, www.actionforhappiness.org.

2. A variety of recent books and reports have drawn attention to the impacts of consumption on the planet: Tim Jackson's *Prosperity without Growth* (2009); Lawrence Smith's *The New North* (2010); and the Royal Society's *People and the Planet* (2012). See also my 2007 book *The Earth Only Endures*, and my 2013 paper "The Consumption of a Finite Planet," in *Environmental and Resource Economics* 55, 475–99. For a narrative on extinction see Challenger 2011, and on collapse see Diamond 2005. David Ehrenfield (2005) has warned that the current form of globalization is "creating an environment that will prove hostile to its own survival."

3. Zen emphasizes the objective of avoiding the many false dichotomies into which we separate the world. This suggests the need for a both-and language rather than either-or, whether referring to technologies (modern, traditional), time (past, future), choices (good, bad). The references contain a list of key books that helped to shape this book, and include those by Aitken, Bashō, Dogen, Govinda, Kapleau, Matthiessen, Santoka, and Snyder. See also poet and gardener Stanley Kunitz's *The Wild Braid* (2005), and Donald Christie's *Blue Sapphire of the Mind* (2013).

4. In *Wisdom of the Mythtellers*, Sean Kane has suggested that myths that evolve in sympathy with nature are different from myths that compete with it.

5. On journeys and paths see list in references, in particular by Robin Hanbury-Tenison, Richard Long, Robert Macfarlane, W. G. Sebald, Iain Sinclair, and Rebecca Solnit.

1. SEACOAST: NGĀI TAHU, AOTEAROA (NEW ZEALAND)

1. For more on sea navigation see Lewis 1972, Gooley 2010, and the comprehensive *Encyclopedia of New Zealand* 2006.

2. For more on Ngāi Tahu tribe see http://www.ngaitahu.iwi.nz/; and on the Centre for Sustainability: Agriculture, Food, Energy, Environment at the University of Otago see http://www.otago.ac.nz/phonebook/dep-csafe.html.

3. For scientific papers by Henrik Moller and colleagues on *māturanga*, *tītī* shearwaters, and climate change see Newman et al. 2009, Moller et al. 2009, Stephenson and Moller 2009, Moller et al. 2010. See also Pretty 2011 for a summary.

4. This line is from Thomas Hardy's *In Time of "The Breaking of Nations"*: Only a man harrowing clods / In a slow silent walk / With an old horse that stumbles and nods / Half asleep as they stalk. / Only thin smoke without flame / From the heaps of couch-grass; / Yet this will go onward the same / Though Dynasties pass.

2. MOUNTAIN: HUANGSHAN, CHINA

1. See Rob Macfarlane's *The Old Ways* (2012) for an account of walking to Minya Konka.
2. The emergence of *shanshui* mountain and water style of landscape painting is well-described in Lin Ci's *The Art of Chinese Painting* (2006).
3. Bashō's haiku on Mount Fuji begins his travel sketch *The Records of a Weather-Exposed Skeleton*, published in *Narrow Road to the Deep North* (1966).
4. For an account of Zen master Dogen's life and work see Tanahashi 1985. For more on the wilderness and cloud poetry of China see Red Pine and O'Connor 1998 and Hinton 2002. Santoka Taneda's *Mountain Tasting* journals contain many fine haiku of the mountains, water, and clouds.
5. See Geoffrey Daniel's haiku: A bitter rain / Two silences / Beneath one umbrella. See Hardy 2002.

3. DESERT COAST: MURUJUGA (BURRUP), AUSTRALIA

1. For a comprehensive archaeological and historical account of the Burrup-Murujuga see Caroline Bird and Sylvia Hallam's 2006 report for the National Trust of Australia (WA).
2. For more on the excellent work of Deborah Bird Rose see *Dingo Makes Us Human* (2000), and *Nourishing Terrains* (1996).
3. On solastalgia see Albrecht et al. 2007 and Albrecht 2010.
4. Bruce Chatwin (1998) called them songlines; Sean Kane (1998) prefers the term mythlines. See also Tim Ingold's *Lines* (2007).

4. STEPPE: TUVA, RUSSIA

1. On spelling and pronunciation: here I use the spelling Tuva, as it is pronounced "Touva" or "Tuva." The local spelling is correctly Tyva. The Way of the White Cloud is a Buddhist theme: see Govinda 1966 for journeys through Tibet.
2. For a comprehensive history of Siberia see Haywood 2010. Both Colin Thubron (1999) and Anna Reid (2002) visit Tuva as part of travels through Siberia, but neither is much impressed.
3. Ted Levin's 2006 account of Tuva's *khöömei* throat-singing is comprehensive and compelling. The music emerges from the land and the elements.
4. The most famous "deer stone" is on the steppe at Ushkin Uver in Mongolia: see Aruz et al. 2006, 188.
5. The best anthropological account of Tuva is by Sevyan Vainshtein, *Nomads of South Siberia* (1980). Vainshtein appears in Ralph Leighton's famed book about Richard Feynman's desire to know more about and even visit Tuva during the period of the Cold War.
6. Many photographs of Scythian gold are on the Internet—see especially the Hermitage exhibition at http://www.hermitagemuseum.org/html_En/03/hm3_10-1_00.html. See also the website of Friends of Tuva at http://www.fotuva.org/history/archaeology.html. The famed kurgan site of Filippovka in the southern Urals is described in full in Aruz et al. 2006. The stags of Filippovka are twenty-six enigmatic figurines from the main kurgan, made of wood overlaid with gold and silver.
7. Wallace Stegner's *Wolf Willow* (1962) account of life on the North American prairies includes reference to the "mythic light in which we have bathed our frontiersmen."

8. To listen to the folk music and throat singing of Chirgilchin see their website at http://www.chirgilchin.com/, where there are embedded videos. The members are Aldar Tandyn, Igor Koshkendey, Mongün-ool Mongush Mirage, and Aidysmaa Koshkendey.

5. SNOW: KARELIA, FINLAND

1. The Snowchange Cooperative links communities of the Arctic together to share pride in long-standing cultural practices, and to develop common approaches to the threat of climate change. See Helander and Mustonen 2009 and Mustonen and Mustonen 2011. See http://www.snowchange.org/.
2. See Keith Bosley's 1989 English translation of *The Kalevala*. Roger Cook's *Tree of Life* (1974) comprehensively presents the cultural importance of trees.
3. For Farley Mowat's accounts of the de-peopling of the Canadian Barrens see *People of the Deer* (1951) and *Walking on the Land* (2000). Hugh Brody's magisterial accounts of the North are in *Maps and Dreams* (1981) and *The Other Side of Eden* (2001).

6. SWAMP: OKAVANGO, BOTSWANA

1. Po Chu-i (772–846) initiated a strand of Chinese poetry that resulted in an interiorization of wilderness (Hinton 2002). The quote is from "Waves Shifting Sand": "A day will no doubt come when dust flies at the bottom of seas / and how can mountaintops avoid the transformation to gravel?"
2. See references to research of Joe Mbaiwa (2005 a, b) and Maitseo Bolaane (2004, 2005) for the Moremi and the Okavango.
3. There are some 30,000 protected areas worldwide, accounting for 8.83% of the world's land area. Of the 7,322 protected areas in developing countries, where many local people still require wild resources for some or all of their livelihoods, 25% are strictly protected in Asia and the Pacific, 28% in Africa, and 40% in Latin America. Some seven million square kilometers are strictly protected. This is a huge area of land from which people are actively excluded. See my *Agri-Culture* (2002) for a discussion on exclusions. See also Bill Adams's *Future Nature* (1996).
4. Laurens van der Post traveled through what is now Botswana in search of so-called lost Bushmen, beginning in the northwest at Chobe and journeying through the Kalahari and Okavango. His accounts and later film drew important attention to the losses the San had suffered.
5. San is a term preferred by San organizations, Basarwa is the official term used in Botswana, and Bushmen tends to be used to describe events and people in the past.
6. For more on the San of the CKGR see Silberbauer 1981 and Lee and Daly, *The Cambridge Encyclopedia of Hunters and Gatherers* (1999). The Survival International website contains many accounts of the San's court actions and subsequent return to the CKGR. See http://www.survivalinternational.org/.
7. See Harry Sharp (1987) for an article on the apparently irrational beliefs of the Chipewyan.

7. MARSH-FARM: EAST ANGLIA, ENGLAND

1. The 1953 floods killed 308 people in the east of the UK on January 31. See Hilda Grieve's *The Great Tide* (1959) for a dramatic account of the long day, night, and subsequent weeks. A chapter in my *This Luminous Coast* (2011) is devoted to the floods.
2. William Dutt visited Breydon in his *Norfolk and Suffolk Coast* (1910).

3. For accounts of P. H. Emerson's life and photographs see McWilliam and Sekules (1986), and Ronald Blythe's essay in *Field Work* (2007).

4. For Patterson, see his *Wildfowlers and Poachers* (1929), and his granddaughter's edited volume, *Tooley* (2004).

5. Three accounts of gypsy life and culture are important: Isabel Fonseca's *Bury Me Standing* (2006) is mainly on the life of continental Europe's communities, and Fraser 1995 and Clark and Greenfields 2006 mainly address life in Britain. See Hugh Brody's *The Other Side of Eden* (2002) for a fresh perspective on the settled and the nomadic.

6. See Deanna Walker's *Basildon Plotlands* (2001) for a personal account.

7. See Morrison 1900 for the life of Cunning Murrell, and Davies 2003 for more on the role of magic, wizard, and witches in English life. Wentworth Day's story of one of the last hunter and gatherers of coastal Essex is in his *Marshland Adventure* (1950).

8. Samuel Bensusan wrote more than five hundred stories set on the Dengie Peninsula of Essex. See his *A Marshland Omnibus* (1954) for a collection.

8. COAST: ANTRIM GLENS, NORTHERN IRELAND

1. There are many guides to the myths and stories of the Antrim coast and its nine glens: Sheane 2010, Donnelly 2000, S. Watson 2004, McAuley 2000, P. Watson 2000. See Young 1910 for more on the role of Celtic tales and myths in all Ireland.

2. I am very grateful to the Larne and District Folklore Society for making me an honorary member.

3. For a fine account of life close to the land across the border in Ireland see Tim Robinson's *Connemara* (2006).

4. The 1953 great winds and floods brought disaster to Northern Ireland and Scotland, when the MV *Princess Victoria* sank with great loss of life. See Hunter 1999, Cameron 2002, and my *This Luminous Coast* (2011).

9. SNOW: NITASSINAN, LABRADOR, CANADA

1. For direct accounts of the lives and history of the Innu see Samson 2003, 2013, sections of Brody 1981, 2002, and Henriksen 2009. The Innu Nation's *Gathering Voices* (1994) contains many rich stories of people's lives from both villages. The website of the Tshikapisk Foundation is particularly rich with images and stories—see http://www.tshikapisk.ca/home/. Barry Lopez's *Arctic Dreams* (1986) remains by far one of the best books about the Arctic and its land, people, and nature.

2. See Meldrum 2006 and Buhs 2009 for differing views on the presence of the sasquatch in the lower American latitudes. See also Peter Matthiessen's *The Snow Leopard* (1978) for observations on the yeti of Tibet. Yuri Rytkheu, in *A Dream in Polar Fog* (2005), makes observations on the *tery'ky* changelings of Siberia. Richard Nelson (1983) reports on the wild men of Alaska, and Georg Henriksen (2009) records Innu hunter Kaniuekutat's own stories about Katshimaitsheshiu.

10. FARM-CITY: AMISH COUNTRY, OHIO

1. See Donald Kraybill's *The Riddle of Amish Culture* (1989, 2001) for an account of culture and history, and David Kline's *Great Possessions* (1990) for stories about farming and nature.

Farming Magazine is published quarterly and contains many articles by small farmers from both Amish and non-Amish communities.

2. For the work of Oberlin's David Orr see Orr's *Design on the Edge* (2006) and *Environmental Literacy* (1993).

3. There are as yet no accounts of the effects of the credit crunch on urban America. Jane Jacobs saw some of this coming in 1961, and Mark Davis sees the downfall of cities in *Dead Cities* (2002). Christopher Woodward's *In Ruins* (2002) addresses the nature of city decline in history.

4. On rural Ohio and small farms see Gene Logsdon's *The Contrary Farmer* (1994) and Louis Bromfield's classic *Malabar Farm* (1948).

11. SWAMP: ATCHAFALAYA BASIN, LOUISIANA

1. See Denevan 1976 for detailed analysis of the native population of the Americas at contact. For powerful and comprehensive studies of the impacts since see James Wilson's *The Earth Shall Weep* (1998), and Dee Brown's *Bury My Heart at Wounded Knee* (1970).

2. On the Cajun people and history see Brasseaux 2005.

3. On swamps and southern culture see A. Wilson 2006. On the bayous and swamps of Louisiana, and the management of water, see Reuss 2004, Davis 1968, Feibleman 1978, and Lockwood 2005.

4. A comprehensive account of a century of water management in the Atchafalaya is by Reuss 2004.

5. A short history of Bayou Chene is contained in the Army Corps of Engineers' booklet by Maygarden and Yakubik 1999.

6. Mike Steinberg's *Stalking the Ghost Bird* (2008) is an excellent account of the ivory-billed woodpecker, and the clashes of knowledge surrounding its assumed extinction or presence. See also Lewis 1988. Audubon's account of the woodpecker is in Rhodes 2006.

7. See C. C. Lockwood's finely illustrated *Marsh Mission* (2005).

8. For more on the United Houma Nation see http://www.unitedhoumanation.org/.

9. For more on the Chitimacha nation see http://www.chitimacha.gov/.

12. DESERT: TIMBISHA (DEATH VALLEY), CALIFORNIA

1. The best book on America's deserts is Edward Abbey's *Desert Solitaire* (1968); see also van Dyke 1907 and Krutch 1951 for fine accounts of the desert habitats of the West.

2. A great deal has been written about the history of what is now called Death Valley. Relatively little recognizes or focuses on the Timbisha Shoshone people. See Crum 1994 for the latter, and Manly 1884, Lingenfelter 1986, and Greene 2009 on the former.

3. Richard Grant (2003) is amusing on the dangers of driving long distances at night, and the emergence of visual disturbances, or jumping jackrabbits.

4. For a modern account of the coyote in America see DeStefano's *Coyote at the Kitchen Door* (2010).

5. Too precious to pick, too precious not to pick: a phrase of Bashō's.

BIBLIOGRAPHY

The references are organized into both chapters and themes. Those cited in each chapter are listed in alphabetical order under their chapter headings. Those relating to common themes across the whole book are also listed under four further headings: Zen Buddhism; Journeys and Paths; Nature, Wild and Place; and Consumption and the Planet.

PREVIOUSLY

Aitken, R. 1978. *A Zen Wave: Bashō's Haiku and Zen*. Washington, DC: Shoemaker and Howard.
——. 1982. *Taking the Path of Zen*. New York: North Point Press.
——. 1996. *Original Dwelling Place*. New York: Counterpoint.
Bashō, M. 1966. *The Narrow Road to the Deep North and Other Travel Sketches*. Translated by Nobuyuki Yuasa. London: Penguin.
Challenger, M. 2011. *On Extinction*. Cambridge: Granta.
Christie, D. 2013. *Blue Sapphire of the Mind*. Oxford: Oxford University Press.
Diamond, J. 2005. *Collapse: How Societies Choose to Fail or Survive*. London: Penguin.
Ehrenfield, D. 2005. "The Environmental Limits to Globalization." *Conservation Biology* 19, no. 2: 318–26.
Frank, R. H. 1999. *Luxury Fever: Weighing the Cost of Excess*. Princeton, NJ: Princeton University Press.
Hanbury-Tenison, R. 2006. *The Seventy Great Journeys*. London: Thames & Hudson.
Jackson, T. 2009. *Prosperity without Growth*. London: Earthscan.
Kane, S. 1998 (2010). *Wisdom of the Mythtellers*. Peterborough, Ontario: Broadview Press.
Kapleau, P. 1965 (2000). *The Three Pillars of Zen*. New York: Anchor Books.
Kasser, T. 2002. *The High Price of Materialism*. Cambridge, MA: MIT Press.
Kunitz, S. 2005. *The Wild Braid*. New York: W. W. Norton.
Layard, R. 2006. *Happiness: Lessons from a New Science*. London: Penguin.
Long, R. 2002. *Walking the Line*. London: Thames & Hudson.
Macfarlane, R. 2003. *Mountains of the Mind*. London: Granta.
——. 2007. *The Wild Places*. London: Granta.
——. 2012. *The Old Ways: A Journey on Foot*. London: Hamish Hamilton.
Matthiessen, P. 1978. *The Snow Leopard*. London: Vintage.
Nettle, D. 2005. *Happiness*. Oxford: Oxford University Press.
Pretty, J. 2007. *The Earth Only Endures: On Reconnecting with Nature and Our Place In It*. London: Earthscan.
——. 2013. "The Consumption of a Finite Planet: Well-Being, Convergence, Divergence, and the Nascent Green Economy." *Environmental and Resource Economics* 55, no. 4: 475–99.
Royal Society. 2012. *People and the Planet*. London: Royal Society.

Santoka Taneda. 2001. *Mountain Tasting: Zen Haiku and Journals.* Translated by John Stevens. Buffalo, NY: White Pine Press.

Sebald, W. G. 2002. *The Rings of Saturn.* London: Vintage.

Sinclair, I. 2002. *London Orbital.* London: Penguin.

Smith, L. C. 2010. *The New North: The World in 2050.* London: Profile.

Snyder, G. 1990. *The Practice of the Wild.* Washington, DC: Shoemaker Hoard.

Solnit, R. 2001. *Wanderlust: A History of Walking.* London: Verso.

———. 2005. *A Field Guide to Getting Lost.* London: Canongate.

Wilkinson, R., and K. Pickett. 2009. *The Spirit Level.* London: Penguin.

1. SEACOAST: NGĀI TAHU, AOTEAROA (NEW ZEALAND)

Allen, O. E. 1980. *The Pacific Navigators.* Alexandria, VA: Time-Life.

Cook, J. 1774. *Hunt for the Southern Continent.* London: Penguin.

Duff, A. 1990. *Once Were Warriors.* London: Vintage Books.

Gooley, T. 2010. *The Natural Navigator.* Virgin Books.

Grimble, A. 1952 (1981). *A Pattern of Islands.* Harmondsworth, UK: Penguin.

———. 1957. *Return to the Islands.* London: John Murray.

Heyerdahl, T. 1950 (1984). *Kon-Tiki.* New York: Pocket Books.

Hulme, K. 1985. *The Bone People.* London: Picador.

Lewis, D. 1972. *We, the Navigators: The Ancient Art of Landfinding in the Pacific.* Honolulu: University of Hawaiʻi Press.

Moller, H., J. C. Kitson, and T. Downs. 2009. "Knowing by Doing: Learning by Sustainable Muttonbird Harvesting." *New Zealand Journal of Zoology* 36:243–58.

Moller, H., J. Newman, P. O'B. Lyver, and Rakiura Tītī Islands Administering Body (RTIAB). 2010. "Fourteen Years On: Lessons for Community-Led Science Partnerships from the Kia Mau te Tītī Mo Ake Tōnu Atu Project." In *Ngā Kete a Rēhua Inaugural Māori Research Symposium Te Waipounamu 2008,* proceedings, edited by R. Taonui, H. Kahi, C. Deeming, K. Kururangi, G. Cooper, L. Ratahi, M. Royal, R. Taonui, M. Haenga, and J. Bray. Christchurch, New Zealand: Aotahi: School of Māori and Indigenous Studies, University of Canterbury.

Newman, J., D. Scott, C. Bragg, S. McKechnie, H. Moller, and D. Fletcher. 2009. "Estimating Regional Population Size and Annual Harvest Intensity of the Sooty Shearwater in New Zealand." *New Zealand Journal of Zoology* 36:307–23.

Pretty, J. 2011. "Interdisciplinary Progress in Approaches to Address Social-Ecological and Ecocultural Systems." *Environmental Conservation* 38, no 2: 127–39.

Stephenson, J., and H. Moller. 2009. "Cross-Cultural Environmental Research and Management." *Journal of the Royal Society of New Zealand* 39:139–49.

Te Ara—the Encyclopedia of New Zealand. 2006. *Māori Peoples of New Zealand: Ngā Iwi o Aotearoa.* Auckland: David Bateman.

Whaanga, M. 2004. *A Carved Cloak for Tahu.* Auckland: Auckland University Press.

2. MOUNTAIN: HUANGSHAN, CHINA

Bashō, M. 1968. *The Narrow Road to the Deep North and Other Travel Sketches.* Translated by Nobuyuki Yuasa. London: Penguin.

Hardy, J. 2002. *Haiku: Poetry Ancient and Modern.* London: Octopus.

Hinton, D., trans. and ed. 2002. *Mountain Home: The Wilderness Poetry of Ancient China.* London: Anvil Press Poetry.

Lin Ci. 2006. *The Art of Chinese Painting.* Beijing: China Intercontinental Press.

Macfarlane, R. 2012. *The Old Ways: A Journey on Foot.* London: Hamish Hamilton.

Red Pine and M. O'Connor, eds. 1998. *The Clouds Should Know Me by Now: Buddhist Poet Monks of China.* Boston: Wisdom Publications.

Santoka Taneda. 2001. *Mountain Tasting: Zen Haiku and Journals.* Translated by John Stevens. Buffalo, NY: White Pine Press.

Tanahashi, K., ed. 1985. *Moon in a Dewdrop: Writings of Zen Master Dogen.* New York: North Point Press.

3. DESERT COAST: MURUJUGA (BURRUP), AUSTRALIA

Albrecht, G. 2010. "Solastalgia and the Creation of New Ways of Living." In *Nature and Culture,* edited by S. E. Pilgrim and J. Pretty. London: Earthscan.

Albrecht, G., G.-M. Sartore, L. Connor, N. Higginbotham, S. Freeman, B. Kelly, H. Stain, A. Tonna, and G. Pollard. 2007. "Solastalgia: The Distress Caused by Environmental Change." *Australasian Psychiatry* 15, no. 1: S95–S98.

Bird, C., and S. Hallam. 2006. *A Review of Archaeology and Rock Art in the Dampier Archipelago.* A report prepared for the National Trust of Australia (WA).

Bird Rose, D. 1996. *Nourishing Terrains.* Canberra: Australian Heritage Commission.

——. 2000. *Dingo Makes Us Human.* Cambridge: Cambridge University Press.

Chatwin, B. 1998. *Songlines.* London: Picador.

Cook, J. 1774. *Hunt for the Southern Continent.* London: Penguin.

Ingold, T. 2007. *Lines: A Brief History.* Oxford: Routledge.

Kane, S. 1998 (2010). *Wisdom of the Mythtellers.* Peterborough, Ontario: Broadview Press.

Wilson, G. J. 1989 (2002). *Pilbara Bushman.* Carlisle, Western Australia: Hesperian Press.

4. STEPPE: TUVA, RUSSIA

Aruz, J., A. Farkas, and E. V. Fino. 2006. *The Golden Deer of Eurasia: Perspectives on the Steppe Nomads of the Ancient World.* New York: Metropolitan Museum of Art.

Bogutskaya, N. G. 2001. "A Revision of Altai Osmans of the Genus *Oreoleuciscus* with a Description of a New Species from River Kobdo System, Mongolia." *Proceedings of Zoological Institute* (Russian Academy of Sciences, St. Petersburg) 287:5–43.

Flesch, E. 2000. "Land of the Shamans." *Moscow Times,* July 22.

Govinda, Lama Anagorika. 1966 (2006). *The Way of the White Cloud.* London: Rider.

Halemba, A., and B. Donahoe. 2008. *Local Perspectives in Hunting and Poaching.* Research report for WWF Russia Altai-Saian Region.

Haywood, A. J. 2010. *Siberia: A Cultural History.* Oxford: Signal Books.

Leighton, R. 1991. *Tuva or Bust! Richard Feynman's Last Journey.* New York: W. W. Norton.

Levin, T. (with V. Suzukei). 2006. *Where Rivers and Mountains Sing.* Bloomington: Indiana University Press.

Matthiessen, P. 1978. *The Snow Leopard.* London: Vintage.

Potapov, L. P. 1969. *Orcherki naradnogo byta tuvintsev* [Studies of the way of life of the Tuvinians]. Moscow.

Reid, A. 2002. *The Shaman's Coat: A Native History of Siberia.* London: Phoenix.

Rinpoche, S. 2008. *The Tibetan Book of Living and Dying*. London: Rider.

Rosshydromet. 2008. *Assessment Report on Climate Change and Its Consequences in Russian Federation*. Moscow: Rosshydromet.

Rytkheu, Y. 2005. *A Dream in Polar Fog*. St. Paul, MN: Archipelago Books.

Sillanpää, L., ed. 2008. *Awakening Siberia*. ActaPolitica 33. Helsinki: University of Helsinki.

Stegner, W. 1962. *Wolf Willow*. London: Penguin.

Thubron, C. 1999. *In Siberia*. London: Penguin.

———. 2006. *Shadow of the Silk Road*. London: Chatto & Windus.

Vainshtein, S. 1980. *Nomads of South Siberia*. Cambridge: Cambridge University Press.

Vitebsky, P. 2005. *Reindeer People: Living with Animals and Spirits in Siberia*. London: Harper Collins.

Zubkov, P. 1985. *Republic in the Heart of Asia: 40th Anniversary of Soviet Tuva*. Moscow: Novosti Press Agency.

5. SNOW: KARELIA, FINLAND

Abraham, R. 1991. *A Place of Their Own: Family Farming in Eastern Finland*. Cambridge: Cambridge University Press.

Bosley, K., trans. 1989. *The Kalevala*. Oxford: Oxford University Press.

Brody, H. 1981. *Maps and Dreams*. New York: Pantheon.

———. 2002. *The Other Side of Eden*. London: Faber and Faber.

Cook, R. 1974. *The Tree of Life*. London: Thames & Hudson.

Helander, E., and T. Mustonen, eds. 2009. *Snowscapes, Dreamscapes*. Finland: Snowchange and Tampere Polytechnic.

Mowat, F. 1951 (1975). *People of the Deer*. Toronto: Seal Books.

———. 2000. *Walking on the Land*. Toronto: Seal Books.

Mustonen, T., and K. Mustonen. 2011. *Eastern Sámi Atlas*. Finland: Snowchange, Selkie.

6. SWAMP: OKAVANGO, BOTSWANA

Adams, W. M. 1996. *Future Nature: A Vision for Conservation*. London: Earthscan.

Barnard, A. 1992. *Hunters and Herders of Southern Africa*. Cambridge: Cambridge University Press.

Bolaane, M. 2004. "The Impact of Game Reserve Policy on the River BaSarwa / Bushmen of Botswana." *Social Policy and Administration* 38:399–417.

———. 2005. "Chiefs, Hunters and Adventurers: The Foundation of the Okavango/Moremi National Park, Botswana." *Journal of Historical Geography* 31:241–59.

Brockington, D., R. Duffy, and J. Igoe. 2008. *Nature Unbound: Conservation, Capitalism and the Future of Protected Areas*. London: Earthscan.

Hinton, D., trans. and ed. 2002. *Mountain Home: The Wilderness Poetry of Ancient China*. London: Anvil Press Poetry.

Isaacson, R. 2001. *The Healing Land: A Kalahari Journey*. London: Fourth Estate.

Lee, R. B. 1979. *The !Kung San*. Cambridge: Cambridge University Press.

Lee, R. B., and R. Daly, eds. 1999. *The Cambridge Encyclopedia of Hunters and Gatherers*. Cambridge: Cambridge University Press.

Mbaiwa, J. 2005. "Enclave Tourism and Its Socio-economic Impacts in the Okavango Delta, Botswana." *Tourism Management* 26, no. 2: 157–72.

—. 2005. "Wildlife Resource Utilisation at Moremi Game Reserve and Khwai Community Area in the Okavango Delta, Botswana." *Journal of Environmental Management* 77:144–56.

Pretty, J. 2002. *Agri-Culture: Reconnecting People, Land and Nature.* London: Earthscan.

Saugestad, S. 2006. "San Development and Challenges in Development Cooperation." In *Updating the San: Image and Reality of an African People in the 21st Century,* edited by R. K. Hitchcock, K. Ikeya, M. Biesele, and R. B. Lee. Osaka: National Museum of Ethology.

Sharp, H. S. 1987. "Giant Fish, Giant Otters, and Dinosaurs: 'Apparently Irrational Beliefs' in a Chipewyan Community." *American Ethnologist* 14, no. 2: 226–35.

Silberbauer, G. B. 1981. *Hunter and Habitat in the Central Kalahari Desert.* Cambridge: Cambridge University Press.

van der Post, L. 1958 (2004). *The Lost World of the Kalahari.* London: Vintage.

7. MARSH-FARM: EAST ANGLIA, ENGLAND

Bensusan, S. L. 1954. *A Marshland Omnibus.* London: Duckworth.

Blythe, R. 1997. *Word from Wormingford.* London: Penguin.

—. 2006. *A Year at Bottengoms Farm.* Norwich, UK: Canterbury Press.

—. 2007. *Field Work: Selected Essays.* Norwich, UK: Black Dog Books.

Brody, H. 2002. *The Other Side of Eden.* London: Faber and Faber.

Canton, J. 2013. *Out of Essex: Re-imagining a History of Landscape.* Oxford: Signal Books.

Chamberlain, M. 1975 (2010). *Fenwomen.* Saxmundham, UK: Full Circle Editions.

Clark, C., and M. Greenfields. 2006. *Here to Stay: The Gypsies and Travellers of Britain.* Hatfield, UK: University of Herts Press.

Davies, O. 2003. *Popular Magic: Cunning Folk in English History.* London: Hambledon Continuum.

Dutt, W. A. 1904. *Highways and Byways in East Anglia.* London: Macmillan.

—. 1910. *The Norfolk and Suffolk Coast.* New York: Frederick Stokes.

Fonseca, I. 2006. *Bury Me Standing: The Gypsies and Their Journey.* London: Vintage Books.

Fraser, A. 1995. *The Gypsies.* 2nd ed. Malden, UK: Blackwell.

Gillingham, D. W. 1953. *Unto the Fields.* London: Country Book Club.

Grieve, H. 1959. *The Great Tide.* Chelmsford, UK: Essex County Council.

McWilliam, N., and V. Sekules, eds. 1986. *Life and Landscape: P. H. Emerson, Art and Photography in East Anglia, 1885–1900.* Norwich, UK: University of East Anglia.

Morrison, A. 1900. *Cunning Murrell.* New York: Doubleday, Page and Co.

Orton, J., and K. Worpole. 2005. *350 Miles: An Essex Journey.* Chelmsford, UK: Essex Development and Regeneration Agency.

Patterson, A. H. 1929 (1988). *Wildfowlers and Poachers.* Southampton: Ashford Press.

Pretty, J. 2011. *This Luminous Coast.* Saxmundham, UK. Full Circle Editions.

Tennyson, J. 1939. *Suffolk Scene: A Book of Description and Adventure.* London: Blackie and Son.

Tompkins, H. 1904. *Marsh Country Rambles.* London: Chatto & Windus.

Tooley, B. 2004. *Scribblings of a Yarmouth Naturalist.* Great Yarmouth, UK: Blackwell John Buckle.

Walker, D. 2001. *Basildon Plotlands.* Chichester, UK: Phillimore.

Wentworth Day, J. 1949. *Coastal Adventure.* London: Harrap.

—. 1950. *Marshland Adventure.* London: Harrap.

8. COAST: ANTRIM GLENS, NORTHERN IRELAND

Cameron, S. 2002. *Death in the North Channel: The Loss of the* Princess Victoria. Newtownards, Northern Ireland: Colourpoint Books.

Donnelly, M. 2000. *The Nine Glens*. Coleraine, Northern Ireland: Impact.

Hunter, J. 1999. *Loss of the* Princess Victoria. Stranraer and District Local History Trust.

McAuley, T. 2000. *Tony McAuley's Glens*. Donaghadee, Northern Ireland: Cottage Publications.

Pretty, J. 2011. *This Luminous Coast*. Saxmundham, UK: Full Circle Editions.

Robinson, T. 2006. *Connemara*. London: Penguin.

Sheane, M. 2010. *The Glens of Antrim*. Ilfracombe, UK: Arthur H. Stockwell.

Watson, P. 2000. *The Giant's Causeway*. Dublin: O'Brien Press.

Watson, S. 2004. *Antrim Coast*. Catrine, Ayrshire, Scotland: Stenlake Publishing.

Young, E. 1910 (1985). *Celtic Wonder Tales*. Edinburgh: Loris Classics.

9. SNOW: NITASSINAN, LABRADOR, CANADA

Anderson, D. G., and M. Nuttall, eds. *Cultivating Arctic Landscapes*. New York: Berghahn.

Bass, R. 2004. *Caribou Rising*. San Francisco: Sierra Club Books.

Berkes, F., R. Huebert, H. Fast, M. Manseau, and A. Diduck. 2005. *Breaking Ice: Renewable Resource and Ocean Management in the Canadian North*. Calgary, Alberta: University of Calgary Press.

Brody, H. 1981. *Maps and Dreams*. New York: Pantheon.

——. 2002. *The Other Side of Eden*. London: Faber and Faber.

Buhs, J. B. 2009. *Bigfoot: The Life and Times of a Legend*. Chicago: University of Chicago Press.

Ehrlich, G. 2002. *This Cold Heaven: Seven Seasons in Greenland*. London: Fourth Estate.

Finkelstein, M., and J. Stone. 2004. *Paddling the Boreal Forest*. Toronto: Natural Heritage Books.

Freestone, J. 2001. *Rowing to Latitude: Journeys along the Arctic's Edge*. New York: North Point Press.

Henriksen, G. 2009. *I Dreamed the Animals: Kaniuekutat, the Life of an Innu Hunter*. New York: Berghahn.

Innu Nation and Mushuau Innu Band Council. 1993. *Gathering Voices: Discovering Our Past, Present and Future*. Sheshatshiu, Labrador: Innu Nation Office.

Lopez, B. 1986. *Arctic Dreams*. London: Harvill.

Matthiessen, P. 1978. *The Snow Leopard*. London: Vintage.

Meldrum, J. 2006. *Sasquatch: Legend Meets Science*. New York: Tom Doherty.

Mowat, F. 1951 (1975). *People of the Deer*. Toronto: Seal Books.

——. 2000. *Walking on the Land*. Toronto: Seal Books.

Nelson, R. 1983. *Make Prayers to the Raven: A Koyukon View of the Northern Forest*. Chicago: University of Chicago Press.

Nuttall, M. 1998. *Protecting the Arctic: Indigenous Peoples and Cultural Survival*. Abingdon, UK: Routledge.

Rytkheu, Y. 2005. *A Dream in Polar Fog*. St. Paul, MN: Archipelago Books.

Samson, C. 2003. *A Way of Life That Does Not Exist: Canada and the Extinguishment of the Innu*. London: Verso.

——. 2013. *A World You Do Not Know*. London: Institute of Commonwealth Studies.

Wheeler, S. 2009. *The Magnetic North: Notes from the Arctic Circle*. London: Vintage.

Wilson J. 1998. *The Earth Shall Weep. A History of Native America*. Grove Press, New York.

10. FARM-CITY: AMISH COUNTRY, OHIO

Bromfield, L. 1948. *Malabar Farm*. Wooster, OH: Wooster Book Co.

Davis, M. 2002. *Dead Cities*. New York: New Press.

Jacobs, J. 1961. *The Life and Death of Great American Cities*. London: Random House.

Kline, D. 1990. *Great Possessions*. Wooster, OH: Wooster Book Co.

Kraybill, D. B. 1989 (2001). *The Riddle of Amish Culture*. Baltimore: Johns Hopkins University.

Logsdon, G. 1994. *The Contrary Farmer*. White River Junction, VT: Chelsea Green Publishing.

Orr, D. W. 1993. *Environmental Literacy: Education as If the Earth Mattered*. Great Barrington, MA: E. F. Schumacher Society.

——. 2004. *The Last Refuge: Patriotism, Politics, and the Environment in an Age of Terror*. Washington, DC: Island Press.

——. 2006. *Design on the Edge: The Making of a High-Performance Building*. Cambridge, MA: MIT Press.

Woodward, C. 2002. *In Ruins: A Journey through History, Art, and Literature*. London: Vintage.

11. SWAMP: ATCHAFALAYA BASIN, LOUISIANA

Angers, T. 1988. *The Truth about the Cajuns*. Lafayette, LA: Acadian House.

Brasseaux, C. 2005. *French, Cajun, Creole, Houma: A Primer on Francophone Louisiana*. Baton Rouge: Louisiana State University Press.

Brown, D. 1970. *Bury My Heart at Wounded Knee*. London: Vintage.

——. 2004. *The American West*. London: Pocket Books.

Cobb, J. C. 1992. *The Most Southern Place on Earth*. Oxford: Oxford University Press.

Dallmeyer, D. G., ed. 2004. *Elemental South*. Athens: University of Georgia Press.

Davis, E. A., ed. 1968. *The Rivers and Bayous of Louisiana*. Baton Rouge, LA: Firebird Press.

Denevan, W. M., ed. 1976. *The Native Population of the Americas in 1492*. Madison: University of Wisconsin Press.

Feibleman, P. S. 1978. *The Bayous of Louisiana*. Amsterdam: Time-Life.

Guirard, G. 1989 (1999). *Cajun Families of the Atchafalaya*. Louisville, KY: G. Guirard.

Jacobs, H., and J. Rice. 1976. *Once upon a Bayou*. New Orleans: Phideaux.

Jacoby, K. 2001. *Crimes against Nature: Squatters, Poachers, Thieves, and the Hidden History of American Conservation*. Berkeley: University of California Press.

Lewis, F. 1988. *Tales of a Louisiana Duck Hunter*. Franklin, LA: Little Atakapas.

Lockwood, C. C. 2005. *Marsh Mission*. Baton Rouge: Louisiana State University Press.

Maygarden, B. D., and J.-K.Yakubik. 1999. *Bayou Chene: The Life Story of an Atchafalaya Basin Community*. New Orleans: U.S. Army Corps of Engineers, New Orleans District.

Nelson, R. 1987. *Heart and Blood: Living with Deer*. New York: Vintage.

Reuss, M. 2004. *Designing the Bayous: The Control of Water in the Atchafalaya Basin, 1800–1995*. College Station: Texas A&M University Press.

Rhodes, R, ed. 2006. *John James Audubon: The Audubon Reader*. New York: Alfred A Knopf.

Roland, G. 2006. *Atchafalaya Houseboat*. Baton Rouge: Louisiana State University Press.

Steinberg, M. K. 2008. *Stalking the Ghost Bird*. Baton Rouge: Louisiana State University Press.

Wilson, A. 2006. *Shadow and Shelter: The Swamp in Southern Culture*. Jackson: University Press of Mississippi.

Wilson, J. 1998. *The Earth Shall Weep: A History of Native America*. New York: Grove Press.

12. DESERT: TIMBISHA (DEATH VALLEY), CALIFORNIA

Abbey, E. 1968. *Desert Solitaire.* New York: Simon & Schuster.

Basso, K. 1996. *Wisdom Sits in Places: Landscape and Language among the Western Apache.* Albuquerque: University of New Mexico Press.

Brown, D. 1970. *Bury My Heart at Wounded Knee.* London: Vintage.

———. 1995 (2004). *The American West.* London: Pocket Books.

Crum, S. J. 1994. *The Road on Which We Came: A History of the Western Shoshone.* Salt Lake City: University of Utah Press.

DeStefano, S. 2010. *Coyote at the Kitchen Door: Living with Wildlife in Suburbia.* Cambridge, MA: Harvard University Press.

Gildart, B., and J. Gildart. 2005. *Death Valley National Park.* Guilford, CT: Falcon Guides.

Grant, R. 2003. *Ghost Riders: Travels with American Nomads.* London: Abacus.

Greene, S. 2009. *Death Valley Books of Knowledge.* New York: iUniverse.

Hunt, C. B. 1975. *Death Valley: Geology, Ecology, Archaeology.* Berkeley: University of California Press.

Krutch, J. W. 1951. *The Desert Year.* Harmondsworth, UK: Penguin.

Lingenfelter, R. E. 1986. *Death Valley and the Amargosa: A Land of Illusion.* Berkeley: University of California Press.

Lopez, B., and D. Gwartney, eds. 2006. *Home Ground: Language for an American Landscape.* San Antonio, TX: Trinity University Press.

Manly, W. L. 1884. *Death Valley in '49.* Hard Press.

van Dyke, J. C. 1907. *The Desert: Further Studies in Natural Appearances.* New York: Charles Scribner's Sons (BiblioLife, Charleston).

Wilson, J. 1998. *The Earth Shall Weep: A History of Native America.* New York: Grove Press.

ZEN BUDDHISM

Aitken, R. 1978. *A Zen Wave: Bashō's Haiku and Zen.* Washington, DC: Shoemaker and Howard.

———. 1982. *Taking the Path of Zen.* New York: North Point Press.

———. 1996. *Original Dwelling Place.* New York: Counterpoint.

Bashō, M. 1968. *The Narrow Road to the Deep North and Other Travel Sketches.* Translated by Nobuyuki Yuasa. London: Penguin.

———. 2008. *Bashō: The Complete Haiku.* Translated by Jane Reichhold. Tokyo: Kodansha International.

Clements, J., trans. 2000. *Zen Haiku.* London: Francis Lincoln.

Govinda, Lama A. 1991. *Insights of a Himalayan Pilgrim.* Oakland, CA: Dharma Publishing.

———. 1966 (2006). *The Way of the White Cloud.* London: Rider.

Hamill, S., trans. 1995 (2000). *The Sound of Water: Haiku by Bashō, Buson, Issa, and Other Poets.* Boston: Shambhala.

Hammill, S., and J. P. Seaton. 2004. *The Poetry of Zen.* Boston: Shambhala.

Hanson, R., and R. Mendius. 2009. *Buddha's Brain: The Practical Neuroscience of Happiness.* Oakland, CA: New Harbinger Publishing.

Hardy, J. 2002. *Haiku: Poetry Ancient and Modern.* London: Octopus.

Hinton, D., trans. and ed. 2002. *Mountain Home: The Wilderness Poetry of Ancient China.* London: Anvil Press Poetry.

Kapleau, P. 1965 (2000). *The Three Pillars of Zen*. New York: Anchor Books.

Matthiessen, P. 1978. *The Snow Leopard*. London: Vintage.

——. 1985 (1998). *Nine-Headed Dragon River*. Boston: Shambhala.

Red Pine and M. O'Connor, eds. 1998. *The Clouds Should Know Me by Now: Buddhist Poet Monks of China*. Boston: Wisdom Publications.

Rinpoche, S. 2008. *The Tibetan Book of Living and Dying*. London: Rider.

Santoka Taneda. 2001. *Mountain Tasting: Zen Haiku and Journals*. Translated by John Stevens. Buffalo, NY: White Pine Press.

Snyder, G. 1990. *The Practice of the Wild*. Washington, DC: Shoemaker Hoard.

——. 1995. *A Place in Space: Ethics, Aesthetics, and Watersheds*. New York: Counterpoint.

Stevens, J., trans. and ed. 1993. *Dewdrops on a Lotus Leaf: Zen Poems of Ryōkan*. Boston: Shambhala.

Suzuki, S. 1970 (2009). *Zen Mind, Beginner's Mind*. Boston: Weatherhill.

Tanahashi, K., ed. 1985. *Moon in a Dewdrop: Writings of Zen Master Dogen*. New York: North Point Press.

JOURNEYS AND PATHS

Bailey, L. 1964. *The Long Walk*. Tucson, AZ: Westernlore Press.

Bryson, B. 1997. *A Walk in the Woods*. New York: Doubleday.

Coverley, M. 2006. *Psychogeography*. Harpenden, UK: Pocket Essentials.

Di Cinto, M. 2012. *Walks: Travels along the Barricades*. London: Union Books.

Fiennes, R. 2003. *Beyond the Limits: The Lessons Learned from a Lifetime's Adventures*. London: Little, Brown.

Hanbury-Tenison, R. 2006. *The Seventy Great Journeys*. London: Thames & Hudson.

Hazlitt, W. 1822. *On Going on a Journey*. London: New Monthly Magazine.

Ingold, T. 2007. *Lines: A Brief History*. Oxford: Routledge.

Leslie, E. E. 1988. *Desperate Journeys, Abandoned Souls*. Boston: Mariner.

Long, R. 2002. *Walking the Line*. London: Thames & Hudson.

Macfarlane, R. 2003. *Mountains of the Mind*. London: Granta.

——. 2007. *The Wild Places*. London: Granta.

——. 2012. *The Old Ways: A Journey on Foot*. London: Hamish Hamilton.

Marples, M. 1959. *Shanks's Pony: A Study of Walking*. London: J. M. Dent.

McKibben, B. 2000. *Long Distance: A Year of Living Strenuously*. New York: Simon & Schuster.

Muir, J. 1911. *My First Summer in the Sierra*. Boston: Houghton Mifflin. Repr. 1988 by Canongate Classics, Edinburgh.

——. 1992. *The Eight Wilderness-Discovery Books*. London: Diadem Books.

Nicholson, G. 2008. *The Lost Art of Walking*. London: Riverhead.

Pretty, J. 2011. *This Luminous Coast*. Saxmundham, UK: Full Circle Editions.

Sebald, W. G. 2002. *The Rings of Saturn*. London: Vintage.

Sinclair, I. 2002. *London Orbital*. London: Penguin.

Solnit, R. 2001. *Wanderlust: A History of Walking*. London: Verso.

——. 2005. *A Field Guide to Getting Lost*. London: Canongate.

Stevenson, R. L. 2011. *Thoughts on Walking*. Read Books, London.

Tait, M. 2003. *The Walker's Companion*. London: Think Books.

Taplin, K. 1979. *The English Path*. Ipswich, UK: Boydell Press.

Thoreau, H. D. 1902. *Walden or Life in the Woods*. London: Henry Frowde, Oxford University Press.

Warner, M. 2012. *Stranger Magic*. London: Vintage.

NATURE, WILD AND PLACE

Abram, D. 1996. *The Spell of the Sensuous*. New York: Vintage Books.

Baker, J. A. 1967 [2005]. *The Peregrine*. New York: New York Review Books.

Barron, D. 2004. *Beast in the Garden*. New York: W. W. Norton.

Basso, K. 1996. *Wisdom Sits in Places: Landscape and Language among the Western Apache*. Albuquerque: University of New Mexico Press.

Bate, J. 2001. *The Song of the Earth*. London: Picador.

Bergman, C. 2003. *Wild Echoes: Encounters with the Most Endangered Animals in North America*. Urbana-Champaign: University of Illinois Press.

Berkes, F. 1999. *Sacred Ecology: Traditional Ecological Knowledge and Resource Management*. Philadelphia: Taylor and Francis.

Callicott, J. B., and M. P. Nelson, eds. 1998. *The Great New Wilderness Debate*. Athens: University of Georgia Press.

Christie, D. 2013. *Blue Sapphire of the Mind*. Oxford: Oxford University Press.

Cocker, M. 2007. *Crow Country*. London: Jonathan Cape.

Cocker, M., and R. Mabey. 2005. *Birds Britannica*. London: Chatto & Windus.

Connors, P. 2011. *Fire Season: Field Notes from a Wilderness Lookout*. London: Macmillan.

Cook, R. 1974. *The Tree of Life*. London: Thames & Hudson.

Deakin, R. 2000. *Waterlog: A Swimmer's Journey through Britain*. London: Vintage.

——. 2007. *Wildwood: A Journey through Trees*. London: Hamish Hamilton.

Dillard, A. 1982. *Teaching a Stone to Talk*. New York: Harper Perennial.

——. 1990. *Pilgrim at Tinker Creek*. In *Three by Annie Dillard*, 2001. New York: Harper Perennial.

Farley, P., and M. S. Roberts. 2011. *Edgelands: Journeys into England's True Wilderness*. London: Jonathan Cape.

Gallagher, W. 1994. *The Power of Place*. New York: Harper Perennial.

Griffiths, J. 2006. *Wild: An Elemental Journey*. London: Hamish Hamilton.

Hoagland, E. 1972. *Red Wolves and Black Bears*. New York: Lyons and Burford.

Hogue, L. 2000. *All the Wild and Lonely Places*. Washington, DC: Island Press.

Jackson, W. 1994. *Becoming Native to This Place*. Lexington: University Press of Kentucky.

Jamie, K. 2012. *Sightlines*. London: Sort of Books.

Jones, K. 2004. *Wolf Mountains: A History of Wolves along the Great Divide*. Calgary, Alberta: University of Calgary Press.

Kastner, J., and B. Wallis. 1998. *Land and Environmental Art*. London: Phaidon Press.

Lopez, B. 1978. *Of Wolves and Men*. New York: Simon & Schuster.

——. 1988. *Crossing Open Ground*. London: Picador.

——. 1998. *About This Life: Journeys on the Threshold of Memory*. London: Harvill.

Louv, R. 2005. *Last Child in the Woods*. Chapel Hill, NC: Algonquin Press.

Mabey, R. 2007. *Beechcombings: The Narratives of Trees*. London: Chatto & Windus.

Marvin, G. 2012. *Wolf*. London: Reaktion Books.

Nabhan, G. 1982. *The Desert Smells Like Rain*. San Francisco: North Point Press.

Nash R. 1973. *Wilderness and the American Mind*. New Haven, CT: Yale University Press.

Posey, D., ed. 1999. *Cultural and Spiritual Values of Biodiversity*. London: IT Publications and UNEP.

Pretty, J. 1995. *Regenerating Agriculture*. London: Earthscan.

——. 2002. *Agri-Culture: Reconnecting People, Land and Nature*. London: Earthscan.

——. 2007. *The Earth Only Endures: On Reconnecting with Nature and Our Place In It*. London: Earthscan.

——. 2011. *This Luminous Coast*. Saxmundham, UK: Full Circle Editions.

Rothenberg, D., and W. Prior, eds. 2004. *Writing the Future*. Cambridge, MA: MIT Press.

Schama, S. 1996. *Landscape and Memory*. London: Fontana Press.

Serpell, J. 1996. *In the Company of Animals*. Cambridge: Cambridge University Press.

Stegner, W. 1962. *Wolf Willow*. London: Penguin.

Stewart, P. J., and A. Strathern, eds. 2003. *Landscape, Memory and History*. London: Pluto Press.

Suzuki, D. 1997. *Sacred Balance*. London: Bantam Books.

Thomas, K. 1983. *Man and the Natural* World. London: Penguin.

Thoreau, H. D. 1837–53. *The Writings of H. D. Thoreau*. Vols. 1–6 (published 1981 to 2000). Princeton, NJ: Princeton University Press.

Tredinnick, M. 2005. *The Land's Wild Music*. San Antonio, TX: Trinity University Press.

Tuan, Y.-F. 1977. *Sense and Place*. Minneapolis: University of Minnesota Press.

Tydeman, W. E. 2013. *Conversations with Barry Lopez*. Norman: University of Oklahoma Press.

Warner, M. 2003. *Signs and Wonders*. London: Vintage.

Wentworth Day, J. 1956. *They Walk the Wild Places*. London: Blandford Press.

Wilson, E. O. 1984. *Biophilia*. Cambridge, MA: Harvard University Press.

Worpole, K. 2003. *Last Landscapes*. London: Reaktion Books.

CONSUMPTION AND THE PLANET

Anderson, E. 1996. *Ecologies of the Heart*. New York: Oxford University Press.

Boyle, D., and A. Simms. 2009. *The New Economics: A Bigger Picture*. London: Earthscan.

Challenger, M. 2011. *On Extinction*. Cambridge: Granta.

Diamond, J. 2005. *Collapse: How Societies Choose to Fail or Survive*. London: Penguin.

Ehrenfield, D. 2005. "The Environmental Limits to Globalization." *Conservation Biology* 19, no. 2: 318–26.

Frank, R. H. 1999. *Luxury Fever: Weighing the Cost of Excess*. Princeton, NJ: Princeton University Press.

Frumkin, H., L. Frank, and R. Jackson. 2004. *Urban Sprawl and Public Health*. Cambridge, MA: MIT Press.

Gray, J. 2002. *Straw Dogs*. London: Granta Books.

——. 2004. *Heresies: Against Progress and Other Illusions*. London: Granta.

Hobsbawm, E., and E. Ranger, eds. 1983. *The Invention of Tradition*. Cambridge: Cambridge University Press.

Intergovernmental Panel on Climate Change. 2007. *Fourth Assessment Report: Climate Change 2007*. Geneva: IPCC.

——. 2013. *Fifth Assessment Report: Climate Change 2013*. Geneva: IPCC.

Jackson, T. 2009. *Prosperity without Growth*. London: Earthscan.

Kane, S. 1998 (2010). *Wisdom of the Mythtellers*. Peterborough, Ontario: Broadview Press.

Kasser, T. 2002. *The High Price of Materialism*. Cambridge, MA: MIT Press.

Kay, J. H. 1997. *Asphalt Nation*. New York: Crown.

Kunitz, S. 2005. *The Wild Braid*. New York: W. W. Norton.

Layard, R. 2006. *Happiness: Lessons from a New Science*. London: Penguin.

Lovelock, J. 2005. *The Revenge of Gaia: Earth's Climate Crisis and the Fate of Humanity*. London: Allen Lane.

McKibben, B. 2007. *Deep Economy: The Wealth of Communities and the Durable Future*. New York: Holt.

McNeill, J. 2000. *Something New under the Sun*. London: Penguin.

Myers, N., and J. Kent. 2004. *The New Consumers*. Washington, DC: Island Press.

Nettle, D. 2005. *Happiness*. Oxford: Oxford University Press.

Pretty, J. 2007. *The Earth Only Endures*. London: Earthscan.

——. 2013. "The Consumption of a Finite Planet: Well-Being, Convergence, Divergence, and the Nascent Green Economy." *Environmental and Resource Economics* 55, no. 4: 475–99.

Rees, M. 2003. *Our Final Century*. London: Arrow Books.

Royal Society. 2012. *People and the Planet*. London: Royal Society.

Smith, L. C. 2010. *The New North: The World in 2050*. London: Profile.

Turner, J. 1996. *The Abstract Wild*. Tucson: University of Arizona Press.

Walker, S. 2011. *The Spirit of Design*. London: Earthscan.

Wapner, P. 2010. *Living through the End of Nature*. Cambridge, MA: MIT Press.

Wilkinson, R., and K. Pickett. 2009. *The Spirit Level*. London: Penguin.

ACKNOWLEDGMENTS

I am grateful to the many people who advised during the organization of these journeys, to those who accompanied me, or allowed me to come with them, and to those who generously gave time to navigate me through their places, memories, and lives. Others offered advice on walking, storytelling, writing, natural and social history, and on passing through landscapes. I hope I told their stories with fairness and accuracy. My deepest thanks to:

Glenn Albrecht, Jill Albrecht, David Allemond, Stephen Andrews, Steve Billington, Tom Bindley, Sheila Blake, Ronald Blythe, Maitseo Bolaane, Patience Buckley, Hugh Campbell, Ricky Carline and Teri-Ann Carline, Nicholas Colloff, Christine Dann, Jaimie Dick, Barbara Durham, Edward Ellison, Pauline Esteves, Hilary van Eyck and Sam van Eyck, John Fairweather, Billy Frosdick, Jay Griffiths, Siua Halavatu, John Hall, Emily Hershberger, Kathleen Hydock, Tony Jenkinson, Dolaana Kadygo, Vladislav Kanzay, Liam Kelly, David Kline and Elsie Kline, Ann Lee, C. C. Lockwood, Michael Lung, Ryan Lynch, Richard Mabey, Rob Macfarlane, Leapetswe Malete, Oliver McCullough, Margaret Rose McSparran, Mary Melnyk, Leah Miller, Shushep Mark, Henrik Moller, Tero Mustonen, Kaisu Mustonen, Kevin North, Basile Penashue, Katnen Pastitchi, Dick Platt, Dominic Pokue, Etienne Pone, Tahu Potiki and Megan Ellison, Esa Rahunen, John Reid, Brenda Dardar Robichaux, Angela Robson, Jim Rokakis, Gwen Roland, Khyla Russell, Colin Samson, Rob Schlabach and Matt Schlabach, Syd Smith and Elvie Smith, Michael Steinberg, Calvin Voisin, James Wilson.

I am very grateful to Glenn Albrecht, Ricky Carline, Barbara Durham, Nicholas Colloff, Billy Frosdick, Tony Jenkinson, Liam Kelly, Leah Miller, Tero Mustonen, Kevin North, John Reid, Gwen Roland, Khyla Russell, and Colin Samson for their comments, advice, and corrections on specific chapters. I also thank Kitty Liu of Cornell University Press for insights and sage guidance. Any errors and misjudgments are mine alone. The photographs were taken by me.

It is a privilege to have had the opportunity to travel the world for these journeys at the edge of extinction. I could say that I offset some of the environmental costs of air travel: I traveled ninety-two thousand kilometers by air for these journeys, resulting in personal emissions of 7.8 tons of carbon (as CO_2e): over the years of these journeys, the solar photovoltaics on our roof at home generated some ten megawatts of electricity, equivalent to about five tons of carbon not emitted. But this is coldly insufficient. There is only one way to tell stories about people in their places, and that is to be with them. The main danger lies in becoming a tourist voyeur; the benefit arises from storytelling if it is both respectful and illuminating. I hope I have been able to do the latter.